TWELVE
AMERICAN POETS
BEFORE 1900

TWELVE AMERICAN POETS BEFORE 1900

by Rica Brenner

Essay Index Reprint Series

Originally published by:
HARCOURT, BRACE AND COMPANY

 BOOKS FOR LIBRARIES PRESS
FREEPORT, NEW YORK

INTERNATIONAL STANDARD BOOK NUMBER:
0-8369-0250-5

LIBRARY OF CONGRESS CATALOG CARD NUMBER:
68-22092

PRINTED IN THE UNITED STATES OF AMERICA

PREFACE

"I do not believe that the verse of the present is better
than the verse of the past, and the verse of one epoch is
superior to that of another: that the Victorian epoch was
necessarily inferior because it was Victorian, or that the
Georgian or neo-Georgian was superior because it was
Georgian or neo-Georgian. I believe great poets are always
exceptional whenever they appear: that when poets or artists achieve great fame there is always some reason for it,
and that once in the temple of fame there is no escape:
they are bound on a wheel which is sometimes in the shade
and sometimes in the sun, and which goes round like a
whirligig; but it is always there, and the famous are always
bound to it: thus it is that great poets are admired by one
generation, forgotten and reviled by the next generation,
and then rediscovered and admired again by a still younger
generation. This happened to Giotto, the painter. It happened to Pope. It happened, is happening, and will hap-
pen to Byron. That good poets have written bad verse as
well as good verse is no matter: those good poets who have
written little or no bad verse are rare, and they have published little. . . . When a great poet, a great master of
verse, expresses the mood of his time with mastery, it is
impossible for those who read his verse to think it will
ever fade or die, or that coming generations will think of
it otherwise than they do themselves."
—MAURICE BARING, *Lost Lectures,*
"Poetry and the Moods of the Public"

"To have great poets, there must be great audiences,
too."

—WALT WHITMAN, *Collect,*
"Ventures, On an Old Theme"

THE FIGURE of the swinging pendulum is much too
good a one to be discarded merely because it has been
used frequently before. So it may be said, not too hesitantly,

v

that with the change in these last few years in fashion, in social habits, and in standards of action and of thought, there has been a return swing, too, of the literary pendulum. The effort of the preceding decades to create new forms in verse, in drama, and in prose has been seen in proper proportion, not as a necessary denial of all that the past has offered but as an enlargement and liberation of that past. Realism in literature, stark and blatant, is now seen to be not the only modern mood, but simply one of a number of possible moods. There has been, furthermore, a more direct return in a renewed interest in those writers of the nineteenth century, whom a young twentieth century cavalierly rejected.

The returning balance retraces, for as long a distance as it may, the path of its going; but, swaying of its own momentum, it never quite returns to its starting point. So, those who are reading again the poets they read when they were younger, who realize that they must not dismiss those writers with the contempt of ten or fifteen years ago and cannot accept them with the blind enthusiasm of their nineteenth century contemporaries, may find in this book a present-day point of departure from which to form their own judgments. The younger generation of readers, those only now being introduced to the "classic" American poets, should find a background of biographical and critical information which may help them to read the poets with sympathy, understanding, critical appreciation, and pleasure. To suggest a present-day point of view toward these writers, rather than to present the results of fresh biographical research, has been the purpose of this book.

One further purpose has been present; and that has been the desire to make clear that the writing of any and of every period has had some roots in the past. No one writing today—no one reading today—can completely escape the

past. The poetry of the earlier American poets has entered
and become a part of American literature and of American
thought. Later writers and readers may have carried the
tradition on unquestioned and unaltered; or they may have
consciously rejected it. But the gesture of rejection is as
definite and significant as that of acceptance. The influence
of these writers, whether positive in the one case or negative
in the other, cannot be denied.

What prompted the choice of these particular twelve
poets? Other names suggested themselves and, regretfully,
had to be omitted. These twelve, it seemed, gave a chrono-
logical picture of poetry in America from the time of the
founding of the republic through the end of the nineteenth
century. Moreover, in their poetry can be found examples
of the various kinds of poetry written today: light newspaper verse and dignified odes; poems of industry and of
the city and those of nature and of the woods; poems of
withdrawn, subjective mysticism and those of rallying patriotism; poems gay, serious, lyrical, philosophical. Finally,
these poets are American poets. Some of them for some of
their poems did find their inspiration in European tradition
and culture. But all of them, including Poe and Emily Dickinson who elude any geographical bounding, were free from
the feeling that Europe and the past could dictate subject
or method. American country and American life entered
into their poetry; and, with varying degrees of success, it
is true, they reflected in their poetry something of American
freedom and spirit.

So far as these poets reflected their own times, they have
an historical significance. But so far as they interpreted
what has proved permanent in American spirit, so far as
they sang what is unchanging in human thought and emotions, they are poets for today.

Any comment that is made upon them as poets gains

point when it may be illustrated by quotations from their poetry. For the privilege thus to quote from the poets included, I acknowledge a pleasant debt of gratitude: to D. Appleton and Company for permission to quote from *The Poetical Works of William Cullen Bryant;* and to Charles Scribner's Sons for their permission to quote from *The Poems of Eugene Field* and from *Poems of Sidney Lanier.* The poems from *Leaves of Grass,* by Walt Whitman, are reprinted by permission from Doubleday, Doran and Company, Inc., to whom I am grateful. Emily Dickinson's poems, quoted from *The Poems of Emily Dickinson,* Centenary Edition, edited by Martha Dickinson Bianchi and Alfred Leete Hampson, are reprinted by permission of Little, Brown, and Company; the excerpts from *Letters of Emily Dickinson,* edited by Mabel Loomis Todd, the original editor of the 1894 edition, are quoted by permission of Mrs. V. W. Bingham and of Harper and Brothers, the publishers. To Houghton Mifflin Company are due my many thanks for their generous permission to use the poems of John Greenleaf Whittier, Henry Wadsworth Longfellow, Ralph Waldo Emerson, James Russell Lowell, and Oliver Wendell Holmes. The quotation from Maurice Baring's "Poetry and the Moods of the Public" is taken from his book, *Lost Lectures,* and is reprinted by permission of and special arrangement with Alfred A. Knopf, Inc., authorized publishers.

There are those whose names have not been mentioned who have patiently and generously helped in the making of this book. They know that I am grateful. To them, here, I repeat my thanks.

R. B.

December 1932.

CONTENTS

TWELVE
AMERICAN POETS
BEFORE 1900

PHILIP FRENEAU

IT IS not without significance that Philip Freneau, "the poet of the Revolution," was by birth and early training identified with New York and New Jersey, two of the Middle Atlantic Colonies. He was thus able to be the spokesman for a larger number of people than if he had represented either the extreme of Puritan New England or that of the cavalier South. But in spite of the fact that he could voice and even mold the opinions of a people gradually growing into a nation, he was never completely at one with his times. An ardent believer in liberty, he could throw his whole soul into the struggle of the Colonies against England:

> If to controul the cunning of a knave,
> Freedom respect, and scorn the name of slave;
> If to protest against a tyrant's laws,
> And arm for vengeance in a righteous cause,
> Be deemed Rebellion—'tis a harmless thing:
> This bug-bear name, like death, has lost its sting.

He could, when the inspiration moved him, express in biting satire the anger of his countrymen against British generals, against the Tories, against those who were felt to be impeding America's progress. But by nature and desire a creative poet, he could not continue his rhymed vituperation when he, himself, felt that the general need for it was past. The public might—and did—demand it. Yet popular request, alone, was not sufficient to compel Freneau to write what he preferred not to write:

3

"Hark ye, my dogs, I have not learned to yelp,
Nor waste my breath on every lousy whelp;
Much less, to write, or stain my wholesome page
In answering puppies—bursting with their rage;
Hence to your straw!—such contest I disdain:
        Learn this ('tis not amiss)
        For Men I keep a pen,
        For dogs, a cane!"

Nor could he identify himself with a world given over, as he thought, too much to material ends and insufficiently hospitable to poetry. The new nation was not yet ready for poetry. Its energies were engrossed in the problems of government and of industry:

        An age employed in edging steel
        Can no poetic raptures feel.

Freneau, himself, was not strong enough to withstand indifference or neglect, or boldly to overcome the difficulties that beset him. He expressed his disappointment in his verse; and when this no longer held comfort for him, time and again he sought escape from his problems in life on the sea.

The essential combination making up Freneau's temperament, that of a strong love of liberty and a delight in the pleasures of fancy, may be attributed to his French Huguenot ancestry. The Huguenots, expelled from France by the revocation of the Edict of Nantes in 1685, sought refuge in more hospitable countries of Europe and in the settlements of the new world across the Atlantic. In their exile, in their founding of new homes and allegiances, they retained their insistence upon freedom, a proverbial honesty and keenness, and withal, a Celtic sprightliness of mind and of spirit.

Among those Huguenots seeking their fortune in America was Andre Fresneau, who arrived in Boston in 1705. In 1707 he settled in New York City, where he conducted a thriving shipping business devoted chiefly to wines. Two sons, Andrew and Pierre, in their turn carried on their father's business. The younger son, Pierre Freneau (the s of the older spelling had been dropped about 1725) in the middle of the eighteenth century married Agnes Watson of Freehold, New Jersey. The birth of their oldest son was duly recorded in the old family Bible which from 1590 had traced the descent of the Fresneau family. He was born January 2 —January 13 after the change in calendar—1752; and he was named Philip Morin Freneau.

The early years of his life were spent in New York City, where the Freneau home, a home of culture and of no small degree of wealth, was a gathering place for men of wit and learning. Shortly after Philip's birth, his father purchased in New Jersey an estate of some thousand acres, which was called Mount Pleasant, the translation of the name of the old French ancestral home, and which, it would seem, was used as a summer residence for the Freneau family. In 1762, the family moved from New York to settle permanently on the New Jersey estate.

Exactly where Philip received his earliest education is not certain. It is probable, however, that until he was ten years old his training was under the direction of his father and of his mother, a woman of education and intelligence and of keen sympathy and understanding. Possibly after the family's removal to New Jersey, there were several years of boarding school for Philip in New York City. At all events, at the age of thirteen, he was enrolled in the Penolopen Latin School to prepare for college. The death of his father two years later did not alter his plans. In November 1768, he entered Nassau Hall at Princeton, so well prepared in his work that President Witherspoon is said to have sent to his mother a highly congratulatory letter in praise of her son. Life at college in Freneau's day was quite different from present college life. The rising bell sounded at five. After a half hour allowed for dressing, attendance was required at prayers. On Sundays, the student body had to listen to two sermons. So, too, the curriculum was in many respects different. There was no large variety of subjects among which a student might fitfully choose. Emphasis throughout the four years was placed upon Mathematics, Latin, Greek, and Philosophy.

At Princeton, Freneau found congenial fellow-students: H. H. Brackenridge, in particular; James Madison, who was to become the fourth president of the United States; and, in the class below him, Aaron Burr. In the Princeton atmosphere of learning and of friendship, Freneau's intellectual interests were further stimulated; he read widely in the classic authors and in the English poets, particularly Pope and Gray. He found that he had a ready pen and during his college years wrote a number of poems that suggested the course of his desires. Among them were "History of the Prophet Jonah"; "The Adventure of Simon Swaugum, a Village Merchant," which gives several pleasantly satirical pictures of the times; and "The Pyramids of Egypt," which, in choice of subject and in treatment, shows the double strain in Freneau, his wandering active fancy and his strong, sometimes moralizing convictions:

> Traveller return—
> There's nought but God immortal—He alone
> Exists secure, when Man, and Death, and Time
> (Time not immortal, but a fancied point
> In the vast circle of eternity)
> Are swallow'd up, and, like the pyramids,
> Leave not an atom for their monument!

With all its academic insistence upon books and the lore of the past, Princeton was not cloistered against contemporary movements and ideas. It was by no means untouched by the political problems then agitating the thirteen Colonies. Its president, John Witherspoon, though born in Scotland, was an ardent champion of the Colonies against England. Its Senior class of 1770 voted to appear at commencement dressed as American manufacturers. Its student body formed partisan political clubs.

Freneau naturally allied himself with the Whigs; and, with Brackenridge and Madison among others, wrote, in the literary war that accompanied the political rivalry of the clubs, heated invectives against the Tories. But more than this, he and Brackenridge, imbued with a patriotic sense of the inherent greatness of America, planned a poem that would chronicle its glory. This work of collaboration, "The Rising Glory of America," was read by Brackenridge at the commencement exercises of September 1771, at which Freneau received his degree although he was himself not present. The poem, most enthusiastically received, seems to have been credited at the time only to Brackenridge. However, he himself acknowledged that the greater and better part was the work of Freneau; and when Freneau, some years later, included the poem in an edition of his writing, it contained only those lines of which he had been the author. In its later version there were many alterations, omissions, and additions; but it retained that early picture of the future which Freneau had seen with the poetic vision that proved to be prophetic:

> I see, I see
> A thousand kingdoms rais'd, cities and men
> Num'rous as sand upon the ocean shore;
> Th' Ohio then shall glide by many a town

Of note: and where the Mississippi stream
By forests shaded now runs weeping on,
Nations shall grow and states not less in fame
Than Greece and Rome of old.

What followed immediately after Freneau's commencement is not known. But there seems to have been a period
of disappointment and disillusionment. He wrote some verse
and was hurt that it did not receive universal approval. He
found that he could not live a life purely of literary activity.
He taught school—for thirteen days—in the town of Flatbush across the river from New York, and hated it. Some of
this hatred—against the work, against the school board,
against the parents of his pupils—he poured out in a poem,
"The Miserable Life of a Pedagogue":

A plague I say on such employment,
Where's neither pleasure nor enjoyment:
Whoe'er to such a life is ty'd,
Was born the day he should have dy'd.

More of it is poured out in a letter which he wrote to Madison in November 1772:
"If I am not wrongly informed by my memory, I have not
seen you since last April. You may recollect I was then
undertaking a school at Flatbush on Long Island. I did
enter upon the business, it is certain, and continued in it
thirteen days—but Long Island I have bid adieu, with all
its brainless crew. The youth of that detested place, are void
of reason and of grace. From Flushing hills to Flatbush
plains, deep ignorance unrivall'd reigns. I am very poetical.
But excuse it."
This letter was written from Somerset County, Maryland,
where, in spite of the fiasco of his Flatbush experiment he
had gone to teach in the school of which his friend Bracken-

ridge was master. But life as a teacher here was no more pleasant than it had been in the North. In the same letter to Madison, Freneau reveals that his only interest is poetry; and with no little pathos suggests his discontent: "I want but five weeks of twenty-one years of age and already feel stiff with age."

The Southern episode was a brief one. By 1775 Freneau was back in New York. The quarrel between the Colonies and the mother country was fast nearing a crisis. Events were moving rapidly about Boston. With his whole heart and soul, Freneau gave himself to the patriotic cause. He issued as pamphlets numerous poems, assailing England and encouraging and urging on the Americans. Among the poems of this period are "General Gage's Soliloquy," "The Midnight Consultations, or, A Trip to Boston," "To the Americans, on the Rumored Approach of the Hessian Forces." Vitriolic pictures of the British army, harsh denunciations of British aims, these poems met with wide popular approval. At the same time, possibly because of their very harshness, they must have aroused some antagonism. For Freneau revived a poem of his college days which flung derision at an adversary, and modifying it to suit his present situation, he published it as "Mac Swiggen, A Satire in Answer to a Hostile Attack." Criticism of his poems he could not stand. Characteristically, he sought escape:

> Sick of all feuds, to Reason I appeal
> From wars of paper, and from wars of steel,
> Let others here their hopes and wishes end,
> I to the sea with weary steps descend.

This escape was to be only the first of many similar ones, in which Freneau set sail either as passenger or as ship master. This time the disillusioned poet embarked for the West Indies. On the journey out, the mate of the vessel died. Freneau was able to fill the vacant position and thus, doubtless, had confirmed his choice of the sea as his second love and his secondary career. Almost three years he spent in the West Indies and in Bermuda, part of the time sailing for a West Indian friend, much of the time giving himself over to poetry. The semi-tropic islands stirred him and, at the same time, soothed away his discontent. The island of Santa Cruz, in particular, pleased him; and in a poem, "The Beauties of Santa Cruz," he lushly described its charms. One discordant note alone antagonized him; his firm belief in human independence revolted at the slavery on the island. The publication of the poem was prefaced by his protest against that institution: "It casts a shade over the native charms of the country; it blots out the beauties of the eternal spring which Providence has there ordained to reign."

Two other poems of this period should be noted: "The House of Night" and "The Jamaica Funeral." The former has been called "the first distinctly romantic note heard in America." With a command over the mysterious and the weird it depicts the death of Death himself.

> Lights in the air like burning stars were hurl'd,
> Dogs howl'd, heaven mutter'd, and the tempest blew,
> The red half-moon peeped from behind a cloud
> As if in dread the amazing scene to view.
>
> The mournful trees that in the garden stood
> Bent to the tempest as it rush'd along,
> The elm, the myrtle, and the cypress sad
> More melancholy tun'd its bellowing song.
>
> No more that elm its noble branches spread,
> The yew, the cypress, or the myrtle tree,
> Bent from the roots the tempest tore them down,
> And all the grove in wild confusion lay.

It ends with Freneau's own conception of death and change:

> Hills sink to plains, and man returns to dust,
> That dust supports a reptile or a flower;
> Each changeful atom by some other nurs'd
> Takes some new form, to perish in an hour.

The second of the poems is a further presentation of Freneau's philosophy of life, an ironically drawn funeral sermon:

> A few short years, at best, will bound our span,
> Wretched and few, the Hebrew exile said;
> Live while you may, be jovial while you can,
> Death as a debt to nature must be paid.

When Freneau returned to the mainland after his years of absence, American independence had been declared. The poet rejoiced. He wrote verses celebrating freedom; he followed closely the events of the war, commemorating the victories, urging the citizens on in defeat. In writing poetry, in editing journals and newspapers, and—when criticism or lack of appreciation overwhelmed him—in flights to the sea, Freneau spent the many remaining years of his life. He vacillated between poetry and voyaging. Now he said a farewell to one:

> Of all the fools that haunt our coast
> The scribbling tribe I pity most:
> Their's is a standing scene of woes,
> And their's no prospect of repose.
> .   .   .   .   .
> Then, Sylvius, come—let you and I
> On Neptune's aid, once more rely:
> Perhaps the muse may still impart
> Her balm to ease the aching heart.

Now, it was a farewell to the other, as in the poem "Never-
sink":

> Proud heights! with pain so often seen,
> (With joy beheld once more)
> On your firm base I take my stand,
> Tenacious of the shore:—
> Let those who pant for wealth or fame
> Pursue the watery road;—
> Soft sleep and ease, blest days and nights,
> And health, attend these favourite heights,
> Retirement's blest abode.

In this life of vacillation, there were several episodes that
were important. In 1780 Freneau sailed on the *Aurora*. Off
the coast of New Jersey on May 25, the boat was captured
by the British ship *Iris*. Freneau, despite his protestations
that he was only a passenger, was taken prisoner; and, because he was accused of having manned one of the *Aurora's*
guns, he was confined in the prison ship *Scorpion*, lying in
the North River off New York. There he suffered great
hardships. He was taken with fever, put on the sick list, and
transferred to the even more horrible hospital ship *Hunter*
in New York harbor. The *Hunter* was overcrowded and
filthy; no proper care was given the invalids. Of all that he
was forced to endure, what Freneau seemed most to resent
was the negligence of the German doctor:

> From Brookland groves a Hessian doctor came,
> Not great his skill, nor greater much his fame;
> Fair Science never call'd the wretch her son,
> And Art disdain'd the stupid man to own.

Finally, worn out, Freneau was released on July 12. Labori-
ously he made his way home, by ferry, by wagon, by walking miles in the hot sun. He neared Mount Pleasant. "When

I came to Obadiah Budleigh's corner," he writes in a prose account of the capture of the *Aurora,* "I turned to the right and came home round about through the woods for fear of terrifying the neighbors with my ghastly looks had I gone thro Mount Pleasant." An even more vivid account he gave in his poem "The British Prison Ship," wherein full rein was given to his bitterness against the British.

During the following years of the war, the verses that flowed from Freneau's rapid pen were widely published; they circulated among the soldiers; they were effective in times of depression. After the war, his pen was turned against the Royalists. There were several years of editorial activity in Philadelphia for one Francis Bailey. Then there came another period of disillusionment; Freneau was unable to live merely by literature; furthermore he preferred not to continue the satiric vein of his poetry, which was the one most popularly appreciated.

Again there was an escape to the sea, which provided him not only a means of living but an inspiration for his beloved verse. The sea in calm and in storms, the hurricanes and drownings that he witnessed, all provided him with poetic material. A paradoxical picture of himself in one of the storms he gives in a letter which he wrote to Bailey: "In the midst of all this vexation the crew endeavoured to keep up their spirits with a little grog, while I had recourse to my old expedient of philosophy and reflection."

While Freneau was voyaging, Bailey in 1786 had brought out a collection of his poems. The book was successful, so successful that plans for a further collection were immediately drawn. These first volumes are landmarks in American literary history. Reflecting the condition of actual life, touched to some degree with fancy and imagination, free in method, they are a distinct break from the traditions of English poetry of the eighteenth century.

Of what Freneau thought of the reception given his work there is no record. He had abandoned a purely literary career—at least, temporarily. Then in 1790 there was a right-about-face; the sea was bidden farewell. Doubtless, the poet's marriage to Eleanor Forman, a New Jersey woman of charm and wit, prompted his decision. At all events, in February 1790, he was again in New York beginning a life of various editorial endeavors that was to continue until 1797.

Some of his activity during this period has become the subject of much controversy. In 1791, the seat of the Federal government was moved from New York to Philadelphia. Freneau made plans to establish a newspaper in the nation's new capital. But before the first issue of his paper, he had been appointed a translator's clerk in the State Department under Jefferson. The appointment was made in August 1791. The first number of Freneau's *National Gazette* appeared in October. Freneau used his journal to engage in active warfare against the *Gazette of the United States*, a Federal organ. He marshaled all his forces against what he considered the monarchial tendencies of the Federalist party, against centralization of government powers, against a national bank, against the neutrality which Washington had proclaimed in the war between France and her enemies. Freneau became the target for most bitter criticism; it was felt that it was dishonest for him to attack the government of which he was an employee; it was thought that the *National Gazette* had been established, with Jefferson's encouragement, merely for the purpose of embarrassing Washington and his party. There were disclaimers; there were explanations. In October 1793, Freneau resigned from his government position. In the same month his paper issued its last number.

It would seem from the evidence of his own character that

Freneau had been unjustly attacked. His personal and life-long antagonism to anything that savored of royalty could, of itself, justify the editorial position which he assumed.

At all events, there was in the whole controversy no personal animosity against Washington. Washington is said to have visited Freneau later at his home; and at the death of the first president, Freneau wrote poems of sincerity and of deep feeling:

> He was no god, ye flattering knaves,
> He own'd no world, he ruled no waves;
> But—and exalt it, if you can,
> He was the upright, Honest Man.

The editorship of further newspapers and journals, additional volumes of verse, did not provide sufficiently for his family. There were five more years on the sea to mend his fortune, and then retirement on the Mount Pleasant estate. Life there was gracious, if not economically efficient. The property had to be mortgaged; its farms were not well managed. But Freneau freed the slaves whom he had owned. He showed a tenderness toward people and animals which is in strong contrast to the bitterness of the fiery partisan of Revolutionary times, but which fits in with the picture that his contemporaries drew of him as a charming man, of great wit, an entertaining conversationalist, unassuming, and withal, a favorite of the ladies.

Life at Mount Pleasant encouraged the writing of further verse. The patriotic spark was fanned again by the War of 1812. New volumes were planned and published. Yet always there is discontent at their reception. "I remained there much longer," he writes a friend in 1819, "than I had intended, not a little out of humour that my two little volumes seemed to have fallen nearly deadborn from the Press, owing to the enmity of some, the politics of others, and the general inattention of all."

America, he felt, had not properly appreciated him. Years before, in "The Rising Glory of America," he had written

> How could I weep that we were born so soon,
> In the beginning of more happy times!

As an old man, he must have felt himself ruthlessly excluded from the hopeful promise of the future.

On December 18, 1832, the eighty-year-old poet set out on some errand to Freehold, two miles from his home. In the evening, he insisted upon returning despite the efforts of some friends to dissuade him. He was overtaken by a blinding snow storm and not until the next morning was his dead, frozen body found.

If Philip Freneau had been merely "the poet of the American Revolution," he and his poems would now be only of historical interest. In his verse, the historian could find a contemporary exposition of the American revolutionary attitude, the rallying enthusiasm of the patriots, the openly personal and bitter attacks on British foes. The historian would find this and few else would read.

But Freneau was something more than the rhyming chronicler of passing events. He was essentially the first American poet—a poet, moreover, who cast off the binding restrictions of poetic tradition imposed by Pope and his followers and from the life about him and his own personality and fancy chose the material for his poems.

Thus, he did not coldly withhold himself from his own writing, content to give a judicious objective expression of opinion. Warmth of feeling permeated all his lines; in them he revealed himself. Restive against all restraints, he was opposed to formal religion. The Puritan custom forbidding travel on the Sabbath is treated humorously in "The New

England Sabbath Day Chace." The hypocrisy of some clergy is denounced, as in "The Jamaica Funeral." Evidently his unorthodox attitude was criticized as the ridiculing of religion. This charge he denied; to it he replied with "To an Angry Zealot," which begins:

> If of Religion I have made a sport,
> Then why not cite me to the Bishop's Court?
> Fair to the world let every page be set,
> And prove your charge from all I've said and writ:—
> What if this heart no narrow notions bind,
> Its pure good-will extends to all mankind:
> Suppose I ask no portion from your feast,
> Nor heaven-ward ride behind your parish priest,
> Because I wear not Shylock's Sunday face,
> Must I, for that, be loaded with disgrace?

If his religion included good-will to all mankind (always excepting those he considered his enemies), it embraced, too, an acceptance of the laws of nature, of Death as simply one of its inevitable changes, a change to be boldly met:

> When Nature bids thee from the world
> With joy thy lodging leave, a fated guest;
> In Paradise, the land of thy desire,
> Existing always, always to be blest.

The same clarity with which he evolved his philosophy made him a keen lover of the truth. One notable example of this is the poem he wrote after Benjamin Franklin's death. Franklin was one of Freneau's heroes, exalted to a place of prominence in the early poem, "The Rising Glory of America." But the exaggerated praise given him at his death provoked the poet to write "Epistle" as though Franklin himself were speaking:

Philosophers are famed for pride;
But, pray, be modest—when I died,
No "sighs disturbed old ocean's bed,"
No "Nature wept" for Franklin dead!

That day, on which I left the coast,
A beggar-man was also lost:
If "Nature wept," you must agree
She wept for him—as well as me.

This love of truth led to the satiric strain in Freneau and
in his verse. Sometimes, frequently indeed, its bitterness is
overwhelming. George III, for example, is made to appear
the supreme coward.

How can I march to meet the insulting foe,
Who never yet to hostile plains did go?

But frequently it is marked by a lightness and a kindliness
that make it most delightful. Such is the wholly absurd account of a trip given in "Slender's Journey." Such, too, are
"Modern Devotion":

Now, pray be wise, no prayers will rise
To heaven—where hearts are not sincere.
No church was made for Cupid's trade;
Then why these arts of ogling here?

and "The Citizen's Resolve," wherein Lysander grows
weary of the city's bustling activity and longs for the calm
repose of the country:

So spoke Lysander, and in haste
His clerks discharg'd, his goods re-cased,
And to the western forests flew
With fifty airy schemes in view;

His ships were set to public sale—
But what did all this change avail?—
In three short months, sick of the heavenly train,
In three short months—he moved to town again.

More than all this, Freneau gave to Americans what they
had never had before, poetry indigenous to the country.
Imported English poetry, however good, however beautiful,
could not satisfy all the needs of the American spirit. What
of the poetic in American life, in the American scene?

Freneau wrote of nature as he found it in America. He
did not transport to these shores the traditional nightingales
of England. He wrote of black-birds, of pheasants, of whip-
poor-wills. He wrote "The Wild Honey Suckle," with its
famous last two lines:

> The space between is but an hour,
> The frail duration of a flower.

And he wrote the utterly delightful "To a Caty-did":

> In a branch of willow hid
> Sings the evening Caty-did:
> From the lofty locust bough
> Feeding on a drop of dew,
> In her suit of green array'd
> Hear her singing in the shade
>   Caty-did, Caty-did, Caty-did!
> .   .   .   .   .
> Tell me, what did Caty do?
> Did she mean to trouble you?—
> Why was Caty not forbid
> To trouble little Caty-did?—
> Wrong, indeed, at you to fling,
> Hurting no one while you sing
>   Caty-did! Caty-did! Caty-did!
> .   .   .   .   .

Stay securely in your nest;
Caty now, will do her best,
All she can, to make you blest;
But, you want no human aid—
Nature, when she form'd you, said,
"Independent you are made,
My dear little Caty-did:
Soon yourself must disappear
With the verdure of the year,"—
And to go we know not where,
With your song of Caty-did.

The Indian, too, Freneau recorded for Americans. In "The Prophecy of King Tammany," the Chief, about to die, admits the growing weakness of his race,

The bow has lost its wonted spring;

he foretells the doom that the Indians are to suffer at the hands of the whites; and then with calm and dignity approaches his own funeral pyre. The same dignity is expressed in "The Dying Indian, Tomo-Chequi." And all that is noble and active and courageous in the Indian is embodied in "The Indian Burying Ground":

In spite of all the learned have said,
I still my old opinion keep;
The posture, that we give the dead,
Points out the soul's eternal sleep.

Not so the ancients of these lands—
The Indian, when from life released,
Again is seated with his friends,
And shares again the joyous feast.

·   ·   ·   ·   ·

By midnight moons, o'er moistening dews;
In habit for the chase arrayed,
The hunter still the deer pursues,
The hunter and the deer, a shade!

One other vast, and before then poetically untraveled, domain Freneau opened up for his American readers—the Atlantic Ocean. The naval victories of the Revolution were acclaimed with particular enthusiasm, as in "The Memorable Victory Obtained by the Gallant, Captain Paul Jones," and in "Song on Captain Barney's Victory." His own delight in the sea colors poem after poem; the lures it holds are suggested in "Captain Jones's Invitation":

But winds must cease, and storms decay,
Not always lasts the gloomy day,
Again the skies are warm and clear,
Again soft zephyrs fan the air,
Again we find the long lost shore,
The winds oppose our wish no more.

If thou hast courage to despise
The various changes of the skies,
To disregard the ocean's rage,
Unmov'd when hostile ships engage,
Come from thy forest, and with me
Learn what it is to go to sea.

It was a vast quantity of verse that Freneau produced in his long life. Much of it may well be ignored; it is scarcely poetry. Much of it was marred by coarseness and by bitterness. Much, too, suffers from carelessness in meter and in grammar. There is in some of it a lack of imagination; the poetic is at times drowned in moralizing.

But much of it is the sheer material of poetry. Furthermore, Freneau must be seen in the light of his own time, the time into which he could never wholly fit. Accepted English poetry was, when he first wrote, cold and studied. The heroic couplet was made to imprison all poetic thought. The subject of poetry was the formal and the correct. Freneau broke away from this dictation. With an amazing facility of rhyme and a variety of verse-form, he used his material as he preferred. His choice of subject was unlimited. At the faint beginning of the romantic movement in poetry in England, Freneau here had already chosen the humble and the familiar as the subject of his poetry. He had introduced the more wildly romantic, as in "The Beauties of Santa Cruz." And he had given expression to the romantic feeling for death and for the mysterious, as in "The House of Night."

He made his own selection of the poetic and he decided for himself how it should be presented. He may, indeed, be said to have issued a second declaration of American independence, not a political but a literary one.

WILLIAM CULLEN BRYANT

THE LITTLE boy who was the very young William Cullen Bryant added to the familiar hymns and prayers of his commonly shared New England religious experience a special prayer of his own. It was a supplication to the God he worshiped that he "might receive the gift of poetic genius and write verses that might endure." For some reason which the mature Bryant could not recall, the boy after a time abandoned the conscious and verbal expression of his desire; but throughout his life, the desire remained.

That the boy should pray and should pray for the gift of song was the not unnatural reflection of his family inheritance. Born in Cummington, Massachusetts, November 3, 1794, the second of seven children of Dr. Peter and Sarah Snell Bryant, William Cullen was the inheritor of the New England insistence upon character training, moral development, and religious devotion. From his father's family came something more, a love of learning and a delight in literature. This family tradition of combining the practice of medicine with a keen fondness for poetry, a tradition three generations old, produced in Dr. Peter Bryant, the poet's father, a most able physician and a man who not only had, himself, a gift for writing verse but was able to give his son poetic direction and training.

It was, however, the mother's family that must have exerted the first and more obvious influence on the boy. When William was about five, he and his family made their home with his grandfather, Ebenezer Snell. Grandfather Snell was for the boy the embodiment of family discipline, an overwhelmingly awe-inspiring person. He it was who led the family in religious devotion. From him and from the community ministers came prayers made up of poetical expressions from the Bible, one of which, repeated again and again, echoed permanently in Bryant's memory: "Let not our feet stumble on the dark mountains of eternal death." Early must the child's thoughts have been turned toward the question of mortality. New England theology touched even the recreation provided by Grandmother Snell. Mild and affectionate, she entertained William and his older brother by drawing with chalk on the kitchen floor, and included in her drawings a portrait of "Old Crooktail," the devil, himself.

Close as his grandparents were to William, still closer, naturally, was his devoted mother. She was endowed with excellent practical sense, necessary in a large family of a poor country doctor. She was interested in matters of public welfare. She possessed keen moral judgment which she transmitted to her family. "Her prompt condemnation of injustice," the poet once wrote in a memoir, "even in those instances in which it is tolerated by the world, made a strong impression upon me in early life, and if in the discussion of public questions I have in my ripe age endeavored to keep in view the great rules of right without much regard to persons, it has been owing in a great degree to the force of her example, which taught me never to countenance a wrong because others did."

It was the mother who taught the children to read and write. It was she who recorded the first step in the formal intellectual development of her poet son. Her diary entry for March 28, 1796, records the fact that William Cullen then knew his alphabet. And he was then not yet a year and a half old! Although there was irregular attendance at school before the boy was four, schooling began in earnest when the family moved to the Snell homestead. It consisted of instruction in reading, spelling, writing, arithmetic, a little grammar, and a little geography. On Saturdays, some time was devoted to studying the Catechism. In this, William made but halting progress; the abstract terms that were employed were beyond his comprehension.

School absorbed but a small part of Bryant's time and interest. There was play with his fellow students: launching rafts on the stream near the school-house, snow forts and snow fights, foot races, and ball playing. There was the social activity of a small country community: "raisings," corn huskings, apple-parings. There was singing school on winter evenings and occasional afternoons. And there was church, three services on Sunday. These all formed a background of life for the young boy. But more significant, because more in evidence as influences in his poetry, were other elements of his existence: long, rambling walks in the woods and quiet evenings devoted to study and to reading the books in his father's library, Milton, Dryden, Pope, Thompson, Byron, Scott. For a long time Pope was the favorite, to be supplanted by Spenser, who, in his turn, yielded to Wordsworth.

In this atmosphere, it did not take long for the boy's inmost desire to express itself. At eight, he began to write verse. At nine, at his grandfather's suggestion, he wrote a rhymed version of the first chapter of the book of Job. Grandfather Snell, primarily interested, doubtless, in religion and in industry, gave Bryant a ninepenny piece as a reward. Dr. Bryant, interested in poetry, gave his son criticism. As a result of the latter, such very limping and awkward lines as:

> His name was Job; evil he did eschew,
> To him were born seven sons; three daughters, too.

were somewhat improved:

> Job, good and just, in Uz had sojourned long,
> He feared his God and shunned the way of wrong,
> Three were his daughters, and his sons were seven,
> And large the wealth bestowed on him by heaven.

When he was ten, he wrote a description of his school, which was printed in the *Hampshire Gazette*, the county newspaper. But even this public glory did not dull Dr. Bryant's critical judgment of his son's poetry. When William wrote a poem in uninspired heroic couplets about the eclipse of the sun in June 1806, the father said, "He will be ashamed of his verses when he is grown up." Unremittingly the father criticized and suggested.

Finally, the boy wrote a poem that did receive his father's approval. It was a political satire directed against President Jefferson. Federalist New England—and Dr. Bryant, staunch Federalist and representative of Cummington in the Massachusetts legislature—were bitterly opposed to the Republican policies adopted to preserve American neutrality in the war between England and France. These policies of non-importation and embargo had resulted in the crippling of New England commerce. New England was enraged. Dr. Bryant reported and discussed the heated political arguments that took place in Boston. Bryant, stirred by the seething bitterness, wrote his poem about Jefferson, the Republican president:

> And thou, the scorn of every patriot name,
> Thy country's ruin and thy council's shame.

He was encouraged by his father to add to his sketch. A poem of some five hundred lines was the result and this Dr. Bryant had printed in Boston in 1808 as a pamphlet: *The Embargo; or, Sketches of the Times, a Satire; by a youth of thirteen.*

Go, wretch, resign the presidential chair,
Disclose thy secret measures, foul or fair.

Thus did the young poet advise. President Jefferson did not resign. But the general public's response to the poem was so approving that a second edition was published in 1809. This answered the question that had been raised by the previous edition as to whether the poem could possibly be the work of so young a person as it purported to be. This new edition appeared with the author's full name and it contained a prefaced statement by friends of the writer: "They, therefore, assure the public that Mr. Bryant, the author, is a native of Cummington, in the county of Hampshire, and in the month of November last arrived at the age of fourteen years."

In the light of Bryant's later development, the publication of this poem was a most significant event. The boy of thirteen tried to combine poetry and public affairs. Could the man continue to do so, or must he separate the two?

Whatever interpretive significance this appearance in print may have had, its immediate effect in the Bryant household must have been to hasten the decision about William's future plans. Ordinarily if but one in a New England family was to have a college education, that one was the oldest son. In this case, however, Austin, the older brother, was provided for; through his grandfather's aid, he was to become a farmer. So William, the next oldest and the poetically endowed, was to go to college, to Williams.

To prepare himself, he studied Latin and French at home. For eight months more he studied Latin with his uncle, Parson Thomas Snell, at Brookfield and in that time completed his Latin entrance requirements. Then for a little more than a year he was in Plainfield, learning Greek

at the "Bread and Milk College" of the Reverend Moses
Hallock, who charged a dollar a week for board and instruction. Finally, in October 1810, Bryant entered Williams in the Sophomore class.

The college was a small one. Its faculty numbered but
four; its scholastic demands were not great. Bryant, whose
literary fame had preceded him, easily accomplished the
daily routine. He was able, moreover, to do a great deal of
reading, to become acquainted with the Greek poets, to
make careful studies in Latin prosody; and to do much
writing of prose and of verse—this latter always under his
father's guidance. Among his writings was a satire against
the college:

> Why should I sing those reverend domes,
>   Where Science rests in grave repose?
> Ah me! their terrors and their glooms
>   Only the wretched inmate knows.

Whatever may have been the cause of his dissatisfac-
tion—whether it was because he felt that the instruction
was poor, whether it was because his room-mate was leaving for Yale, or whether because there was some other more
basic and more hidden restlessness—at the end of the third
term of the Sophomore year, in May 1811, he asked and
received his honorable dismissal. He returned to Cummington, his hopes set on entering Yale.

In this he was disappointed. After a summer of work on
the farm, when the beginning of the collegiate year approached, he was told by his father that the family means
did not permit of his being sent to the Connecticut college.
What was he to do? Evidently, at one time, it had been
hoped that he might carry on the family tradition and become a doctor. Wasn't his very name, William Cullen, the
name of a famous Scotch physician? But his father knew

only too well how hard was the life of a doctor and how small were its financial rewards. A life devoted wholly to literature was not to be thought of. Finally it was decided that Bryant should become a lawyer.

But before this decision was reached, there were months of inquietude and of unhappiness. Bryant sought solace in his father's library. He read his books on medicine; he became profoundly interested in chemistry and in botany. He read again in the poets and particularly in those of the "graveyard school." "The melancholy tone which prevails in them," Bryant later wrote, "deepened the interest with which I read them, for about that time I had, as young poets are apt to have, a liking for poetry of a querulous cast." Books alone did not suffice. Bryant turned to the source to which in later life he was to turn again and again for refuge and comfort; he turned to nature, to the country about him, and went on long, meditative rambles through the woods. Somehow, out of his desires, his questioning, his reading, and his meditation a new creation was fused. About this time, he wrote his first great poem, "Thanatopsis," his reaction to the thought of man's mortality, the poem that several years later was to be published and to startle the world into the knowledge that America had produced a poet. For the time being, significantly enough, Bryant showed these verses to no one, not even to his father, but laid them away in a to-be-forgotten desk drawer.

This period had a lasting effect upon Bryant. The realization of his poverty, the regret for his interrupted scholastic training—a regret he was never to lose—made him feel inferior to others, and drove him, diffident and reticent, in upon himself.

So it was a shy, ill at ease boy of 17 who, in December 1811, entered the law office of a Mr. Howe at Worthington, about five miles from Cummington. Here, relieved at least from the pressure of farm duties, he began his study of law and, at the same time, found an increasing opportunity to write poems.

After two and a half years, which saw the beginning and ending of a love affair, about which very little is known, Bryant left Worthington for the somewhat larger town of Bridgewater, where he continued his legal studies in the office of Mr. William Baylies. Mr. Baylies was a member of Congress and during his absences in Washington used his young law clerk to keep him informed on local political sentiment.

This sentiment soon crystallized into deep opposition to the War of 1812. As for Bryant, his individual reaction made him wish to become a soldier, not in the federal army to fight against England but in the state militia to protect Massachusetts against national action. In addition to his local patriotism, there was a still more personal motive behind his desire. In a letter to his father urging the desirability of his plan, he suggests that he does not wish to enter the legal profession "in all the greenness of a secluded education," that it would be easier to begin life as a lawyer "with my excessive bashfulness and rusticity rubbed off by a military life." He received his commission as adjutant in July 1816; but since peace had meanwhile been declared, he gave it up. Meanwhile, too, after successfully passing his law examinations, he had become of age and in 1815 had been admitted to the bar.

Studying law did not for Bryant preclude his continued interest in poetry. He wrote, experimenting with one verse form and another; and finally evolved for himself a simple, straight-forth manner of expression. To this period belong such poems as "The Yellow Violet" and "Inscription for the Entrance to a Wood" (originally known only as "Fragment"), poems which in method and mood set the key for much of Bryant's later work.

"Inscription" extols the woods as a haven from the world's hurts:

> Thou wilt find nothing here
> Of all that pained thee in the haunts of men,
> And made thee loathe thy life.

What of the world's "sorrows, crimes, and cares" had Bryant encountered? True, he declared that "no school of long experience" is needed to know these evils. But Bryant's contacts with the world had been so very, very short that one wonders whether the poem so much reflected his past life as it suggested the timidity with which he apprehended his future in "the haunts of men."

For only in a world of activity could his legal profession be useful. Where was he to practice law? The first choice of location, an unfortunate one, was Plainfield, a very small farming settlement about seven miles from Cummington. He went there in December 1815. The future to him appeared dark; he was despondent. As he walked over the hills to his new home and his new life, his spirits sank lower and lower. Then a flash!—a bird sailed across the sky. As in a previous crisis, Bryant found solace in nature's revelation. That night, comforted, he wrote "To a Waterfowl":

> Whither, midst falling dew,
> While glow the heavens with the last steps of day,
> Far, through their rosy depths, dost thou pursue
> Thy solitary way?
>
> .   .   .   .
>
> Thou'rt gone, the abyss of heaven
> Hath swallowed up thy form; yet, on my heart
> Deeply has sunk the lesson thou hast given,
> And shall not soon depart.

He who, from zone to zone,
Guides through the boundless sky thy certain flight,
In the long way that I must tread alone,
Will lead my steps aright.

Eight months were more than enough to prove that Plainfield had not been a wise selection. When a suggestion came that Bryant join the law firm of Mr. George H. Ives of Great Barrington, Massachusetts, it was accepted. In October 1816, Bryant entered his new work, acting at first as a partner in the firm, and then shortly taking over the entire practice.

At Great Barrington, he evidently played an active part in the town's life. He made a large number of personal and literary friends, among whom was Catharine M. Sedgwick, the writer, who lived in the near-by town of Stockbridge.

His literary powers were acknowledged: he was asked to give a Fourth of July oration, and to contribute to a book of hymns. He was made a tithing man of the church. At a salary of $5 a year, he was elected town clerk—the only public office he ever was willing to hold.

Curiously enough, in the records he kept, there are only two flaws: a blot on the recording of his own marriage, and an interlineation made necessary by the neglect to insert the mother's name in recording the birth of his own child. His wife was Fanny Fairchild. He had met her in Great Barrington. In his courting, he wrote her many poems, only one of which, "O Fairest of the Rural Maids," he ever permitted to be published. He had married her on June 11, 1821, in Great Barrington and there his first child was born.

It was while Bryant was in Great Barrington that *The North American Review* published "Thanatopsis." In June 1817, his father wrote him that Willard Phillips, an old Cummington acquaintance connected with the newly estab-

lished magazine, wished contributions to the review. Before
Bryant had the opportunity to prepare anything for publication, Dr. Bryant had found the verses written long before and, delighted with them, had left them merely with
his name at Mr. Phillips's home in Boston.

> Yet a few days, and thee
> The all-beholding sun shall see no more
> In all his course.

So the poem began in its original form. Phillips read and
was impressed. Another editor, Richard H. Dana, was more
than impressed. He was skeptical. "Ah! Phillips, you have
been imposed upon; no one on this side of the Atlantic is
capable of writing such verses." But the poem was published, together with "Inscription for the Entrance to a
Wood," in the September number.

Once the authorship of these poems was established,
Bryant's ability was recognized and acclaimed. In July
1818, he contributed to the magazine, as a review of a book
of poems, "An Essay on American Poetry," wherein he
urged greater independence from English models. In 1822,
he delivered the Phi Beta Kappa poem at Harvard, "The
Ages," and in it sketched the pageant of history in such a
way as to make it give promise of greater future happiness
to man:

> A thousand cheerful omens give
> Hope of yet happier days, whose dawn is nigh.

On the visit to Boston to deliver his poem, he met people
of importance, Harvard professors, the men publishing the
Review. A new world was opened to him. He was urged to
bring out a collection of his poems. He consented. A few
days after his return home to Great Barrington, the proofs
of his forty-four-page booklet reached him. In September

1821, *Poems* appeared. It was favorably reviewed in *The North American Review* for October and in the following year its poems, included in an English publication, *Specimens of English Poetry*, brought Bryant to English notice.

In *Poems*, "Thanatopsis" had a new form. In 1820, Bryant's father had died and in his grief, Bryant once again sought consolation in nature. What comfort he found, he again put into verse, enclosing the original lines of "Thanatopsis" in a frame of nature's words. The idea of the universality of death became nature's message; so, too, became the final note of trust, trust not in immortality but in righteous living. Nature proudly bids man:

> So live, that when thy summons comes to join
> The innumerable caravan, which moves
> To that mysterious realm, where each shall take
> His chamber in the silent halls of death,
> Thou go not, like the quarry-slave at night,
> Scourged to his dungeon, but sustained and soothed
> By an unfaltering trust, approach thy grave,
> Like one who wraps the drapery of his couch
> About him, and lies down to pleasant dreams.

The years at Great Barrington, devoted to law, had produced but few poems. Yet the desire to write persisted and grew stronger. With that increased desire, the practice of his profession became more and more irksome. How was he to escape?

In 1824, chiefly through the offices of Miss Sedgwick's brothers, Bryant paid a brief visit to New York. Henry Sedgwick urged that he make it his home; literary work would be open to him and his income from writing could be increased by teaching foreigners. The visit stimulated him so that, though returning to Great Barrington and law, he wrote a large number of poems. He had made connections with *The United States Literary Gazette* which paid him $2 a poem until the publishers arranged to pay him $200 a year for an average of one hundred lines of poetry a month. Through the *Gazette,* Bryant's fame became more general; the possibilities of success in a literary career seemed greater.

Should he give up the law? He hesitated; he consulted with his friends. A decision was rendered in one of his cases not in accordance with his ideas of fundamental justice. There were several other visits to New York. Bryant finally decided to try himself in the literary field.

In the spring of 1825, again in New York, he was made an editor of *The New York Review and Athenæum Magazine.* He returned to Great Barrington to put his affairs in order and to say his farewell in "A Forest Hymn":

> The groves were God's first temples.
>
> .   .   .   .   .
>
> . . . Be it ours to meditate,
> In these calm shades, thy milder majesty.
> And to the beautiful order of thy works
> Learn to conform the order of our lives.

While his family remained for the summer in Massachusetts, Bryant began his editorial labors in New York. However much he may have wondered about the possibility of future success, he knew only relief at having abandoned distasteful work. "In the meantime," he wrote to his wife, "I am not plagued with the disagreeable, disgusting drudgery of the law." In the fall, his family joined him and from that time New York was to become their permanent home.

The *Review* passed through various vicissitudes. It was merged with several other magazines. Its limited public grew still smaller. Bryant, fearful lest he lose all means of livelihood, applied for admission to the New York bar and, in one case at least, was associated with Henry Sedgwick. Opportunely, he was asked to serve as temporary assistant editor on the New York *Evening Post*. The position became a permanent one, Bryant still acting as an editor of the *Review*. Finally that magazine expired; and in 1829, Bryant became editor-in-chief of the *Post*.

Whether Bryant was ever consciously aware of the problem presented at the time of the publication of "The Embargo" years before, the problem of combining poetry and public life, one can never know. But the problem was there for him. Eager to escape from one profession in order to have freedom to write poetry, Bryant entered another, equally demanding. Bryant, the journalist, engrossed in making a living, ardent in the molding of public opinion, yielding to the demands of public life in New York, quite overwhelmed Bryant, the poet. The desire to write great poetry still existed. There was frequently expressed irritation at the exactions of his daily work: "But here am I a draught-horse, harnessed to a daily drag. I have so much to do with my legs and hoofs, struggling and pulling and kicking, that if there is anything of the Pegasus in me, I am too much exhausted to use my wings." Yet, even after he had acquired an ample fortune and might have retired, he continued his editorial work. Possibly only thus could he ease that early hurt of poverty and inferiority. It was not that he ceased to write poetry. He continued to write; but with a few exceptions, his poems seemed to be the product of a fugitive, detached life.

Although from the time of the *Post* connection, Bryant's life was much more the life of the journalist than of the poet, some knowledge of this aspect of him is necessary to an understanding of the man and of those later poems that are significant. Throughout his journalistic career, he insisted unquestioningly upon freedom, freedom of speech and of action, freedom in religion and in politics. Government, its machinery and operation, he believed should be reduced to the barest minimum to allow the greatest amount of individual liberty. He felt that slavery in the United States would, of itself, die out; but he finally allied himself with the Abolitionists on the principle of free speech. And when the Civil War broke out, he stood unalterably opposed to the South and uncompromisingly behind the Union cause. His editorial comment was always outspoken and fearless, devoted ever to what he thought right and just.

The demands of the times and of his career were wearing. Bryant needed escape, relief. The country home which he had bought at Roslyn, Long Island, gave him for many months of the year a happy refuge from New York life. There were, too, frequent trips to Europe. The letters that he wrote on these European trips were printed and eventually published in book form. For the most part they are matter of fact recounting of what any tourist might see. Bryant, on these trips, met the great of the world, the writers, the artists, the leaders of men; but his own innate sense of privacy and of reticence prevented his making them the subject of his comments.

He, in his turn, however, is described by Hawthorne, who met him in Rome in 1858. In *French and Italian Notes,* Hawthorne wrote:

"He presented himself now with a long white beard, such as a palmer might have worn as the growth of his long pilgrimages, a brow almost entirely bald, and what hair he has quite hoary; a forehead impending, yet not massive; dark, bushy eyebrows and keen eyes, without much softness in them; a dark and sallow complexion; a slender figure, bent a little with age, but at once alert and infirm. . . .

"He uttered neither passion nor poetry, but excellent

good sense, and accurate information, on whatever subject transpired; a very pleasant man to associate with, but rather cold, I should imagine, if one should seek to touch his heart with one's own."

Again, after meeting him in Florence, Hawthorne commented on the essential goodness of the man and then went on to say: "He is not eminently an affectionate man. I take him to be one who cannot get closely home to his sorrow, nor feel it so sensibly as he gladly would; and in consequence of that deficiency, the world lacks substance to him. It is partly the result, perhaps, of his not having sufficiently cultivated his emotional nature. His poetry shows it, and his personal intercourse, though kindly, does not stir one's blood in the least."

In addition to such geographically removed retreats as Roslyn and Europe, there was a more subjective one, that of his creative writing. In the most stressful times of the Civil War, he voiced his soul's longing for peace in such emotionally controlled poems as "The Return of the Birds" and "My Autumn Walk." A more satisfying escape from the war and greater protection from the world's blows were provided by those other poems, "Sella," and "The Little People of the Snow," fanciful poems, completely out of touch with reality.

If the specific events of the world of affairs seldom were made the subject of his poems, so too the events of his life were seldom thus signalized. His poetry was the poetry of thought after reflection, rather than the poetry of emotion evoked by a person or incident. There are, of course, occasional exceptions. "The Life That Is," for example, is a tender poem written when his wife was critically ill. But after Mrs. Bryant's death in 1866, it was characteristic that Bryant should set himself methodically to writing a new poetical translation of Homer: to write simply and fluently the Greek heroic narratives. That was intellectual, rather than emotional, employment.

There was a further reason for such literary activity. Bryant was now an old man and felt that there would be less drain on his energy and capacity if he devoted himself to the problem of method of expression rather than to that of method and material. His *Iliad* and *Odyssey* were well received, fitting culmination to a long literary career.

The *Odyssey* was published in 1871. In the seven years of life remaining, Bryant wrote some twelve or fifteen more poems. He had seen since the first collection, in 1821, various editions of his poetry published and popularly approved. As dean of American poets he held a secure literary position. His poems were simple, direct, unaffected, and easily understood.

Thus, too, could his life be characterized. Sincere, honest, good, his life as much as his works established him in general respect and deep esteem. He received many honors. He was elected to honorary societies, American and foreign. His seventieth and eightieth birthdays were made the occasions of nation-wide celebration, producing sincere tributes from the great of the country.

He remained in touch with events. A directness of manner and a felicity of address had made him a speaker in demand at public meetings of eulogy or dedication. On May 29, 1878, he was asked to dedicate a bust of the Italian patriot Mazzini in Central Park, New York. The closing words of his address were: "Remain for ages yet to come where we place thee, in this resort of millions; remain till the day shall dawn—far distant though it may be—when the rights and duties of human brotherhood shall be acknowledged by all the races of mankind."

These were the last words he ever spoke in public. At the close of the exercises he was taken ill. On June 12 he died. Two days later, in fulfillment of a wish he had once expressed,

> 'Twere pleasant, that in flowery June,

he was buried in Roslyn.

It is true that at no time did Bryant ever give himselt completely to his art, make any sacrifice to his poetry. But that part of him which he felt could be free to be the poet, that part which was withdrawn from studies, from the court, and from the editorial desk, was always loyal to the theory of poetry as he had developed it. "I don't invoke the muse at all," he once wrote. Poetry, which to him thus seemed no more divinely inspired than any other intellectual activity, he explained in a preface written for *A New Library of Poetry and Song:*

"The elements of poetry lie in natural objects, in the vicissitudes of human life, in the emotions of the human heart, and the relations of man to man. He who can present them in combinations and lights which at once affect the mind with a deep sense of their truth and beauty is the poet of his own age and the ages that succeed him."

He did not deny the necessity for the presence of truth and beauty; but he emphasized—overemphasized—the importance of an intellectual appeal. How was this appeal to be made? Negatively, in telling what to avoid, he elaborated his theory.

"There are two tendencies by which the seekers after poetic fame in our day are apt to be misled, through both the example of others and the applause of critics. One of these is the desire to extort admiration by striking novelties of expression, and the other, to distinguish themselves by subtleties of thought, remote from the common apprehension."

One other exposition of his theory should be noted, that in his own poem, "The Poet."

Deem not the framing of a deathless lay
The pastime of a drowsy summer day.
.   .   .   .
The secret wouldst thou know
To touch the heart or fire the blood at will?
Let thine own eyes o'erflow;
Let thy lips quiver with the passionate thrill;
Seize the great thought, ere yet its power be past
And bind, in words, the fleet emotion fast.

If one would write of tempests or of battles, he goes on to say,
                    make thyself a part
Of the great tumult.

It was for the very reason that Bryant could not make his own self a part of the great tumult that his own poetic range was limited. Once, in "Hymn of the City," Bryant shows his sympathy with the active world; but even here it is not with man's activity that he is concerned so much as it is with the city as an expression of the Divinity's presence:
                    Even here do I behold
Thy steps, Almighty!

For the rest, his attitude is more nearly that of the poem, "I Cannot Forget With What Fervid Devotion." Once he "worshipped the visions of verse and of fame"; but

Bright visions! I mixed with the world, and ye faded.

Only by withdrawal, could he keep his visions bright. The result is a lack of warmth and of richness. But those visions which he did retain, he expressed with a fidelity and simplicity that make them memorable.

Truth to experience was the keynote of his poetry. One of his brothers ventured to write a poem about a skylark. Bryant was indignant.

"Did you ever see such a bird? Let me counsel you to draw your images, in describing Nature, from what you observe around you, unless you are professedly composing a description of some foreign country, when, of course, you will learn what you can from books."

This material of observation and of reflection Bryant handled with an accuracy of rhyme and of meter. His early studies in prosody enabled him to use with ease a variety of verse forms: the modified ballad as in "Song of Marion's Men"; the Spenserian stanza as in "The Ages"; his favorite iambic tetrameter as in "To the Fringed Gentian"; blank verse with a masterly handling of the cæsura as in "Thanatopsis," "An Evening Revery," and "The Fountain."

There are occasional threadbare expressions, "verdant steeps," for example. There are manufactured words: "*whelm* from sight." There are even pedestrian lines which, except for the fact that they are divided into even lengths, might well be prose:

> Near our southwestern border, when a child
> Dies in the cabin of an Indian wife,
> She makes its funeral-couch of delicate furs,
> Blankets and bark.

But offsetting these are such expressions as,

> A silence, the brief sabbath of an hour;

and stanzas like this from "The Evening Wind":

Go—but the circle of eternal change,
Which is the life of Nature, shall restore,
With sounds and scents from all thy mighty range,
Thee to thy birthplace of the deep once more;
Sweet odors in the sea-air sweet and strange,
Shall tell the home-sick mariner of the shore;
And, listening to thy murmur, he shall deem
He hears the rustling leaf and running stream.

It was in such direct exposition of his thoughts that Bryant was at his best. His imagination was at best the imagination of a child building castles in fairyland, as in "Sella" or in "Castles in the Air." His handling of narrative was never very adroit. His tales proceed unexcitingly. The framework of the narrative is often heavy and pointless, as in "Children of the Snow." And, as must be obvious, there is little passion in his verse. (So cold did they seem to one critic that he suggested they be bound in fur.)

In fact, so removed does he seem from feelings and emotions that the world of his poetry appears a world without men and women. It is a world of ideas and these center primarily about nature. It is from this restricted field must come Bryant's claim to permanence.

True, from the time of "Thanatopsis" to that of "The Flood of Years," the extent of his creative activity, there was little development of ideas. The latter poem reëchoes the thought of the former; the boy was the man. But this is an indication not so much of immaturity as it is of the narrow range to which he restricted himself.

Primarily, Bryant was a poet of American nature. "The Yellow Violet,"

When beechen buds begin to swell,
And woods the blue-bird's warble know,

> The yellow violet's modest bell
> Peeps from the last year's leaves below.

"Robert of Lincoln,"

> Robert of Lincoln is telling his name:
> Bob-o'-link, bob-o'-link,
> Spink, spank, spink.

"To the Fringed Gentian,"

> Thou waitest late and com'st alone,
> When woods are bare and birds are flown,
> And frosts and shortening days portend
> The aged year is near his end.—

these poems, and many like them, are poems of the woods
he knew well. That there should be an American interpreta-
tion to these observations of nature, he suggests in "The
Painted Cup." Do not consider, he says, these bright flowers
cups for fairies:

> Call not up
> Amid this fresh and virgin solitude
> The faded fancies of an elder world.—
>
> .   .   .   .
>
> Let then the gentle Manitou of flowers,
> Lingering amid the bloomy waste he loves,
> Though all his swarthy worshippers are gone—
> Slender and small, his rounded cheek all brown
> And ruddy with the sunshine; let him come
> On summer mornings, when the blossoms wake,
> And part with little hands the spiky grass,
> And touching, with his cherry lips, the edge
> Of these bright beakers, drain the gathered dew.

In these poems there is the record of keen observation
of flowers and birds, keenness that must have been devel-

oped by those scientific studies of early manhood. But
tucked into such objectivity—sometimes, indeed, obtru-
sively inserted—there is almost inevitably some moral
teaching.

The yellow violet, for example, welcome as first of the
spring's flowers but forgotten in the richer bloom of May,
reminds him:

> So they, who climb to wealth, forget
> The friends in darker fortunes tried.
> I copied them—but I regret
> That I should ape the ways of pride.

There was for Bryant a parallel between the natural and
the moral world. Nature, for him, was something more than
a delight for the senses.

It was, in addition, a symbol of God's greatness and goodness. Because it revealed God to man it gave the opportunity for worship, for meditation, and for comfort.

It did one thing more: it suggested the mortality of all
things. In "The Fountain," "The Prairies," "Thanatopsis,"
the great cycles of nature and of race roll on; nature becomes the grave of the past and, at the same time, the cradle
of the future. All things are subject to the inexorable law
of change. Bryant, in thus making death simply a part of
movement and development, took it out of the realm of
theology where the New England religious attitude would
have wished it to remain to serve as goad or as punishment.
Bryant made it natural, a thing not to be feared.

If in "Thanatopsis," for example, this results in a pagan
attitude toward death, there is still evidence of Bryant's
belief in immortality of the soul. He expresses it in "The
Flood of Years." He expresses it in "The Future Life."

> Shalt thou not teach me, in that calmer home,
> The wisdom that I learned so ill in this—

> The wisdom which is love—till I become
> Thy fit companion in that land of bliss?

Bryant was essentially an ethical poet. Truth and justice were the qualities he emphasized; and nowhere did he extol them more exultingly than in the line of "The Battle-field," that often quoted line:

> Truth, crushed to earth, shall rise again.

Truth and justice were the admired virtues; and one other —freedom. "The Greek Partisan," "William Tell," "The Antiquity of Freedom," all bear witness to his staunch belief:

> Thy birthright was not given by human hands:
> Thou wert twin-born with man.

In America he saw the potentiality for the unhindered development of freedom. So a quiet form of patriotism is manifested in some of his poems, as in "Not Yet" and in "Oh Mother of a Mighty Race":

> Oh, fair young mother! on thy brow
> Shall sit a nobler grace than now.

Yet, somehow, there is something lacking in his manifestation of Americanism. One misses the vitality of the typical American spirit. There is no reflection of the contemporary great movements of American life, social and political. The institution of slavery, for example, is the immediate subject of only one poem, "The Death of Slavery"; the "Death of Lincoln" is one of the very few poems reflecting the waves of feeling that swept the country. In fact, Bryant as a poet seems only partially to belong to the nineteenth century.

Yet he cannot be brusquely thrust aside. Among the poems written for his seventieth birthday was one by Whittier:

> We praise not now the poet's art,
> The rounded beauty of his song;
> Who weighs him from his life apart
> Must do his nobler nature wrong.

Possibly the dignity and force of his life have in the past magnified his stature, evoking homage to the man. But any estimation of him as a poet must not overlook the fact that in his time Bryant was a vital force in American literature. With him poetry achieved an honored place in American life. As for the present—and the future—some few of his poems, "Thanatopsis," "A Forest Hymn," "To a Waterfowl," "To the Fringed Gentian" among them, will undoubtedly—and rightly so—continue to be part of America's poetic heritage.

RALPH WALDO EMERSON

THE LITTLE boy grew restless. The Sunday church service was long and the sermon dull. To amuse himself, to distract his mind from his aching body, he invented a game. He would take the word *black* and repeat it to himself over and over, twenty times, thirty times. Or the word *white*. Or some other equally common word, like *board*. "Board, board, board," the repetition continued until the word completely lost all significance. Stiff pews were forgotten; the sermon was unheard.

Years later, when the boy had grown up, he described this Sunday relaxation in his journal, adding to his description these sentences: "and I began to doubt which was the right name for the thing, when I saw that neither had any natural relation, but were all arbitrary. It was a child's first lesson in Idealism."

The young metaphysician was Ralph Waldo Emerson; the time, the beginning of the nineteenth century. In those days, there was no question that the place for any child on Sunday was in church with its long and many services. With Emerson, particularly, there was not room for even the shadow of a questioning. For behind him were there not generations of New England ancestors with their stern ideas of morality and of conduct, ancestors among whom were many ministers? Hadn't his grandfather, William Emerson, been a minister? Wasn't his step-grandfather, Ezra Ripley, a minister? And his own father, William Emerson? The Emerson theological strain was strong.

But in the case of his own father, the strain was somewhat tempered. William Emerson, a Harvard graduate of 1789, with a love for music and a strong desire for social life, had no very strong predilection for the ministry. Tradition, however, had chosen his profession for him. In the spring of 1799, about three years after his marriage to "the pious and amiable Ruth Haskins, fifth daughter of Mr. John Haskins of Rainsford's Lane, Boston," he was installed as minister of the First Church of Boston. There his services became known for his rich-voiced reading and the eloquence of his speech. There his own disposition inclined him toward liberalism in religion, leading him at one time to the point of planning a church without formal ritual. But the church did not claim all his interests. He was a member of a number of Massachusetts learned societies, a founder of Boston's Athenæum Library, and editor of *The Monthly Anthology,* a periodical liberal in religion, but conservative in politics and in literature.

In this atmosphere of religion and of culture, the atmosphere of what Oliver Wendell Holmes was to call the "Brahmin caste," William Emerson and his wife brought up their family. On May 25, 1803, the father casually noted in his diary the birth of his fourth child and third son: "Mr. Puffer preached his Election Sermon to great acceptance. This day also, whilst I was at dinner at Governor Strong's, my son Ralph Waldo was born. Mrs. E. well. Club at Mr. Adam's."

The Reverend William Emerson planned for Ralph, as for all his children, a well-grounded education. Instruction began early. He was disappointed that Ralph, not yet three, "does not read very well yet." When he was at home, the father heard each of his children recite a sentence of English grammar before breakfast. When he was away, he urged his wife to continue the practice, writing to her on one occasion that if she had not time to teach all the children and could attend to only one, Ralph, who had by then passed his third birthday, "should be that one."

Other children were born. The family grew larger and larger, far outpacing the father's income from the ministry. "We are poor and cold," William Emerson wrote, "and have little meal, and little wood, and little meat, but, thank God, courage enough." There was, as a matter of fact, a conscious rejection of material things when there was a necessary choice between them and intangible qualities of spirit and of character. So it was with an awareness of his situation that William Emerson wrote to his sister Mary Moody Emerson, a woman of strong character and of strange personality, "Our family, you know, have so long been in the habit of trusting Providence, that none of them ever seriously thought of providing a terrestrial maintenance for themselves and household."

True to this Emerson family tradition, the father died in May 1811, leaving his widow with six children, all under the age of ten, and with no financial provision for their future. The church of which he had been pastor came to his family's relief. It continued his salary for six months and for seven years gave $500 annually to Mrs. Emerson. This scant income Mrs. Emerson supplemented by taking boarders into her home.

The years that followed were marked by removals from one house to another, by gaunt poverty that necessitated Ralph and a brother sharing one overcoat between them, by hard work in which Ralph was called upon to do his part of the household labors. But though there was little time or opportunity for play, there were the adventures of the fields and woods about their homes.

> They took this valley for their toy,
> They played with it in every mood.

Something of memory for what he had enjoyed, and something more of regret for what had been denied him must have entered into that note on "Education" which Emerson wrote in his later years:

"Don't let them eat their seed-corn; don't let them anticipate, antedate, and be young men, before they have finished their boyhood. Let them have the fields and woods, and learn their secret and the base- and foot-ball, and wrestling, and brickbats, and suck all the strength and courage that lies for them in these games; let them ride bare-back, and catch their horse in his pasture, let them hook and spear their fish, and shin a post and a tall tree, and shoot their partridge and trap the woodchuck, before they begin to dress like collegians and sing in serenades, and make polite calls."

To the courageous poverty of his boyhood Emerson felt he owed the point of view that colored his later life. In his lecture on "Domestic Life," he said, "What is the hook that holds them staunch? It is the iron hand of poverty, of necessity, of austerity, which, excluding them from the sensual enjoyments which make other boys too early old, has directed their activity in safe and right channels and made them, despite themselves, reverers of the grand, the beautiful, and the good."

One other influence during these formative years must not be overlooked—the influence of Ralph's Aunt Mary. She paid frequent visits to the Emerson household and, even in her absences, maintained constant supervision over her nephews' well being. She it was who stiffened their souls with stern injunctions; to whom problems of thought and of conduct were presented; who laid down the guiding principle, "Always do what you are afraid to do." So when Aunt Mary said of her nephews, "They were born to be educated," sacrifices were made that they might have the proper schooling.

Ralph's schooling began in March 1806, when he first attended the Dame School of Mrs. Whitwell. In 1813 he entered the Boston Latin School and, at the same time, spent part of the school day at a private school where he received further instruction in writing and in ciphering.

While he was in the Latin School, echoes of the War of 1812 reached Boston. At one rumored threat of danger, the boys of the city, Ralph among them, were called upon to help build dirt breast-works. The martial note was seized upon as the subject of the verse that Ralph was then writing, high-flown conventionalized verse based on formalized eighteenth-century models. One result was an epic poem, "The History of Fortus, a Chivalric Poem, in one volume, complete; with Notes, Critical and Explanatory, by R. W. Emerson, LL.D." Something of its manner may be judged from a brief quotation:

> Fortus beholds—recovers breath,
> Then arms to do the work of death,
> Then like a Lion bounding o'er his foes
> Swift as the lightning he to combat goes.

Again, with the end of the war, Ralph wrote to his brother about the celebration of peace:

> Fair Peace triumphant blooms on golden wings,
> And War no more of all his victory sings.

Themes of a more familiar nature, however, soon stirred him to verse. One brother or another was away at preparatory school. To them Ralph would write the news of home, frequently putting some of it in verse form. After a year with Dr. Ripley in Concord, the family had moved to a new home in Boston, which Ralph thus described in a letter:

By boards and dirt and rubbish marr'd,
Upon the right a wicket gate,
The left appears a Jail of State.
Before, the view all boundless spreads,
And five tall chimneys lift their lofty heads.

A letter written in 1815 to his older brother ends:

And now, dear William, with a rhyme I'll close,
For you are tired, I may well suppose.
Besides, we soon shall hear the nightly bell
For prayers—so now farewell.

Ralph stayed on in Boston. He continued attendance at the Latin School until, at the age of fourteen, he was considered adequately prepared for college. In August 1817, he entered Harvard. It was necessary that he help defray the costs of his college education. He was appointed President's Freshman, an appointment which, in exchange for acting as the President's official messenger, gave him free lodgings. He was a waiter at Commons, and so saved his board bills. He did some tutoring, in addition, and between the college sessions taught school.

His work at Harvard was satisfactory, rather than brilliant. He heartily disliked mathematics; but enjoyed particularly his courses in Greek, in rhetoric, and in philosophy, building up for himself a vague dream of future renown in oratory. To encourage him in his hopes were the facts that his essays on "The Character of Socrates" and "The Present State of Ethical Philosophy" had won two Bowdoin prizes and that a declamation had won him a $30 Boylston Prize. This prize money, incidentally, he sent home hoping that with it his mother would buy a new shawl; instead it was used to pay food bills for the Emerson household. He was a member, too, of the Pythologian Club, a college club that offered opportunities for speaking and for writing. And he was reading widely on his own initiative,—Shakespeare, Montaigne, Swift, Addison, Steele, Milton, and Plato. His classmates recognized his interests and his ability by making him class poet. He expected, in fact, to be given the class poem on the Commencement program; but his only average standing in his work entitled him to a less conspicuous part and he was given instead the rôle of John Knox in a "Conference on the Characters of Knox, Penn, and Wesley." Graduating, at the age of eighteen, he felt that college had done little for him.

But one thing college did do for him. For it was while he was at Harvard that he began his habit, which he continued for more than fifty years, of keeping journals—his "wide worlds" or "savings banks," he called them—in which he wrote whatever came into his mind. In the earlier volumes are records of his readings, "phrases for use poetical," evidences of a conscious effort to build a literary style. Thus, an entry for June 1820 gives a glimpse of Emerson's reading:

"Have been of late reading patches of Barrow and Ben Jonson; and what the object—not curiosity? no—nor expectation of edification intellectual or moral—but merely because they are authors where vigorous phrases and quaint, peculiar words and expressions may be sought and found, the better 'to rattle out the battle of my thoughts.' "

Another in the same year indicates the florid and ornate style toward which current modes of expression and his own natural tendencies led him: "Spring has begun to unfold her beautiful array, to throw herself on wild-flower couches, to walk abroad on the hills and summon her songsters to do her sweet homage."

But in addition to such evidences of a conscious striving for literary expression, the early journals contained the record of Emerson's thoughts on life and action, a self-analysis that was frank, a revelation of the hopes and fears and disappointments that made up his life.

For despair and disappointment were to mark the years following his graduation. He suffered from the feeling that his abilities were not equal to his ambition. The profession he was to follow, the ministry, was one into which he drifted rather than one that he deeply desired. To achieve it, furthermore, he had to earn money and he did it by teaching school, an occupation that he disliked. In addition, he suffered from ill health, part of it to be traced to a family inheritance and part of it, doubtless, to the strain of his childhood's poverty. It is this dark picture that he draws of himself:

"The dreams of my childhood are all fading away and giving place to some very sober and very disgusting views of a quiet mediocrity of talents and condition—nor does it appear to me that any application of which I am capable, any efforts, any sacrifices, could at this moment restore any reasonableness to the familiar expectations of my earlier youth."

It was at the school of his brother William, held in his mother's home, that Ralph taught after his graduation from Harvard. For two years he acted as an assistant to his brother; then, when William left for study in Göttingen, he was in sole charge for six months. In school he was not at ease. The presence of his young women students embarrassed him, for except for his mother and his aunt the atmosphere in which he had grown up since the early death of his sister was wholly masculine. He confessed later that the real work of this period did not consist of his teaching, but of the reading and journal writing that he did at night; and that the glow and enthusiasm enkindled then he was unable to transmit to his pupils.

Indicative somewhat of the mental unrest of this period of his life was Emerson's request that his name be changed. Henceforth he wished to be called not Ralph, but Waldo. It was an evidence of that same desire for change and for escape that he manifested in a letter to his aunt: "Every man has a fairyland just beyond the compass of his horizon. . . . The poet yearns for . . . all unearthly things." Aunt Mary suggested that he needed seclusion in which to think calmly and constructively and reach a solution of his difficulties. Her suggestion and his own natural preferences led him to take long, solitary walks through the country, finding solace in his contacts with nature. At this time, in 1823, Mrs. Emerson moved to a farmhouse in Roxbury, about four miles from Boston. This change of home from the city to the country, although the Boston teaching continued, delighted Emerson. He seized the opportunity to bid a disillusioned farewell to Boston in the poem, "Good-Bye."

Good-bye, proud world! I'm going home:
Thou art not my friend, and I'm not thine.
Long through thy weary crowds I roam;
A river-ark on the ocean brine,
Long I've been tossed like the driven foam;
But now, proud world! I'm going home.

. . . . . .

O, when I am safe in my sylvan home,
I tread on the pride of Greece and Rome;
And when I am stretched beneath the pines,
Where the evening star so holy shines,
I laugh at the lore and the pride of man,
At the sophist schools and the learned clan;
For what are they all, in their high conceit,
When man in the bush with God may meet?

Behind the teaching that continued for several years, motivating Emerson to follow an occupation which he disliked, was the necessity to earn a living and to save enough money so that he might study for the profession on which he had decided. His journal for April 24, 1824, announces his decision: "I am beginning my professional studies. In a month I shall be legally a man; and I deliberately dedicate my time, my talents, and my hopes to the church." The ministry called him. He abandoned his earlier hopes that some college might offer him a professorship of rhetoric and elocution. He analyzed his capabilities. He possessed a strong imagination and "consequently a keen relish for the beauties of poetry." His reasoning faculty he declared "proportionably weak," but this weakness he considered no handicap to the ministry. "For, the highest species of reasoning upon divine subject is rather the fruit of a sort of moral imagination, than of the Reasoning Machines." In this declaration is the key to Emerson's decision and to the philosophical thinking that characterized his life; discovery of spiritual truth is dependent rather upon individual moral intuition than on coldly logical thought. The defects of his personality and abilities made him reject law and medicine as possible professions. The dictates of the Brahmin caste of New England left the ministry as the only remaining choice; Emerson's family tradition pointed to it; and he, himself, felt that he could follow it as well as, possibly better than, any other.

There were some preliminary questionings, puzzles of religious and moral points of view, that he wished answered. He went to his Aunt Mary for help; he went to Dr. Channing, one of the most noted ministers of the time. But these failed him. For his own solutions, he found, he had to depend upon himself and upon himself alone.

By the very beginning of 1825 he had planned to close his

school and to study at the Divinity School in Cambridge. In February, he took a room in Divinity Hall. But a month later, ill health forced him to leave and to seek recuperation at the farm of an uncle. Somewhat restored to health, he taught school again, and attended lectures at the Divinity School, but did not resume regular work there. In October 1826, without having formally finished his course, he was "approbated to preach" by the Middlesex Association of Ministers of Massachusetts.

Still he was not ready to begin his career. Ill health again upset his plans and in November 1826 he sailed south for Charleston, South Carolina. His Southern journey took him as far south as St. Augustine, Florida. It widened the field of his contacts and deepened his interests. He had his first glimpse of the horrors of Southern slavery and in Achille Murat, Napoleon's nephew, first met a religious unbeliever whose unbelief was founded on reasoned intelligence.

The return North was made in the spring. Emerson preached in various cities on the way. But that his sole interest did not lie in his profession is indicated by a letter to his brother, in which he wrote, "Shall I commence author? Of prose or of verse? Alack of both, the unwilling Muse."

Requests came to him from New England that he temporarily fill various pulpits. Preaching in Concord, New Hampshire, in December 1827, he first saw Ellen Tucker. A year later his engagement to her, then only seventeen, was announced. Before they could marry, his fiancée's ill health necessitated a trip to the South. The separation stimulated him to poetic expression. He wrote "Lines to Ellen" and "To Ellen at the South." In these, tenderly and simply, he expressed his personal feelings, creating delicate love poems, as he did in those other poems of this period, "Thine Eyes Still Shined":

When the redbird spread his shining wing,
  And showed his side of flame;
When the rosebud ripened to the rose,
  In both I read thy name.

and "To Ellen":

And Ellen, when the graybeard years
  Have brought us to life's evening hour,
And all the crowded Past appears
  A tiny scene of sun and shower,

Then, if I read the page aright
  Where Hope, the soothsayer, reads our lot,
Thyself shalt own the page was bright,
  Well that we loved, woe had we not,

When Mirth is dumb, and Flattery's fled,
  And mute thy music's dearest tone,
When all but Love itself is dead
  And all but deathless Reason gone.

In the fall of 1829 the two were married.

A few months before that, Emerson had been made minister of the Old North Church in Boston, the Second Congregational Church. He had for a time served as assistant to the minister, Dr. Ware; on the latter's retirement, however, he was appointed to fill his place. But his tenure was short and, in its brevity, troubled. He did not easily fill the pastoral duties of his office, the calling upon and making of personal contacts with the members of his congregation. Soon, too, the theological aspects of his office disturbed him. He found himself more interested in ethical principles than in doctrine. He felt that each moment of the universe was a new creation, a new miracle, a new revelation; and so he questioned the authority of the past. He objected to the rigidity of set prayers. And he found, at last, that he could not regard the Lord's Supper as a sacrament, urging that it be merely an act of commemoration. He set forth his views in a sermon to his congregation and awaited its decision as to whether or not he should continue in office.

The year before, his wife, again ill, had made another trip to the South. There she had died in the spring of 1831. The death of his wife, the removal of his responsibility to her, must have increased Emerson's sense of independence of action. For in the summer of 1832, after delivering his views to his congregation, he left Boston for the White Mountains to reconsider his position. He realized the necessity of a sense of proportion, of putting emphasis on the important. "I will not," he wrote in his journal, "because we may not all think alike of the means, fight so strenuously against the means, as to miss of the end which we all value alike." But he came to feel that the matter of attitude toward the Lord's Supper was the crux of a religious attitude in general and so he continued:

"I know very well that it is a bad sign in a man to be too conscientious, and stick at gnats. The most desperate scoundrels have been the over-refiners. Without accommodation society is impracticable. But this ordinance is esteemed the most sacred of religious institutions, and I cannot go habitually to an institution which they esteem holiest with indifference and dislike."

On his return to Boston, he offered his resignation and on October 28, 1832, it was accepted.

The emotional strain of his wife's death and of his own religious adjustment had its effect. Once again Emerson's health failed. This time he sought healing in a trip to Europe. On Christmas Day 1832 he sailed.

In the story of Emerson's intellectual development, this

European trip is most significant. His moral and spiritual views were beginning to crystallize. Nature, conceived as a continually opening book of revelation, offered in her laws the moral laws of the universe. Man, himself, held the key to them. "This strong-winged sea-gull," Emerson wrote in his journal, "and striped shear water that you have watched as they skimmed the waves under our vault,—they are works of art better worth your enthusiasm, masterpieces of eternal power; strictly eternal, because now active, and ye need not go so far to seek what ye would not seek at all if it were not within you." If Emerson, developing his views, had not yet complete reliance in himself, that was to come later. For the present, he felt that in the great men of Europe whom he wished to meet, Landor, Carlyle, Wordsworth, and Coleridge, he would find the elucidators of nature's truths.

He went to Italy and visited Naples and Rome. His poems, "Written in Naples," and "Written at Rome,"

And ever in the strife of your own thoughts
Obey the nobler impulse; that is Rome.

recall his visits. He went on to France. A visit in Paris to the Jardin des Plantes impressed upon him the unity, the essential harmony of composition in nature. "Not a form so grotesque, so savage, nor so beautiful but it is an expression of some property inherent in man the observer,—an occult relation between the very scorpions and man. I feel the centipede in me,—cayman, carp, eagle, and fox. I am moved by strange sympathies; I say continually, 'I will be a naturalist.' "

From France Emerson went to England and then to Scotland. He had on his journey met his four great men. The day when first he saw Carlyle he called a "white day in my life"; on it began a friendship that lasted throughout his life. But in each of his great men he recognized some weakness, some element of common humanity.

His traveling experiences cured him of an earlier provincial reverence for Europe and for England, particularly. They cured him, too, of whatever remained of a reverential attitude toward other people. Henceforth, he, himself, was to be his own authority for thought and conduct. "I shall judge men justly, less timidly of wise men forevermore." On the return voyage in September 1833, he wrote out his own Declaration of Independence, a creed that included these definite and ringing statements:

"A man contains all that is needful to his government within himself. He is made a law unto himself. All real good and evil that can befall him must be from himself. He only can do himself any good or any harm. . . . The purpose of life seems to be to acquaint a man with himself. He is not to live to the future as described to him, but to live to the real future by living to the real present. The highest revelation is that God is in every man."

On his return to America, he joined his mother at Newton near Boston. He resumed occasional preachings and he began his career as a lecturer with a series of lectures in Boston for the Society of Natural History. The purpose of this course was to explain man to himself. There followed a series on great men, two of the lectures, those on Michelangelo and on Milton, seeing publication later in *The North American Review*. In these first efforts to express his views to a public, Emerson was carefully feeling his way. In November 1834, however, he recorded his determination to be outspoken, unafraid. "Henceforth I design not to utter any speech, poem or book that is not entirely and peculiarly my work." Thereafter he found that he could say from the platform—and have eagerly accepted—things that he could not say from the pulpit.

One of Emerson's visits had taken him to Plymouth, where he met Miss Lydia Jackson. Shortly after, he became engaged to her. At Concord, seventeen miles from Boston, he bought a house, where he and his bride could begin their married life. He planned, too, that his mother and a younger brother should live with them. Concord, founded by one of Emerson's ancestors, welcomed its new citizen. Though he was retiring and found it difficult to mingle in the casual social life of the town, he soon filled a respected place in the community. In September he was asked to make the address commemorating the two hundredth anniversary of Concord. Two days later, he married Miss Jackson, whose name for the sake of euphony he asked her to change from Lydia to Lidian.

Married, he made his home in the house he had bought. Thereafter, his life was to be identified with Concord. Community responsibility was to appoint him to the office of "hog-reeve." Social activity was to make him a member of Concord's Social Club. But the life he was to lead in Concord was to be primarily a life of the mind and the spirit, a working out of his thoughts in prose and in verse.

For now, more than ever, he clung to his idea of the function of a poet. In a letter written to Miss Jackson during their engagement, he had made clear his attitude:

"I am born a poet,—of a low class without doubt, yet a poet. That is my nature and vocation. My singing, be sure, is very husky, and is for the most part in prose. Still I am a poet in the sense of a perceiver and dear lover of harmonies that are in the soul and in matter, and specially of the correspondence between these and those."

There now began, with his establishment at Concord, the period of Emerson's greatest literary productivity. To realize in any degree its import, it is necessary to see Emerson, however sketchily, against a background of his time. It was a period of growing industrialism and of increasing wealth in America. Side by side with the increase in physical wealth and a material well-being, there arose a steady challenging of the past, of traditions of religion and of loyalties, and a questioning of the future with its trends and potentialities. It was a time for reforms of all sorts, for furious idealism, and for considered thought-testing.

By 1836 Emerson had some of his views in a form ready for publication. In that year appeared his essay *Nature*. Nature, Emerson explained, in addition to its outward, objective beauty, served another function; it, together with man, was the expression of Divinity. Natural facts thus became the symbols of spiritual facts; and nature became the means through which Universal Spirit—or God—speaks to the individual. When man's will submits to the divine inspiration, man too becomes a creator; and, in so far as he does, he becomes part of divinity, a goal which he is constantly seeking.

The book, it is true, aroused at the time but little interest. Yet Emerson was becoming better known. The following year he was asked to give the Phi Beta Kappa address at Harvard where, two years before, he had read the Phi Beta Kappa poem. He chose as his subject "The American Scholar" and issued his proclamation of intellectual independence. The Present is the all-important, he declared; for inherent in it are the Past and the Future. Examine and reject the out-worn relics of the past. Develop self-reliance. "If the single man plant himself indomitably on his instincts, and there abide, the huge world will come round to him."

Where would such principles finally lead Emerson? Could they be logically applied in every field of human activity? In 1838, when Emerson addressed the graduating class of the Divinity School at Cambridge, he made it clear that this principle of independence, of rejection of obsolete authority,

was to be carried into religion itself. Moral laws execute
themselves; "he who does a good deed is instantly enno-
bled." Man is not a depraved creature, he challenged orthodox theology, but is born to be good and in so far as he is
good and just, then so far "is he God." Jesus, instead of
being the founder of a ritualistic religion, was simply one of
a long line who were "true to what is in you and in me."
Gradually, Emerson led his audience to his climax. "Let me
admonish you, first of all, to go alone; to refuse the good
models, even those which are sacred in the imagination of
men, and dare to love God without mediator or veil." Such
a complete casting off of tradition and authority was a challenge to established churches and their creeds. Emerson and
his views became the center of bitter controversy. A reflection of the bitterness, of the upheaval, of the effect upon
Emerson of this crisis in his intellectual life, is caught in
"Uriel," his parable-poem:

> As Uriel spoke with piercing eye,
> A shudder ran around the sky;
> The stern old war-gods shook their heads,
> The seraphs frowned from myrtle-beds;
> Seemed to the holy festival
> The rash word boded ill to all;
> The balance-beam of Fate was bent;
> The bounds of good and ill were rent;
> Strong Hades could not keep his own,
> But all slid to confusion.

Gradually Emerson's ideas and views were developed,
added to, and modified. The notes he made in his journal he
collected, classified by subject, knitted them together—
sometimes strongly, sometimes weakly—and made them the
material for his lectures. These in turn he worked over so
that they might appear in printed form. As *Essays* they

were published—the first series in 1841, the second in 1844. "Self-Reliance," "Compensation," "Love," "Friendship," "The Over-Soul," "Circles," "The Poet," "Experience," "Character"—these are some of the subjects which he elaborated.

As his residence in Concord continued, as his place in intellectual and literary America became more securely established, Emerson drew around him a circle of thinkers, among whom were Alcott, Thoreau, Margaret Fuller, Elizabeth Peabody. He was a member, too, of the Hedge Club, or Symposium, a discussion club, whose members had in one way or another been influenced individually by current German philosophical thought. The belief that ultimate truth could be learned through Understanding or Intuition, rather than through Reason, earned for this group the name of Transcendentalists. From this group sprang *The Dial,* a magazine edited for a time by Margaret Fuller and later by Emerson, himself, and one which was the vehicle for much of his poetry.

If Emerson did identify himself with this group of people, he was nevertheless chary of other groups. He suspected all organizations and institutions. So the attempt on the part of some of the Transcendentalists to put their abstract ideas into concrete form in the Brook Farm experiment did not receive Emerson's coöperation. Brook Farm Emerson called "a room in the Astor House hired for Transcendentalists." His insistence upon individualism and, very possibly too, his Yankee canniness, kept him aloof from the experiment. "So I stay where I am, even with the degradation of owning bank-stock and seeing poor men suffer whilst the universal genius apprises me of this disgrace and beckons me to the martyr's and redeemer's office."

It was not that Emerson was an airy idealist, content simply to see his theories in the form of words. He tried in his own household to break down class lines between master and servant; he tried in his own garden, with Thoreau's help, to carry out his ideas of simple manual labor. But when these plans failed, he acknowledged the force of reality and realized that in the universe a sense of proportion is necessary, that the whole is made up of a number of varying, but all necessary, parts. "When the terrestrial corn, beets, onions, and tomatoes flourish, the celestial archetypes do not." And Emerson's concern was with the archetypes. "The writer shall not dig. To be sure, he may work in the garden, but his stay there must be measured, not by the need of the garden, but of the study."

There was, however, one social movement in which Emerson did take part. The Abolition cause had not at first aroused his active enthusiasm; but when Judge Hoar, the father of his dead brother's fiancée, was compelled in 1844 to leave Charleston because of his Abolition sympathies, Emerson definitely allied himself with the movement. In August 1844 he delivered a lecture on Abolition. When the Fugitive Slave Law was passed, he declared it one "which no man can obey or abet the obeying without loss of self-respect and of forfeiture of the name of a gentleman." His attitude at first was not the urging of emancipation; he believed rather that slavery should be confined to the slave states and that the states should be helped to end it. But when the Union was threatened, Emerson's views changed; all his sympathies were thrown on the Northern side. "Let us respect the Union to all honest ends, but let us also respect an older and wider union: the laws of nature and rectitude." The day that the Emancipation Proclamation went into effect, January 1, 1863, Emerson's "Boston Hymn" was read in the Boston Music Hall:

> I break your bonds and masterships,
> And I unchain the slave:
> Free be his heart and hand henceforth
> As wind and wandering wave.
>
> .   .   .   .   .
>
> To-day unbind the captive,
> So only are ye un-bound;
> Lift up a people from the dust,
> Trump of their rescue, sound!

The Civil War had caused his income to shrink. The lectures which he had been giving yearly since 1834 were relied upon more and more as sources of financial gain. His early fame had resulted in an invitation to lecture in England. In 1847 he had sailed again to Europe. He had lectured in England, met Carlyle once again, gathered material for a book on *English Traits,* had seen the Revolution in France, and returned to America bringing with him a "contentedness with home."

From 1850 on for twenty years, for two months in the year, he lectured through the country, his travels taking him as far west as St. Louis. The absurdities of his trips he enjoyed, the discomforts of his travels he bore patiently. His lectures he saw in the nature of a wager. " 'I'll bet you fifty dollars a day that you will not leave your library, and wade and ride and run and suffer all manner of indignities and stand up for an hour each night reading in a hall,' and I answered, 'I'll bet I will.' I do it and win the $900."

These lecture trips introduced Emerson to vast numbers of people who might otherwise not have known him or his writings. For his part, they supplemented his income and helped him provide for his family at Concord. They were, after all, interludes in his Concord life, the life of thought and of family relations.

The Concord household had gone through many changes. Emerson had seen the deaths of two brothers and had mourned for them as for a part of himself. His mother died. To him and his wife, four children were born, two boys and two girls. The death in 1842 of the oldest son Waldo, a child of five, was a terrific blow from which Emerson recovered only with great difficulty. "Threnody" is the poet's lament for his son:

> The South-wind brings
> Life, sunshine and desire,
> And on every mount and meadow
> Breathes aromatic fire;
> But over the dead he has no power,
> The lost, the lost, he cannot restore;
> And looking over the hills, I mourn
> The darling you shall not return.

In it he expresses the consolation which finally came to him:

> *"What is excellent,*
> *As God lives, is permanent;*
> *Hearts are dust, hearts' loves remain;*
> *Heart's love will meet thee again."*

Emerson's poetry had become sufficiently well known to produce in 1843 a request for a volume of verse. His poems were collected, made ready for the press and in 1846 appeared in book form, *Poems*. There followed several volumes of essays, made up of his travel observations and his lecture materials. His writings stimulated people; but they never offered a complete philosophy nor formed the basis for an organized school of thought. Such would indeed have been a contradiction of all that Emerson held vital.

But in his own lifetime Emerson as a thinker touched the lives of many and influenced them in thought and action.

His position in the country was acknowledged. In 1863, President Lincoln appointed him to the Board of Visitors to West Point. In 1866, Harvard, whose doors had been shut to him since his Divinity School address, gave him the degree of LL.D. and made him an Overseer. In 1867, he was once more invited to deliver the Phi Beta Kappa address and to conduct a course of lectures in Philosophy. That same year saw the publication of his second book of poems, *May Day*.

Emerson was now growing old. He confessed to the feeling of age in his poem, "Terminus":

It is time to be old,
To take in sail:—

Then, in the summer of 1872, he received a shock that seriously affected him. One July night, during a rainstorm, his house burned. The excitement, the strain of rescuing his books and papers, the exposure, all had their effect in undermining his health. Friends rallied to his aid. Funds were raised for rebuilding his home; they were graciously offered and as graciously accepted. While work was going on, Emerson and his daughter sailed once again for Europe and for a visit to Egypt. On their return, Emerson received a soul-heartening welcome from Concord.

But it was a very old man who returned, one who clearly showed his age. His memory failed him; words, even for the most common objects, eluded him. He continued his lectures, including one before a not altogether reconciled Southern audience at the University of Virginia; but in these he needed constant help in keeping his place in his notes, in providing the right words in his speech. He grew weaker and weaker, "fading out like an old photograph." On April 27, 1882, he died.

Emerson, as has been said, did not perfect a system of

philosophy; nor did he gather about him a group of disciples. "It did not go," he wrote in his journal, "from any wish in me to bring men to me, but to themselves." His influence was a personal one, a challenge to the best in the individual man. Hawthorne gives a picture that suggests the force not only of his thoughts, but of his personality:

"It was so good to meet him in the woodpaths or sometimes in our avenue, with that pure intellectual gleam diffusing about his presence like the garment of a shining one; and he, so quiet, so simple, so without pretension, encountering each man alive as if expecting to receive more than he would impart."

No less revealing is the story that some humble working woman announced that she was going to one of Emerson's lectures. She was asked whether she understood him. "Not a word," she replied, "but I like to go and see him stand up there and look as if he thought every one was as good as he was."

This belief in essential goodness is fundamental to his poetry. If one remembers this and recalls, too, those other most important beliefs of his, such poems as have won for him the reputation of being hazy, vague, muddled, or unintelligible, will take on a greater degree of clarity; for his poems, as much as his essays, were the expressions of his philosophical beliefs.

Emerson believed that the Divine Will was continually creating, continually revealing itself to man. Since this is so, he went on, the present is the all important, holding within it both the past and the future.

Shines the last age, the next with hope is seen,
To-day slinks poorly off unmarked between;
Future or Past no richer secret folds,
O friendless Present! than thy bosom holds.

The constantly renewing miracle of creation is, according to Emerson, the manifestation of a single force; an essential unity underlies the universe; man and nature are simply different manifestations of the same power. This idea Emerson expressed in "The Sphinx":

> Sea, earth, air, sound, silence,
> Plant, quadruped, bird,
> By one music enchanted,
> One duty stirred,—

The same thought he developed further in "Brahma," the poem which evoked so many ridiculing parodies, the poem which to one without some conception of Emerson's philosophy appears almost incomprehensible:

> If the red slayer thinks he slays,
> Or if the slain thinks he is slain,
> They know not well the subtle ways
> I keep, and pass, and turn again.
> .   .   .   .   .
> They reckon ill who leave me out;
> When me they fly, I am the wings;
> I am the doubter and the doubt,
> And I the hymn the Brahmin sings.

The correspondence between man and nature is so close that in the latter man can seek and find the same moral laws that govern his life.

> Out from the heart of nature rolled
> The burdens of the Bible old.

Truth is to be found in the smallest as well as in the great:

> As sings the pine-tree in the wind,
> So sings in the wind a sprig of the pine;

Her strength and soul has laughing France
Shed in each drop of wine.

But, Emerson added with what at first might seem a contradiction, the small, the isolated, reveals the truth only because it is part and only in so far as it is part of the "perfect whole." In "The Fable" both the mountain and the
squirrel have a part to play; in "Each and All" the same
idea is expressed:

All are needed by each one;
Nothing is fair or good alone.

Operating throughout this universe, the balance-beam of
seeming opposites and contradictions, is the law of compensation. Every action carries within itself its own immediate effect; goodness has its own reward, evil its punishment.

And Nemesis,
Who with even matches odd,
Who athwart space redresses
The partial wrong,
Fills the just period,
And finishes the song.

Nature, as the theatre of the operation of such laws, the
laws themselves—all these are secondary to man. And by
man Emerson meant any man, every man. It was the "in-
finitude of the private man" that Emerson preached; each
one must look to himself for authority and for sanction:

Go where he will, the wise man is at home.

And what is the seal of truth in understanding the laws
of the universe, the seal of goodness in yielding to them?
Emerson answered "Beauty"; the beauty of his poem "The

Rhodora," the beauty of the dipping paddles in "Wood-notes," the beauty in "Each and All":

> Beauty through my senses stole;
> I yielded myself to the perfect whole.

Misused, such doctrines could be pernicious, could be made the excuses for excess in conduct. Rightly interpreted, however, they were stimulating calls to lofty thinking and to right conduct. For they were to be interpreted in the light of Emerson's belief: "My creed is very simple, that Goodness is the only Reality, that to Goodness alone can we trust, to that we may trust all and always; beautiful and blessed and blessing is it, even though it should seem to slay me."

There is little wonder that America, hearing this creed expressed in Emerson's lectures, or reading it in his essays or poems, was stimulated and uplifted. However much Emerson's personality may have added to the force of his lectures, there is no question that the field of his influence was widened by his printed works. Lectures—and essays as their revised form—and poems were all the reworked version of his journal entries. How close is the correspondence between poem and journal can be illustrated by comparing the poem "Each and All" with the entry for May 16, 1834. "I remember when I was a boy going upon the beach and being charmed with the colors and forms of the shells. I picked up many and put them in my pocket. When I got home I could find nothing that I gathered—nothing but some dry, ugly mussel and snail shells. Thence I learned that composition was more important than the individual forms to effect. On the shore they lay wet and social by the sea and under the sky."

If his essays provided Emerson with a medium of expression, why, then, did he resort to verse at all? In the first place, he wrote some few lyrics, like his poems to Ellen and

"Give All to Love," which could have verse as their only possible form. But there was, furthermore, a definite belief in the poet's function that made Emerson write. For him it was the poet, rather than the reasoner, who was the right philosopher.

> The gods talk in the breath of the woods,
> They talk in the shaken pine,
> And fill the long reach of the old seashore
> With dialogue divine;
> And the poet who overhears
> Some random word they say
> Is the fated man of men
> Whom the ages must obey.

This is the poet of "Merlin," the poet of "Saadi." True, this poet is a being somewhat different from a mere master of prosody; he uses not "metres, but a metre-making argument." Yet always the language of the poet has been something other than prose; and Emerson modified to his use the meters and rhymes of the poets.

But, in keeping with his basic conception of the poet's purpose, he began with ideas rather than emotions. Poetry was his instrument rather than his end.

Blank verse would be the meter naturally suited to such a purpose. But this Emerson used only infrequently and then not most happily. More usually it was a shorter line that he employed; and if it was not always so short as in the following quotation from "Ode Inscribed to W. H. Channing," still that poem is typically Emersonian in effect:

> 'Tis fit the forest fall,
> The steep be graded,
> The mountain tunnelled,
> The sand shaded.

Sometimes, indeed, the line seems too short to bear the dignity of the idea. And sometimes, as in "May Day," the inspiration is not sustained throughout the poems.

Weaknesses in the mechanics of poetry are unquestionably present. Forced rhymes are numerous: rhymes like *mourn—return; art—bard; coats—spots*. Inversions, such as

> In plains that room for shadows make
> Of skirting hills to lie.

are annoying. Meters are frequently halting. One hesitates in reading

> None save dappling shadows climb,
> Under clouds, my lonely head,
> Old as the sun, old almost as the shade.

or

> And ever by delicate powers
> Gathering along the centuries.

But if Emerson had small ear for music, "the lack of *musical ear* is made good to me through my eyes; that which others hear, I see." He was able thus to pick out unerringly picture-creating words:

Wings of time are pied with morning and with night.

The bumble-bee is a "yellow-breeched philosopher." This instinct for the exact word led him to the creation of such completely perfect expressions as "tumultuous privacy of storm," "frolic architecture of the snow."

Nor was it only in details that Emerson showed his skill. He wrote true poetry, sustained poetry, and perfect poems in "The Rhodora," "Concord Hymn," "The Snow-Storm," and "Days,"

Daughters of Time, the hypocritic Days,
Muffled and dumb like barefoot dervishes,
And marching single in an endless file,
Bring diadems and fagots in their hands.
To each they offer gifts after his will,
Bread, kingdoms, stars, and sky that holds them all.
I, in my pleached garden, watched the pomp,
Forgot my morning wishes, hastily
Took a few herbs and apples, and the Day
Turned and departed silent. I, too late,
Under her solemn fillet saw the scorn.

If some few poems are memorable in their entirety, it is more usually a thought succinctly expressed in a line or two that remains unforgettable. Lines like

For there's no rood has not a star above it

or

Line in nature is not found;
Unit and universe are round.

are so entirely right that they have passed into the common currency of expression. Emerson's poetic gift was at his best in such epigrammatic form, in poems like the following quatrain:

Teach me your mood, O patient stars!
Who climb each night the ancient sky,
Leaving on space no shade, no scars;
No trace of age, no fear to die.

Words for the sake of words, even ideas for the sake of ideas, were to Emerson idle.

That book is good
Which puts me in a working mood.

So, by the standards which he himself set, one must judge Emerson not only in himself but as he influenced others. It is not simply that he gave a courageous lift to the thought of his contemporaries. It is rather that he unmistakably helped establish a point of view for modern thinkers, helped clear the way to freedom of expression for those writing today.

One must recognize first his underlying independence of soul. That impelled him to cast off allegiance to European countries and to European literary models. Always he insisted upon Americanism in American writers. His poetry is colored not only with references to purely American scenes but with intensely American spirit.

His independence led him, furthermore, to individuality of method. "I wish to write such rhymes as shall not suggest a restraint, but contrariwise the wildest freedom," he wrote in his journal. And again, "I do perceive that the finest rhythms and cadences of poetry are yet unfound." In his search for them, indeed in his creation of them, he definitely rejected the rules of meter and of rhyme that earlier prosody had dictated. He used, when it suited him, indefinite verse forms, unrhymed, and rhythmic rather than metric. In this the *vers-libre* of a later generation found a definite forerunner.

So modern a note is but intensified by his general attitude toward the poetic. In his essay on "Poetry" he wrote:

"Readers of poetry see the factory-village and the railway, and fancy that the poetry of the landscape is broken up by them—for these works of art are not yet consecrated in their reading; but the poet sees them fall within the great order not less than the beehive or the spider's geometrical web. Nature adopts them very fast into her vital circles, and the gliding train of cars she loves like her own."

> But in the mud and scum of things
> There always, always something sings.

Thus he expressed the same idea in a fragment of his poem, "The Poet." Thus he showed the way to those who sang after him, the way to a greater field of the poetic.

To include in the poetic the lowly as well as the great, the factory as well as the beehive, was an absolutely necessary result of his philosophic belief in the essential unity of the universe. Since all were the results of one cause, they must have something in common with that cause. For Emerson this was part of his religious faith.

In this point of view, he was no less scientific than the scientist who today seeks a single universal principle. Emerson had no quarrel with science. "The Religion that is afraid of science dishonors God and commits suicide." As there was no conflict between religion seeking the good and science seeking the truth, so there was no conflict between science and poetry. The modernity of Emerson cannot be better suggested than it was when Samuel McChord Crothers wrote of him,[1] "What the scientist discovered to be true, the poet saw to be beautiful."

[1] *Ralph Waldo Emerson; How to Know Him,* Bobbs-Merrill Co.

HENRY WADSWORTH
LONGFELLOW

BETTER, perhaps, than any other poet, Henry Wadsworth Longfellow expressed the feelings, thoughts, and ideals of the average American of his generation. A belief in the homely virtues, a sentimental romanticism, a simple faith, these colored—or, possibly, bleached—by a didactic morality were the substance of many of the poems by which he rose to fame and through which he became his countrymen's accepted spokesman. Later, as styles in thought as well as in verse changed, it became the fashion to ridicule this unassuming poet, to criticize and condemn him for those very qualities for which an earlier generation had admired him. At the present, a fresh evaluation may not be amiss.

That Longfellow chose the simple rather than the magnificent as theme for most of his poetry is scarcely valid ground for criticism. He, himself, felt his place to be among the minor poets. *The Waif*, a collection of verse which he edited, had as its proem his own poem, "The Day is Done," the poem which includes these stanzas:

> Come, read to me some poem,
>   Some simple and heartfelt lay,
> That shall soothe this restless feeling,
>   And banish the thoughts of day.
>
>   .   .   .   .   .
>
> Read from some humbler poet,
>   Whose songs gushed from his heart,
> As showers from the clouds of summer,
>   Or tears from the eyelids start;

Who, through long days of labor,
And nights devoid of ease,
Still heard in his soul the music
Of wonderful melodies.

These stanzas come very close to self-characterization. In one respect, however, his own poems fall short of this description: they lack that force and inevitability which one might expect of songs that "gush from his heart." They appear rather to be the refined and worked-over—even if simple—expression of feelings that have been restrained; the response to emotion that one has been taught should be made rather than the response one would naturally make.

"Be bold! be bold!" and everywhere, "Be bold;
Be not too bold!" Yet better the excess
Than the defect; better the more than less;
Better like Hector in the field to die,
Than like a perfumed Paris turn and fly.

Thus Longfellow wrote in his "Morituri Salutamus." But thus, he, himself, did not live. His life—and it is revealed in his poetry—was a life of restraint, of retreat. It was a life of reflection rather than of activity, of shade rather than of sunlight:

From the cool cisterns of the midnight air
My spirit drank repose;
The fountain of perpetual peace flows there,—
From those deep cisterns flows.

It was a life that made the title of his first book, *Voices of the Night,* peculiarly appropriate as a key to his personality and to his writings.

His early life was that of a beloved and carefully tended son in a well-to-do New England family. Longfellows had been in Massachusetts since 1676 and had produced a fam-

ily of teachers, lawyers, and judges. The Wadsworths, Longfellow's maternal ancestors, had first come to Boston in
1632. In both families was the tradition of education and
culture; Harvard figured frequently as the college of their
sons. Stephen Longfellow, the poet's grandfather, was a
surveyor; he represented his town in the General Court of
Massachusetts and was a Judge of the Court of Common
Pleas. Peleg Wadsworth, the poet's other grandfather, had
been a general in the Revolution, Adjutant-General of State,
and was a wealthy merchant of Portland. In 1804 the latter's daughter, Zilpah, married Stephen Longfellow, a lawyer. The young couple made their home in Portland which,
together with what is now all the state of Maine, was then
part of Massachusetts.

On February 27, 1807, their second son was born, Henry
Wadsworth Longfellow, named for his uncle Henry Wadsworth, who had lost his life in the expedition against Tripoli.
The Longfellow family grew; there were four sons and
four daughters. An aunt, Lucia Wadsworth, made her home
with them. But the household, though large, was one of
plenty and of gracious order. The father was an upright
dignified man, noted for his old-fashioned courtesy; the
mother was known for her tenderness, her love of nature
and of poetry. In both parents, the old rigid New England
Puritanism had yielded to the more generous Unitarianism.
A religious atmosphere was not lacking; moral right living
was insisted upon and Sundays were days of "meetings"
and of family hymn singing. But the traditional sternness
was gone. The children played joyous games. They attended
singing school and dancing school. A well-supplied library
was theirs to enjoy.

Life in Portland was in those days an adventure in itself.
The city, a seaport, suffered for a time from Jefferson's em-

bargo policy. But with the War of 1812 came renewed commercial activity. Its harbor was filled with ships. In constant touch with the world abroad, it was busy, hustling, alive. It formed a background to Longfellow's boyhood memories:

> I remember the black wharves and the slips,
>   And the sea-tides tossing free;
> And Spanish sailors with bearded lips,
> And the beauty and mystery of the ships,
>   And the magic of the sea.
>   And the voice of that wayward song
>   Is singing and saying still:
>   "A boy's will is the wind's will,
> And the thoughts of youth are long, long thoughts."

In that harbor, Longfellow saw the sea fight between the *Enterprise* and the *Boxer* in the War of 1812. The martial atmosphere of the town did not leave the little boy untouched. In May 1812, his Aunt Lucia wrote of him: "Our little Henry is ready to march; he had his tin gun prepared and his head powdered a week ago." A year and a half later, his strongest desire was for a drum, for which he asked in the first letter he ever wrote his father.

"Dear Papa—

Ann wants a little Bible like Betsey's. Will you please buy her one, if you can find any in Boston. I have been to school all the week, and got only seven marks. I shall have a billet on Monday. I wish you to buy me a drum.

Henry W. Longfellow."

Tin guns and drums, however, must have been his concession to the stress of the times. They do not fit into the consistent picture that is drawn of him—a brown-haired, blue-eyed boy with delicate complexion, a boy who is sensitive, and conscientious, who is neat, and who dislikes loud noises and excitement.

As a matter of fact, it was because of the roughness of the boys at the public town school that Henry Longfellow's stay there was limited to one week. Before that, when he was but three, he had gone to Ma'am Fellows's school. "She," he afterwards wrote, "inspired me with one trait,— that is, a genuine respect for my elders." The public school proving impossible—an early instance of the poet's attitude in the face of difficulty—the boy at the age of five was sent to the private school of Nathaniel H. Carter and, when that teacher was made head of the Portland Academy, followed him to the larger school. At school, Longfellow's conduct was exemplary. In June 1813, his teacher sent home this report:

"Master Henry Longfellow is one of the best boys we have in school. He spells and reads very well. He also can add and multiply numbers. His conduct last quarter was very correct and amiable.

N. H. CARTER."

His goodness was one that continued throughout his life. In 1817, another report declares that with the exception of "Monday morning's lessons and occasional levity," he "has during the week distinguished himself by his good deportment."

Formal education, with its insistence upon lessons and upon model conduct, was supplemented by the informal education of life outside of school. The boy read widely in the family library, Irving's *Sketch Book,* in particular, opening new delights to him.

"Every reader has his first book; I mean to say, one book among all others which in early youth first fascinates his imagination, and at once, excites and satisfies the desires of his mind. To me, this first book was *The Sketch Book* of Washington Irving."

There were, too, between school-terms, visits to the farms of the two grandfathers, to the Longfellow farm at Gorham and to the Wadsworth farm at Hiram. Near the Hiram farm was Lovell's Pond, the scene of an early fight between colonists and Indians. The story of the encounter stirred Longfellow's imagination. That he was moved to express his feelings in verse may have been due to the influence of Grandfather Wadsworth who, as a Harvard student, had demonstrated his own poetic ability by writing a poem, "On the Decay of Virtue and Increase of Politeness and Servility at Harvard College." What the immediate impulse may have been, one is not sure; but at all events, Henry at the age of thirteen wrote a poem, "The Battle of Lovell's Pond," which appeared in *The Portland Gazette* of November 17, 1820. It was signed "Henry," the poet and one of his sisters alone knowing the identity of the author.

> Cold, cold is the north wind and rude is the blast
> That sweeps like a hurricane loudly and fast,
> As it moans through the tall waving pines lone and drear,
> Sighs a requiem sad o'er the warrior's bier.
>
> .   .   .   .
>
> They died in their glory, surrounded by fame,
> And Victory's loud trump their death did proclaim;
> They are dead; but they live in each Patriot's breast,
> And their names are engraven on honor's bright crest.

The anonymous poem was criticized. Among others, a Judge Mellen, a friend of the Longfellow family, pronounced it "very stiff, remarkably stiff; moreover, it is all borrowed, every word of it." However much such adverse criticism may have hurt the sensitive poet, still it failed to check his interest in poetry and his desire to write it.

His college years served chiefly to intensify his literary interests. It was in 1822, after a year of study at home, that Longfellow entered the Sophomore class of Bowdoin College, then a small college about twenty years old, of which the poet's father was one of the trustees. In addition to this probable reason for its choice in preference to Harvard, local pride may also have directed its selection; for in 1820, Maine had become a separate state and Bowdoin in Brunswick had thus become a Maine college.

At college, Longfellow found himself one of a very small number of Unitarians in a Calvinist atmosphere. He was, moreover, the son of a well-to-do trustee and so distinguished in a student body that was far from wealthy. Whether he was therefore set apart by others or whether he, himself, withdrew from his fellow students, he apparently created the impression of being aloof and reserved.

In his studies, he was more than merely adequate. Although weak in mathematics, he graduated fourth in a class of thirty-eight. In the light of his future, it seems strange that on the commencement program he was not assigned the commencement poem. Instead, he was given the third oration for which, after rejecting the idea of writing on the poet Chatterton, he chose as his subject "Our Native Writers."

"We are a plain people," he declared in it, "that have had nothing to do with the mere pleasures and luxuries of life; and hence there has sprung up within us a quicksightedness to the failings of literary men, and an aversion to everything that is not practical, operative, and thoroughgoing."

Obviously, by the time of his graduation, Longfellow's sympathies were identified with literary men.

This is not strange in view of his interests during his college years. He was an eager and assiduous reader, particularly of the English poets. In his regular correspondence with his parents were frequent comments on the works that engrossed his attention. In one letter, he wrote of Gray's poems and to it received an answer from his mother that must have affected his attitude toward his own writing:

"I am much better pleased with those pieces which touch the feelings and improve the heart than those which excite the imagination only and raise perhaps an indistinct admiration,—that is, an admiration of we know not exactly what."

Naturally enough, his close contact with books moved Longfellow to write. Together with his brother Stephen and some other classmates he contributed a series of prose articles to *The Portland Advertiser*. He wrote also a number of poems, which were printed in the *Advertiser* and in *The United States Literary Gazette,* and which, for the most part, showed that tendency to "touch the feelings and improve the heart" that pleased his mother and that was to characterize much of his later poetry.

At this time, one of the strongest literary influences upon Longfellow was the poetry of William Cullen Bryant, an influence which the mature Longfellow acknowledged: "When I look back upon my earlier years I cannot but smile to see how much in them is really yours." "Thanksgiving," which with the initials H. W. L. appeared in *The United States Literary Gazette* for November 15, 1824, had, as its ending, lines generally reminiscent of the older poet and particularly reminiscent of "Thanatopsis":

> Let him that in the summer day of youth
> Keeps pure the holy fount of youthful feeling,
> And him that in the nightfall of his years
> Lies down in his last sleep and shuts in peace
> His dim pale eyes on life's short wayfaring,
> Praise Him that rules the destiny of man.

Longfellow's early poems were well received. Bryant in a critical article in 1825 mentions with praise "April Day," "Hymn of the Moravian Nuns," and "Sunrise in the Hills," "all by H. W. L., we know not who he is." The editor of the *Gazette*, breaking his customary rule of not paying for poetry, paid Longfellow two dollars for each of his poems. This payment, together with the one dollar a column which he received for his prose contributions, earned for Longfellow the sum of seventeen dollars from the first volume of the magazine.

The financial returns from literature were not great; but it was toward a writing career that Longfellow felt himself drawn. The question of a profession, not so much what he wished to do as what it would be possible for him to do, was one that bothered him for several years at college.

Early in his college course he had formulated for himself this piece of philosophy: "I find it most profitable to form such plans as are least liable to failure." Realizing that his father's approval would be important in his choice of a career, he cautiously approached the question in a letter in March 1824.

"And now, as somehow or other this subject has been introduced, I am curious to know what you do intend to make of me,—whether I am to study a profession or not; and if so, what profession. I hope that your ideas upon this subject will agree with mine, for I have a particular and strong prejudice for one course of life, to which you, I fear, will not agree. It will not be worth while for me to mention what this is, until I become more acquainted with your wishes."

To his father's suggestion that he follow law he demurred: "But in thinking to make a lawyer of me, I fear you thought more partially than justly"; and then declared that he was "altogether in favor of the farmer's life."

Farming must have been only a forced choice for him. For six months later he wrote to his father that after graduation from Bowdoin he should like one year to study at Cambridge where he might read history and literature and learn Italian. He admitted what dictated this desire:

"The fact is—and I will not disguise it in the least, for I think I ought not—the fact is, I most eagerly aspire after future eminence in literature; my whole soul burns most ardently for it, and every earthly thought centers in it. There may be something visionary in *this*, but I flatter myself that I have prudence enough to keep my enthusiasm from defeating its own object by too great haste."

The elder Longfellow reminded his son that there was "not wealth enough in the country to afford encouragement and patronage to merely literary men"; and to dampen further his ardor pointed out several flaws in one of his poems that had just been published!

Finally a compromise was reached and a decision made. If health and finances permitted, Longfellow was to have his year at Cambridge; he was then to study law since "this will support my real existence, literature an ideal one."

But the bar was, after all, not to number Longfellow among its followers. Fate intervened in the person of Madame Bowdoin who, by a gift of $1,000 to Bowdoin College, established there a Chair of Modern Languages. The new professorship was to be Longfellow's after a year's study of languages in Europe.

This news reached Longfellow in the fall of 1825. Since he could not sail for Europe until the spring, he spent the intervening months reading law in his father's office. Besides his studying, he wrote an occasional paper for *The Portland Advertiser*.

Toward the end of April 1826, he left Portland to sail from New York. On his way, he stopped at Cambridge where George Ticknor, the Harvard professor of modern languages, gave him a letter of introduction to his early idol, Irving, and advised him to study at Göttingen.

This advice was disregarded until very late in the European trip. France, Spain, Italy were all visited before he entered Germany. It was, indeed, scarcely as the profound student that Longfellow approached Europe, but rather as an interested tourist, keen, alert, with a flair for and a facility in acquiring languages.

He had, as most tourists do, periods when he longed for home. When he was worried about finances, when he felt he was not making sufficient progress in his studies, he grew despondent and homesick. Particularly did he feel dejected and alone when he lacked contact with people he knew well. "My own part in this world's comedy," he wrote to his mother, "is so connected with the parts my friends have to act upon the same stage that without their presence I am not sure of my own identity."

It was with a somewhat desperate clinging to that sense of identity that he first permitted Europe to impress him. Sights and customs different from his New England ones moved him to "divers fits of laughter." Usages that were not consistent with his New England morality offended him and led him to brand them as "dissolute manners."

In spite of this disturbing sense of difference, Europe moved him deeply and in such a way as to influence all his later life and writing. He became a link between the old world and the new, an exponent for America of European culture and tradition. Very early in his trip, with his first sight of the Cathedral at Rouen, was he touched by a sense of the past. But it was Spain especially that stirred him. He arrived in Madrid in March 1827. There he met and was cordially received by Washington Irving. He enjoyed good Spanish society. He felt at ease.

With a visit to the Alhambra his trip reached a climax. "There are moments in our lives in which we feel that romance could add nothing, and which poetry itself could not beautify. Such were those I passed in lingering about the Alhambra and dreaming over the warlike deeds of other days." After eight months in Spain, he was never to visit that country again. Yet its memory colored all his life. Years later he wrote in "Castles in Spain":

> How much of my young heart, O Spain,
>   Went out to thee in days of yore!
> What dreams romantic filled my brain,
> And summoned back to life again
> The Paladins of Charlemagne
>   The Cid Campeador!
>
>   .   .   .   .   .
>
> It was these memories, perchance,
>   From annals of remotest eld,
> That lent the colors of romance
> To every trivial circumstance,
> And changed the form and countenance
>   Of all that I beheld.

Despite the significance which the European scene had for him, it was towards America that his thoughts turned when he planned a piece of writing, a series of New England sketches. Obviously, he had not decided that poetry was his proper medium; in fact, he came almost to reject it. "My poetic career is finished. Since I left America, I have hardly put two lines together."

Very little writing, indeed, was accomplished during his European sojourn. His time and energy were, for the most part, engrossed by his language studies. At the end of three years, he was able to read Portuguese, to speak and write

French, Spanish, and Italian, the last so fluently that he was at times mistaken for a native Italian.

One can imagine the disappointment that engulfed Longfellow when, after years of study, he heard that the Bowdoin professorship had been withdrawn. He was thought to be too young to fill the position. Despondent, he went on to Germany, to study seriously at Göttingen. He wrote to his father that if no position was open to him, he could lecture on literature. Finally, after a short trip to England, he was called back to America by the illness of one of his sisters. In Paris, he learned that she had died. He went on, sailing from Liverpool in August 1829. Meanwhile, he heard that the Bowdoin trustees had reconsidered their decision; beginning with the fall term of 1829, he was to serve as professor of languages with a salary of $800 a year. In addition, he was to be college librarian for $100.

The young man of twenty-two entered seriously upon his duties. He was popular with his students and much interested in his teaching. For his classroom work, he edited French and Spanish books and translated a French grammar.

Although his desire for literary eminence had not disappeared, it still was not poetic eminence that he sought. In June 1830, he wrote, "Since my return I have written one piece of poetry but have not published a line." Instead, he was writing articles for *The North American Review* on such subjects as the origins of the French language; and for the *New England Magazine* a series of articles called "The Schoolmaster," evidently those which he had planned in Europe and which later he was to revise and form into his first prose book, *Outre-Mer,* 1833.

In September 1831, Longfellow married Mary Storer Potter. Life at Brunswick was pleasant; but Longfellow was restless and not content. So when Harvard offered him the chair of modern languages, then held by Professor Ticknor, he welcomed the opportunity for change. Again there was to be a European study trip before he entered his new position.

The journey that began in April 1835 was to prove a most significant one. Germany, Switzerland, and the Scandinavian countries were the countries visited. They aroused in him an interest that became permanent, an interest that is reflected in such poems as "Nuremberg," "The Belfry of Bruges," "The Golden Legend," and the devotedly told tales of the Musician in *Tales of a Wayside Inn:* "The Saga of King Olaf," "Ballad of Carmillian." Germany, however, did more than enrich his knowledge of legends and of places: it introduced him to the romantic literary wave that was sweeping the country. So, when his wife died in Rotterdam in November 1835, and when, soon after, he heard of the death of his brother-in-law, his closest friend, he sought solace in the German romanticism that was to characterize so much of his later verse.

This period marks an important stage in Longfellow's poetic development. His emotions had been aroused and required expression. So he turned to poetry, finding in it the satisfaction that he sought. He yielded to the prevailing romantic sentiment; and he had deepened within him that desire to find and formulate permanent moral truths that resulted in the marked didactic strain of his verse. Typical of this period is the poem "Footsteps of Angels," in which he alludes to the deaths of his two dear ones and in which he finds comfort in what would seem to others an only mildly comforting conclusion:

> Oh, though oft depressed and lonely,
>   All my fears are laid aside,
> If I but remember only
>   Such as these have lived and died!

The didacticism of "The Village Blacksmith," "The Builders," "The Singers," continued through to his later writing,
as in the poem "Loss and Gain." One of its earliest expressions, its most characteristic and best remembered, is "A
Psalm of Life":

> Let us, then, be up and doing,
>   With a heart for any fate;
> Still achieving, still pursuing,
>   Learn to labor and to wait.

This poem meant much to the poet; to him it was an expression of faith wrung from his own experience. "I kept
it some time in manuscript," he wrote, "unwilling to show
it to any one, it being a voice from my inmost heart at a
time when I was rallying from depression."

The poems of this period were written after he had assumed his duties at Harvard. There he was head of the
department of modern languages, himself lecturing and
superintending the recitations of his assistants. He lived in
the Craigie House, the old Washington headquarters. In
Cambridge, he was caught in the social life of a college
town. Two of his most intimate friends were Cornelius Fel-
ton, professor of Greek, and Charles Sumner, who was then
lecturing at the Law school. With them and some others he
formed a mildly Bohemian club, which met frequently. But
his social life was not limited to the companionship of men.
Young, traveled, a person of position, and very much of a
dandy, Longfellow was considered something of a "catch"
by the young ladies of the town and was present at many
of the Cambridge dances and parties.

In 1839, about three years after his coming to Cambridge,
two books were published: *Hyperion*, a romantic version of
his travels, based, as Longfellow said, on fictitious events
but on true feelings; and *Voices of the Night*, his first vol-

ume of poetry. The latter book, which included a few of the poems written while he was in college, was gently sentimental and melancholy in tone, a tone which seems at variance with the general tenor, at all events the superficial tenor, of his Cambridge life, but one which struck immediately the public fancy.

America, after years of struggle and effort, was beginning to find the opportunity to enjoy the more delicate emotions that come with ease and leisure; but it had not yet completely rid itself of the idea that poetry was, at best, weak and effeminate and time-wasting. If in some cases the indulgence of reading poetry was accompanied by twinges of conscience, such self-accusation was not necessary in the enjoyment of Longfellow's poems; for his poetry still conserved the old moralistic attitude; it still maintained the alliance between beauty and truth. It presented the virtues of life in pleasing form. It vocalized American thought.

Some few critics adversely criticized the poetry. But from such criticism Longfellow characteristically turned away. "I never read what is written against me," he wrote to his friend Samuel Ward. "Therefore it is to me as if it had never been written, and I am saved the momentary pang arising from abuse."

Undeterred then, he continued his writing. His interest was awakened in native material. His purpose he defined for himself as "working upon the people's feelings."

In 1841 appeared *Ballads and Other Poems,* containing those poems, still so often memorized and recited: "The Wreck of the Hesperus," "The Skeleton in Armor," "The Village Blacksmith," and "Excelsior."

The following year the now well-known poet went to Europe for the health cure at Marienbad. The one poem which he wrote while in Europe, "Mezzo Cammin," expressed his own sense of lack of accomplishment; at the same time it revealed that the very injunction which meant so much to his readers:

Act—act in the living Present.

was one which he, himself, was unable to follow.

Half of my life is gone, and I have let
The years slip from me and have not fulfilled
The aspiration of my youth, to build
Some tower of song with lofty parapet.
Not indolence, nor pleasure, nor the fret
Of restless passions that would not be stilled,
But sorrow, and a care that almost killed,
Kept me from what I may accomplish yet;
Though, half-way up the hill, I see the Past
Lying beneath me with its sounds and sights,—
A city in the twilight dim and vast,
With smoking roofs, soft bells, and gleaming lights,—
And hear above me on the autumnal blast
The cataract of Death far thundering from the heights.

On the return voyage, Longfellow's poetic impulse was stirred by thoughts of slavery and of the Abolition movement in America. He wrote eight poems which were later published as a thirty-page pamphlet, *Poems on Slavery*. They expressed no depth of feeling, no indignation. They were merely romanticized pictures, as in "The Slave's Dream," "The Slave in the Dismal Swamp," "The Quadroon Girl." Of a subject that moved other men to decided action, the poet declared, "I have attempted only to invest the subject with a poetic coloring." From the reality of this social and political issue he escaped by writing the romantic drama, "The Spanish Student."

Longfellow's personal thoughts had for some time been turning toward the great love of his life. On his second European trip, he had met the Appleton family and had been attracted by the daughter, Frances Elizabeth. The relationship begun then continued. Finally, on July 13, 1843, the two were married.

Mr. Appleton bought the Craigie House for his daughter and son-in-law. There they took up their married life. There their children were born and there Longfellow was to live the rest of his life.

He was socially and financially secure. Possibly because his teaching was not a matter of necessity, it grew more and more irksome. In October 1850 he was already seriously thinking of resigning his professorship. In February 1854, he was "pawing to get free." In April he gave his last lecture.

Henceforth he was able to devote all his time to the writing which for the past few years had been absorbing him more and more. This was the period that produced the three long poems which are most familiar. "Evangeline," begun as "Gabrielle" in 1845, was finished in 1847. The suggestion of the story had come from Hawthorne; the Mississippi scenic background was built up of pictures from a Boston exhibit. Although the details may not have been authenticated, the plot not original and most certainly not dramatically handled, still in "Evangeline" Longfellow succeeded in giving an American idyll that was true to feeling. Moreover, he did introduce the startling novelty of a hexameter line, a meter that was the subject of much theoretical discussion.

The second long poem was "The Song of Hiawatha." The Indians had long interested Longfellow as a subject for his poetry. In college, he had read Heckwelder's *Account of the History, Manners and Customs of the Indian Natives of Pennsylvania* and had found it a vindication of Indian character which had been "barbarously maltreated by the whites, both in word and deed." He further evidenced his interest in his Junior year when in a "Dialogue between a North American Indian and a European," he, himself, assumed the part of King Philip. The Indian poem which he now wrote presented an idealized picture with a wealth of Indian legend. Rich with color and music, insistent with its frequent repetition and its meter derived from the Finnish poem, the "Kalevala," it rapidly took hold of popular fancy.

1858 saw the publication of the third of the long poems, "The Courtship of Miles Standish," a pleasant tale, a romance of the Puritans with one of Longfellow's own ancestors, John Alden, as its hero; but a story without any force of action or depth of character.

These three poems were not the sole achievement of this period. There was a book of shorter poems, *The Seaside and the Fireside;* there were two collections of poems edited by him; and there was a novel, *Kavanagh.* There were, too, the beginnings of that series of poems making up *Christus,* the epic of Christianity, which Longfellow hoped, but hoped vainly, would prove the lasting foundation of his fame.

Longfellow had now reached the point for which he had always longed. Recognized as one of the leading American poets, he was able to give himself entirely to his writing. He had a devoted and interesting circle of friends. He was a member of the Saturday Club, the outgrowth of the newly established *Atlantic Monthly.* His home life was warmly rich. So it was with doubly felt force that tragedy entered it. Longfellow had known sorrow in the death of his first wife and in that of a small daughter. But the death of his second wife was a blow from which he never recovered. On July 9, 1861, she was sealing some packages of their children's hair. A breeze fanned the candle's flame which ignited her dress. Longfellow helped to fight the flames; but his wife was so severely burned that she died of her injuries. Longfellow, himself, was so hurt that he was unable to attend her funeral.

Only rarely, and then with difficulty, did Longfellow ever allude to this event. But the grief and desolation that he felt were deep. Eighteen years later he wrote the sonnet, "The Cross of Snow," which was published only after his own death.

> In the long, sleepless watches of the night,
> A gentle face—the face of one long dead—
> Looks at me from the wall, where round its head
> The night-lamp casts a halo of pale light.
> Here in this room she died; and soul more white
> Never through martyrdom of fire was led
> To its repose; nor can in books be read
> The legend of a life more benedight.
> There is a mountain in the distant West,
> That, sun-defying, in its deep ravines
> Displays a cross of snow upon its side.
> Such is the cross I wear upon my breast
> These eighteen years, through all the changing scenes
> And seasons, changeless since the day she died.

Painfully, Longfellow took up the burden of daily existence. He devoted much time to his children, particularly to his daughters, who in "The Children's Hour" became familiar to his sympathetic and admiring readers. As refuge from his feelings, he began his translation of Dante, which was finished in 1867. And for release, he wrote and wrote copiously. In addition to Dante and the finally completed *Christus,* were numerous volumes of verse: *Tales of a Wayside Inn,* the two collections with their stories of "Paul Revere's Ride," "King Robert of Sicily," "The Bell of Atri," "The Legend Beautiful," and their one entirely original tale, "The Birds of Killingworth"; *Three Books of Songs,* "Morituri Salutamus," *Aftermath, Masque of Pandora, Kéramos, Flower de Luce, Ultima Thule,* and *In the Harbor.*

His poetic position was secure. In 1862 he had gone to England and was hailed as literary ambassador between that country and the United States. Oxford and Cambridge gave him honorary degrees. Queen Victoria summoned him to an audience. In his own country, he was held in affectionate esteem. His appeal was wide. His poems were without mystery and complication and so were easily understood. His feelings, if not deep and involved, were simple and readily appreciated. An evidence of his appeal to children and to the childlike in the Americans of his time was the gift on his seventy-second birthday: from the chestnut tree under which the village blacksmith had stood, a chair was made and presented to Longfellow by the children of Cambridge. In response the poet wrote "From My Arm-Chair":

> And thus, dear children, have you made for me
> This day a jubilee,
> And to my more than threescore years and ten
> Brought back my youth again.

Toward the end of 1881 Longfellow was taken ill. Though he regained his strength, he never fully recovered. On March 24, 1882, he died. Only nine days before, he had written the concluding stanza of his last poem, "The Bells of San Blas":

> O Bells of San Blas, in vain
> Ye call back the Past again!
> The Past is deaf to your prayer;
> Out of the shadows of night
> The world rolls into light,
> It is daybreak everywhere.

Only with his own death did the shadowy twilight of Longfellow's life appear to end. Characteristic of that life is the
frequently repeated statement of Emerson. Himself old and
mentally weakened, the philosopher and poet attended
Longfellow's funeral. He looked upon the coffin. "I cannot
recall the name of our friend," he said, "but he was a good
man."

Frequently the personal virtues of a literary man have
in America been wrongly used to form the basis of a literary
judgment. The sweetness and goodness of Longfellow's life
did undoubtedly affect the public's attitude toward his
poetry. Yet with this statement one cannot dismiss either
Longfellow's influence or his literary position.

He came to hold a peculiar place in American life. A visiting Englishman startled him with the statement that since
there were no ruins in America, he had chosen to call upon
the poet instead. Longfellow was a literary landmark, a
conspicuous personality.

This is all the more strange in view of Longfellow's own
aloofness from public affairs.

> The scholar and the world! The endless strife,
> The discord in the harmonies of life!
> The love of learning, the sequestered nooks,
> And all the sweet serenity of books;
> The market-place, the eager love of gain,
> Whose aim is vanity, and whose end is pain!

Longfellow's natural tendency was to withdraw from the
discord. His own poems on slavery, as a concession to the
anti-Abolitionists, were omitted from one edition of his collected poems. To Whittier he declined a nomination for
Congress: "Partisan warfare becomes too violent, too vin-
dictive for my taste." It was, then, not the Longfellow of

social activity, but the Longfellow of the poems, who was known to the public.

The outstanding characteristic of these poems is their acceptance of the lessons of life: abnegation of self, patience in despair, reliance in an ever-present God. It is a calm, quiet acceptance. Sorrow and grief are present in his poetry; but there is no suggestion of conflict or of truth that has been achieved through struggle. Sometimes the moral significance of the poems is merely suggested; frequently it makes the poems rhymed sermons as in "A Psalm of Life."

> Nothing useless is, or low;
>   Each thing in its place is best;
> And what seems but idle show
>   Strengthens and supports the rest.

Thus he preaches in "The Builders"; and again, in "In the Churchyard at Cambridge":

> Hereafter?—And do you think to look
> On the terrible pages of that Book
>   To find her failings, faults, and errors?
> Ah, you will then have other cares,
> In your own shortcomings and despairs,
>   In your own secret sins and terrors!

Moral injunctions, however permanently valid, are not the material of lasting poetry. But Longfellow was something more than a didactic moralist. He was a lyric interpreter of the simple emotions. One misses depth of feelings, even in a love story like that of Evangeline; but one does find the expression of tender, delicate emotions in such poems as the "Serenade" from *The Spanish Student,* or "The Hanging of the Crane," or "Daybreak," or "Song":

> Then stay at home, my heart, and rest;
> The bird is safest in its nest;

O'er all that flutter their wings and fly
A hawk is hovering in the sky;
To stay at home is best.

While Longfellow's gift was eminently lyric and not dramatic, he still could tell in pleasant, even tones, delightful tales. The Wayside Inn collections are rich treasuries of stories, humorous, pathetic, religious. "The Ballad of Carmihan," one of that series, "The Wreck of the Hesperus," "The Skeleton in Armor," suggest his ability to tell a story succinctly with a minimum of detail.

Some of these narratives used American themes. The long poems of "Evangeline," "Hiawatha," and "Miles Standish" were native in material. So were "Paul Revere's Ride," "Lady Wentworth," and "The Birds of Killingworth." The final section of *Christus,* "The New England Tragedies," used as its subject the intolerance and bigotry of the New England Puritans. Among his shorter poems are a number essentially American in subject, Indian poems, for example, like "The Burial of Minnesink," and "The Revenge of Rain-in-the-Face." The sea, too, so essential to American life and development, is a subject close to Longfellow and one which he lovingly expressed. "The Building of the Ship," with its double allegory, "Twilight," "The Secret of the Sea," "The Light-House," "The Sound of the Sea," "The Tides," are examples of his use of this subject. So, too, is "Seaweed":

> When descends on the Atlantic
>   The gigantic
> Storm-wind of the equinox,
> Landward in his wrath he scourges
>   The toiling surges
> Laden with seaweed from the rocks.

Longfellow could not have written as he did if he had not been an American. His country dictated some of his subjects and, in its moralistic aspect, some of his point of view. But judged by the great mass of his writing, Longfellow was not completely, or essentially, American. European subjects are more numerous than American ones. And in his treatment of even these latter, his spirit is far from what is considered typically American. These poems lack the force and power and elemental vigor of the America that was growing up about him and appear rather the reflection of a retiring spirit that had been touched by cosmopolitan culture.

In poetic technique, however, Longfellow was willing to be more positive and definite. Objecting to elaboration and ornamentation, he consciously strove for simplicity in his writing. "I like simplicity in all things, but above all in poetry." This simplicity, carried to an extreme, often resulted in banality, as in such lines as

> All are scattered now and fled,
> Some are married, some are dead.

An obvious and inflexible adherence, moreover, to the requirements of fixed meter and rhyme resulted in awkward lines, like:

Wrapped in thy scarlet blanket, I see thee stalk through the city's

His, not mine, are the gifts and only so far can I make them Mine, as in giving I add my heart to whatever is given.

It was against just such effects of discord between idea and expression that the poets of a later generation rebelled. Longfellow was criticized as a stilted follower of outgrown poetic methods. But in such criticism was forgotten the fact that Longfellow was, himself, an innovator. An age which is accustomed to the use by poetry of whatever meter is suited to the subject of the poem, can scarcely understand the discussion provoked by the meter of "Evangeline" and that of "Hiawatha." Longfellow did not hesitate to employ a variety of experimental forms. "To an Old Danish Song Book" uses a rhymeless verse-form:

> There are marks of age,
> There are thumb-marks on thy margin,
> Made by hands that clasped thee rudely,
> At the alehouse.

"Rain in Summer," as another example of experimentation, in its variety of meter and of stanza form suggests the varying beat and sound of a rainstorm. There is throughout his poetry an unusual freedom in metric and rhyme schemes.

Still another aspect of his poetic skill lies in the aptness of his figures. Sometimes a simple simile adds beauty to his lines:

And the hooded clouds like friars

When she had passed, it seemed like the ceasing of exquisite music

Sometimes the figure is sustained throughout a poem as in "Daylight and Moonlight" or in that most skillfully designed poem, "The Fire of Drift-Wood," wherein there is drawn a comparison between the fire and the thoughts and words of a group of friends who know that their future contacts are to be less intimate than their past:

> O flames that glowed! O hearts that yearned!
> They were indeed too much akin,
> The drift-wood fire without that burned,
> The thoughts that burned and glowed within.

The perfection of Longfellow's technique shows itself in his sentimental poems which were the most natural expression of his spirit, in poems like "The Hanging of the Crane" and "My Lost Youth"; and in his sonnets, as in the "Divina Commedia" sequence, and in "The Fiftieth Birthday of Agassiz," "Keats," and "Nature":

As a fond mother, when the day is o'er,
Leads by the hand her little child to bed,
Half willing, half reluctant to be led,
And leave his broken playthings on the floor,
Still gazing at them through the open door,
Nor wholly reassured and comforted
By promises of others in their stead,
Which, though more splendid, may not please him more;
So Nature deals with us, and takes away
Our playthings one by one, and by the hand
Leads us to rest so gently, that we go
Scarce knowing if we wish to go or stay,
Being too full of sleep to understand
How far the unknown transcends the what we know.

Longfellow had formulated for himself the poet's function; his it was to sing the song:

Out of the heart of Nature, or the heart
Of man, the child of Nature.

But in doing so, he was the agent of some greater, some uncontrollable force which at times gave its favor and at times withheld it:

His, and not his, are the lays
He sings, and their fame
Is his, and not his; and the praise
And the pride of a name.

> For voices pursue him by day,
>   And haunt him by night,
> And he listens, and needs must obey,
>   When the Angel says, "Write!"

Too frequently Longfellow felt his own inadequacy as a poet. Too frequently, the inspiration eluded him:

> But when I would enter the gate
>   Of the golden atmosphere,
> It is gone, and I wonder and wait
>   For the vision to reappear.

This timidity, this lack of certainty, results in an attractive sweetness and humility; but at the same time it produces a weakness of feeling and of expression which ought not to be present in poetry. When Longfellow, however, did have the courage to lay bare his heart and write as he spontaneously felt, then did he write those poems which will have lasting value.

It was Longfellow's fate to suffer from the over-praise of his time. His sympathetic appeal to his own generation dulled its critical power; the bad was accepted with the good. A later generation, aware of the bad, saw only that. And so Longfellow was ruthlessly cast among the writers outworn and outgrown.

For two distinct reasons he must not be relegated to that position. In the first place he was essential historically in the development of American poetry. He did use American subjects as his themes. But he also introduced into American poetry a European attitude and atmosphere. This was due partly to his temperament and taste. It may have been the result, too, of a conscious artistic creed. In *Kavanagh* Longfellow wrote: "Nationality is a good thing to a certain extent, but universality is better. All that is best in the great poets of all countries is not what is national in them, but what is universal."

Universality may be achieved by a penetrating and thorough understanding of the particular; and by such an understanding a thoroughly American poet could become universal. This, however, was not the way of Longfellow. Yet his insistence was one needed by America. America, become self-conscious, aware of its self in the arts, was in danger of becoming provincial. Longfellow taught it to accept what it could of other civilizations, not to reject it simply because it was foreign.

Even without considering this historical position, Longfellow still has claim to attention. His field is narrow, but it is a lasting one. The simpler things and the simple emotions of life endure. As long as they continue to move one to smiles or to tears, so long will the simply sung poems of Longfellow seem their adequate expression.

JOHN GREENLEAF
WHITTIER

And one there was, a dreamer born,
  Who, with a mission to fulfil,
Had left the Muses' haunt to turn
  The crank of an opinion-mill,
Making his rustic reed of song
A weapon in the war with wrong,
Yoking his fancy to the breaking-plough
That beam-deep turned the soil for truth to spring and grow.

IT IS thus that John Greenleaf Whittier in his poem "The Tent on the Beach," sketched his own portrait. To complete the picture, one other piece of self-delineation should be added, an extract from an article, "The Training":

"Without intending any disparagement of my peaceable ancestry for many generations, I have still strong suspicions that somewhat of the old Norman blood, something of the grim Berserker spirit, has been bequeathed to me. How else can I account for the intense childish eagerness with which I listened to the story of old campaigners who sometimes fought their battles over again in my hearing? Why did I, in my young fancy, go up with Jonathan, the son of Saul, to smite the garrisoned Philistines of Michmash, or with the fierce son of Nun against the cities of Canaan? Why was Mr. Greatheart, in *Pilgrim's Progress*, my favorite character? What gave such fascination to the narrative of the grand Homeric encounter between Christian and Apollyon in the valley?"

Dreamer and writer, devout Quaker of "peaceable ancestry," battling humanitarian—these were his basic elements. The resolution of these sometimes conflicting forces is the story of the development of Whittier, the man and the poet.

The first Whittier to come to America was one Thomas, who settled near Haverhill, Massachusetts, in 1638. He appears to have been conspicuous in the community for having brought with him from England a hive of bees. More significant, however, for his poet descendant were two characteristics: keen justice, which made him even in his unbarricaded home always secure from Indian raids; and an independence and strength of belief, which made him champion the unpopular cause of some Quakers, though he, himself, was not a member of the Society of Friends.

It was through the marriage of John's son Joseph to Mary Peaslee, a Quaker, that Quakerism entered the Whittier family. Some knowledge of the distinctive tenets of that faith is necessary for an understanding of Whittier and of his poetry. According to the Quakers, the Bible is not the sole or final source of authority for conduct and belief; further revelation comes from the "Light Within," a spiritual force operating supernaturally within the individual. Since any and all may cultivate this force, there is no place for priesthood, for class distinctions, for the superiority—except spiritually—of any one man above his fellows. So in its perfection, Quakerism implies sympathy with mankind, the dignity of the individual, independence, and democracy.

It was in a devout Quaker household that John Greenleaf Whittier was born on December 17, 1807. His father John at the age of 44 had in 1804 married Abigail Hussey. The poet was the second of their four children; Mary was the oldest child, and younger than Greenleaf, as his family called him, were Matthew Franklin and Elizabeth Hussey, to the latter of whom the poet was always most tenderly devoted.

The Whittiers were simple, farming folk, living a life of poverty and of toil in Haverhill, making their home in the very house which the pioneer Whittier had built. The poet Whittier was the representative of this native, rural stock; his roots clung deep to his birthplace; his experiences and feelings were those of his neighbors; their commonly shared possession was the material of his poetry.

Haverhill was surrounded by green mountains; it was within sound of the Atlantic Ocean. Sufficiently close to the nearest city to keep in touch with public events and public movements, it was still far enough removed to be able to maintain its own individuality. Boston was only forty miles away. Yet that city evidently exercised no influence on the growing boy and was apparently visited by him but once before he was twenty.

It was Haverhill, and more particularly, it was the Whittier household that influenced the young poet. His father, "a prompt decisive man," trustworthy and respected; his mother, sensitive and sympathetic; his sisters and brother; a bachelor uncle Moses, "innocent of books," yet well versed in the lore of nature; a tender and loving maiden aunt— these made up the family circle. They are vividly described in "Snow-Bound," Whittier's genre painting in verse of his New England home, a poem which unforgettably depicts the color and atmosphere and life of his boyhood home. Within the circle of that home, Whittier felt a security, to which even in his later years he clung in retrospect.

"I think at the age of which thy note inquires,"[1] he wrote to a little girl, "I found about equal satisfaction in an old

---

[1] *Life and Letters of John Greenleaf Whittier,* by Samuel T. Pickard, Houghton Mifflin and Co., Boston.

rural home, with the shifting panorama of the seasons, in reading the few books within my reach, and dreaming of something wonderful and grand somewhere in the future. Neither change nor loss had then made me realize the uncertainty of all earthly things. I felt secure of my mother's love, and dreamed of losing nothing and gaining much."

With his sister Mary, Whittier first attended school; but district schooling was a brief twelve-week winter interlude in a farmer's year. The farm which his father and uncle cultivated demanded more and more of the boy's attention and assistance. Although he had never been very strong, he had by fifteen reached man's size and so was required to do his full share of the farm work. At seventeen, he was hurt in such a way as to handicap him in performing the physical labors of a farmer and as to darken the rest of his life with the cloud of ill-health.

But long before this, farming had irked him.

> And must I always swing the flail,
> And help to fill the milking pail?
> I wish to go away to school;
> I do not wish to be a fool.

The world of books had opened before him and urged him to explore. For a time it was but a small world that invited him. The family library consisted of some twenty or thirty volumes, mostly sermons and the biographies or journals of Friends. From a rhymed catalogue which the boy made some idea may be obtained of the reading available to him:

NARRATIVES

> How Captain Riley and his crew
> Were on Sahara's desert threw,
>
> .   .   .   .   .   .

RELIGIOUS

The Bible towering o'er the rest,
Of all the other books the best.
Old Father Baxter's pious call
To the unconverted all.

. . . . . .

A book concerning John's baptism,
Elias Smith's "Universalism."

JOURNALS, LIVES, ETC.

The Lives of Franklin and of Penn,
Of Fox and Scott, all worthy men.

There was, in addition, a Waverley novel which, as a work of fiction, had to be concealed from disapproving eyes. There was a copy of Shakespeare, bought on the memorable visit to distant relations in Boston when even his pride in the "boughten" buttons on his new coat failed to compensate him for the loneliness with which that city overwhelmed him. When the home library was exhausted, Whittier borrowed from the neighbors' store, walking miles to secure some book of travel or a biography. One other source of reading material presented itself, the newspapers which came into the home and which frequently printed poems of popular appeal in their "Poet's Corner."

The boy, absorbed in books, was at fourteen ready for a momentous event, his schoolmaster's reading to him the poems of Robert Burns, one of whose songs he had heard sung by a peddler, a "pawky auld carle of a wandering Scotchman," who had stopped at the Whittier home.

"When I was fourteen years old," Whittier wrote in a brief autobiographical letter, "my first schoolmaster, Joshua Coffin, the able, eccentric historian of Newbury, brought with him to our house a volume of Burns' poems, from which he read, greatly to my delight. I begged him to leave the book with me, and set myself at once to the task of mastering the glossary of the Scottish dialect at its close. This was about the first poetry I had ever read (with the exception of that of the Bible, of which I had been a close student), and it had a lasting influence upon me. I began to make rhymes myself, and to imagine stories and adventures. In fact, I lived a sort of dual life, and in a world of fancy, as well as in the world of plain matter-of-fact about me."

The verses that the boy took to writing imitated in form those that he read in his school readers or in the newspapers. The significance of his introduction to Burns lay not so much in the fact that it prompted Whittier to write verse as in the fact that it showed him a new source of poetic material; the poetic was close to him, in the country about him, in his own life and in the life of his neighbors:

> I saw through all familiar things
>   The romance underlying;
> The joys and griefs that plume the wings
>   Of Fancy skyward flying.

The boy wrote unceasingly. At school, his slate was covered with verse more frequently than it was with sums. At home, the writing continued, but with greater secrecy. Indeed it is said that only when the rubbish was removed from the garret which he had made his hiding place, was much of his writing discovered. For John Whittier, the father, a stern Quaker who insisted on the plain things of life, was not sympathetic toward his son's versifying. But if the father was not enthusiastic, other members of the family were. Among these was Mary who, one day, found a poem which Whittier had written and, without his knowledge, sent it to *The Free Press*.

The Free Press was a weekly established by William

Lloyd Garrison at Newburyport, Massachusetts, in 1826. Its humanitarian and liberal tone won the favor of the elder Whittier, who subscribed to it.

One can imagine the young poet's delighted surprise when he discovered in the "Poet's Corner" of the June 8, 1826, issue his own verses, "The Exile's Departure":

> Fond scenes, which delighted my youthful existence,
>   With feelings of sorrow I bid ye adieu—
> A lasting adieu! for now, dim in the distance,
>   The shores of Hibernia recede from my view.

Shortly after, *The Free Press* printed a second poem, "The Deity":

>   His face he veiled
> Within his mantle, and in meekness owned
> The presence of his God, discovered not in
> The storm, the earthquake, or the mighty flame
> But in the still small whisper to his soul.

The flood of poetry was let loose! Poem after poem flowed from his pen. Much of it was imitative, using for models the sentimental, often saccharine, verse that was currently popular. Such, for example, was "The Willow," obviously patterned after "The Old Oaken Bucket":

> Oh, dear to my heart are the scenes which delighted
> My fancy in moments I ne'er can recall,

with its repeated line

> The storm-battered willow, the ivy-bound willow, the water-
>   washed willow, that grew by its side.

However faulty such verse was, it was yet of sufficient quality to impress the young editor of *The Free Press*. He became curious about the identity of his Haverhill contributor and determined to become acquainted with him. He rode over one day to Haverhill. Immediately a bond of sympathy was forged between the farmer-poet and the editor, himself but two years older than Whittier. Garrison, aware of Whittier's yearnings and potentialities, tried to persuade the father that his son's formal education should be continued. The elder Whittier was at first unwilling; but when to Garrison's pleas were added those of Abijah W. Thayer, the editor of *The Haverhill Gazette,* he finally consented, provided that sufficient money could be raised from some source other than the impossible one of his heavily mortgaged farm.

Whittier applied himself to financing his education. From a farmhand he had learned to make a light shoe. These shoes were sold for twenty-five cents a pair, of which eight cents went to the maker. During the winter and spring of 1827, the shoemaking went on until Whittier had accumulated enough money to cover his expenses for one term and, by close calculation, to leave at the end of the school year a balance of a quarter. Actually, at the end of the term, that was the amount which the poet had. With the shoemaking continued the verse-making, the poems being kept in the little low drawer of the shoemaker's table.

On April 30, 1827, the new Haverhill Academy was dedicated. The exercises included the singing of an ode that had been written by Whittier:

> Hail, Star of Science! Come forth in thy splendor,
>   Illumine these walls—let them evermore be
> A shrine where thy votaries offerings may tender,
>   Hallowed by genius, and sacred to thee.

The next day, Whittier entered the Academy.

During the following six months, he boarded with Mr. Thayer, returning to the farm for week-ends. A new life was beginning for him. There was his work at the Academy where, in addition to the usual studies, French was taught. Libraries were more freely available to him. A pleasant social life was his to enjoy. Tall and slender, with piercing dark eyes, with gracious courtesy, ready wit, and love of fun, he was popular with both the young men and the young women.

It is doubtful that Whittier had at this time any definite plans for a future career. His main interest, however, was directed toward writing both prose and verse. He wrote articles for *The Haverhill Gazette,* the first on Burns, the next on Temperance. That same paper in 1827 and 1828 published about one hundred of his poems, the first to appear with his own name being "The Outlaw" on October 28, 1828. His verses appeared, too, in *The Boston Statesman,* edited by a distant relative, and in *The National Philanthropist,* which Garrison was then editing. They were reprinted by other papers throughout the country. Yet, somehow, there is the suggestion that the world did not receive his poetry in too kindly a fashion and that with it he could not win fame or fortune, a suggestion made in the poem, "I Would Not Lose That Romance Wild," written during the Haverhill first term:

> And though the critic's scornful eye
>   Condemn his faltering lay,
> And though with heartless apathy,
>   The cold world turn away—
> And envy strive with secret aim
> To blast and dim his rising fame;
> .   .   .   .   .   .
> Come then, my lyre, although there be
>   No witchery in thy tone;
> And though the lofty harmony
>   Which other bards have known,

Is not, and cannot e'er be mine,
To touch with power those chords of thine.

Yet thou canst tell, in humble strain,
    The feelings of a heart,
Which, though not proud, would still disdain
    To bear a meaner part
Than that of bending at the shrine
Where their bright wreaths the muses twine.

During the winter of 1827-1828, Whittier taught at the Birch Meadow School, an experience little to his liking but necessary for earning money for the further education which he so much desired. There was an additional plan for raising money, the publication of Whittier's poems under the title of *The Poems of Adrian*, Adrian being one of his pseudonyms. The plan was outlined in *The Gazette* in January 1828.

"It is believed by his friends that these poems indicate genius of a high order, which deserves all possible culture. The design of thus offering his juvenile writings to the public is to raise money to assist him in obtaining a classical education. He is a worthy member of the Society of Friends, and it is hoped that from them the volume will receive a liberal patronage."

But though the plan had so worthy a purpose, and though the terms of sale were liberal—each copy to cost seventy-five cents and to any one selling six copies, a seventh to be given—the scheme failed. These early poems that were to have been collected were the fair, promising poems of a schoolboy; but they were not great poetry. Whittier, himself, in later years, exercising judgment and discrimination retained but few of them for the collected edition of his poems.

In spite of the abandonment of this publishing plan,

Whittier was able to have a second term at the Haverhill Academy. At its end he was confronted with the question of his future. He disliked farming and was, furthermore, not strong enough to stand its rigorous labor. Further study and a college education meant years of inevitable poverty. Teaching, tried once, was still distasteful. Shoemaking—? At this time, Garrison appeared once again as a friend in need.

He was about to resign as editor of *The Philanthropist,* a journal devoted to the cause of temperance, so that he might give himself zealously and completely to the Abolition movement. He suggested to the paper's publisher, the Rev. William Collier, that Whittier be chosen as his successor. The invitation was given. But before Whittier, himself, decided to accept it, he wrote to his Haverhill friend, Mr. Thayer, a letter, quoted in Pickard's *Life and Letters of John Greenleaf Whittier,* outlining the situation with the clarity, and sanity, and dignity that were so characteristic of him.

"I have renounced college for the good reason that I have no disposition to humble myself to meanness for an education—crowding myself through college upon the charities of others, and leaving it with a debt or an obligation to weigh down my spirit like an incubus, and paralyze every exertion. The professions are already crowded full to overflowing; and I, forsooth, because I have a miserable knack of rhyming, must swell the already enormous number, struggle awhile with debt and difficulties, and then, weary of life, go down to my original insignificance, where the tinsel of classical honors will but aggravate my misfortune. . . .

"What, then, remains for me? Schoolkeeping—out upon it! The memory of last year's experience comes up before me like a horrible dream. No, I had rather be a tin-peddler, and drive around the country with a bunch of sheepskins hanging to my wagon."

Finally, a decision having been reached, Whittier arrived in Boston in December 1828 to initiate his journalistic career. But through some change in plans, it was not *The Philanthropist* that he was to edit, but a second Collier publication, *The American Manufacturer*, a publication "devoted to the interests of manufacturers, mechanics, agriculture, internal improvements, literature, education, and general intelligence." Terms were arranged; Whittier was to receive $9 a week and to board with Mr. Collier, his employer. Volume I, No. 14 of the paper appeared on January 1, 1829, with the name of the new editor.

Here began that interest in politics which Whittier was to maintain throughout his life. That strain in him which made him an ardent champion of public causes and of humanitarian principles was here stirred. The paper was an advocate of temperance. Its chief editorial policy, however, was the championing of Henry Clay and the advocation of a protective tariff in the interest of American industry. There was no lack of political and economic reasoning behind Whittier's editorials; but, more than that, there was an understanding, personal, sympathetic note. A series of editorials addressed to young mechanics opened in the April 16th number. In it the editor thus expressed himself:

"He has felt, in common with you all, the injustice of that illiberal feeling, which has been manifested toward mechanics by the wealthy and arrogant of other classes."

That Whittier, in spite of his Quakerism, was sensitive to the class distinctions that others might draw, is quite apparent. For the most part he could conceal it from others by a gay social air. So to a friend he writes of his Boston stay: "I have become a notable fellow in gallantry of late; I mean old-fashioned gallantry, however. I have given my whiskers a more ferocious appearance, and take the liberty of frightening into good nature those who will not be complaisant of their own accord." That this was, however, a pose covering timidity is suggested by a later comment: "At that very time I was in reality a shy, timid recluse, afraid of a shadow, especially the shadow of a woman. There is a period in life—a sort of tadpole state, between the boy and the man—when any sort of pretense, egotism, and self-conceit may be expected."

In August 1829, the editorship ended for Whittier. His father's illness called him back to the farm and, however disturbing was the reason for his return, it must be imagined that Whittier welcomed the security that his home always meant for him. For almost a year, Whittier helped manage the farm. His spare hours were given over to study. His political ambitions were aroused. In July 1830, the month after his father's death, he left Haverhill for Hartford, Connecticut, to become editor of *The New England Review,* an important political journal.

Its former editor, George D. Prentice, a gay, dashing young man, was engaged to go to Kentucky to write a biography of Henry Clay. Whittier, from his Haverhill farm, had written to the Hartford paper letters that had so interested Prentice that he suggested the letter-writer as his successor. The Hartford residence was interrupted in March 1831 by a visit to Haverhill to settle his father's estate. After a brief return to Hartford, Whittier's own poor health necessitated his leaving that city. Despondent, worn, ill, he went back to the farm and in January 1832 resigned his editorial position.

The Hartford period, though not long, was a significant one for Whittier. His paper was nationally important in politics; Whittier met the influential men of his party. His position as editor was important in the social and literary life of the city. He was one of a large circle of eager, interested people. Mrs. Sigourney, the writer, became his friend and confidante. He was welcomed in the homes of the leading Hartford families; there is evidence that he courted, though unsuccessfully, Miss Cornelia Russ, the daughter of a judge. Boston had been too large and overwhelming to affect him otherwise than with a sense of his own insignificance. Hartford encouraged him and aroused in him strong personal ambition.

For *The Review* of October 18, 1831, he had written a poem, "New England," which voiced his longings:

> Land of my fathers!—if my name,
>   Now humble and unwed to fame,
>   Hereafter burn upon the lip
>
> .   .   .   .   .
>
>   Thine be the bard's undying lay,
>   The murmur of his praise be thine!

"I would have fame with me *now*—or not at all," he wrote at this period.

But in the refuge of the Haverhill farm the road to fame did not appear clearly marked. There was his old interest in poetry; there was his more newly acquired interest in politics. He felt that he must choose between them. Possibly with some defiance, undoubtedly with much regret, he chose the latter.

What he thought he was giving up for ever was very precious to him: "The truth is I love poetry, with a love as warm, as fervent, as sincere, as any of the more gifted worshipers at the temple of the Muses. I consider the gift as something holy and above the fashion of the world." What he chose in its stead he knew was at best but second choice. In January 1833, he wrote to Mrs. Sigourney:

"Of poetry I have nearly taken my leave, and a pen is

getting to be something of a stranger to me. I have been compelled again to plunge into the political whirlpool; for I have found that my political reputation is more influential than my poetical: so I try to make myself a man of the world—and the public are deceived, but I am not. They do not see that I have thrown the rough armor of rude and turbulent controversy over a keenly sensitive bosom,—a heart of softer and greater emotions than I dare expose."

The ambition motivating his conduct plunged him into local politics. The Whig party at Haverhill was divided into factions. Whittier applied his political knowledge to the situation; he used a practical, clear-sighted common sense, characteristic of his New England and his Quaker training. Finally, in 1835, after several years of advising and managing while he was still too young to be eligible for office, he was elected to the Massachusetts legislature. In 1836 he was reëlected, but his poor health prevented his serving.

Political activity, however, had not completely quieted his pen. In 1831, *Legends of New England* was published, seven prose sketches reprinted from *The New England Magazine.* In 1833 appeared *New England Superstitions.* And the writing of poems continued. Toward the work of this period, Whittier was most severe. Only five of the poems, among them "The Vaudois Teacher" and "The Star of Bethlehem," were kept in the final collected edition of his poetry; and only fifteen more were included in the appendix.

Yet during this period, Whittier was consciously achieving what so many other writers, with varying success, were attempting—the production of a native American literature. In the preface to *Legends,* he commented on the richness of local material and said, "The field is a new one—and I have but partially explored it." Again, in an introduction to a volume of poetry, he wrote: "The great forests which our fathers penetrated—the red men—their struggle and their disappearance—the Powwows and the War-dance—the savage inroad and the English sally—the tale of superstition, and the scenes of Witchcraft—all these are rich materials of poetry." These were the subjects that Whittier, himself, was to select for his own poems, so that he was to become preëminently the poet of New England, the narrator of its legends and folk tales.

While Whittier was formulating his literary creed in spite of his determination to abandon poetry, and while he was engaged in Haverhill politics, he met the crisis of his career; and, meeting it, unquestionably unaware of its personal significance, he resolved the conflicting elements of his life. "My lad," in his later years he advised a young boy, "if thou wouldst win success, join thyself to some unpopular but noble cause." This was exactly his own procedure when the crisis presented itself and he joined the Abolition movement. In joining it, he gave up his personal ambition for the sake of an unselfish championing of the negro slave. He gave up the hope of literary and political fame. "For twenty years," he said, "my name would have injured the circulation of any of the literary or political journals in the country." He gave up all this; but, with fitting poetic justice, he received much more. For his ardent labors in the Abolition movement won for him recognition and esteem both in this country and abroad. And the spirit and fervor and feeling which this activity released he was able to put into his verses—first in his anti-slavery poems and then in his others —so that his poetry was deepened and enriched in a way that it had not been before.

That the Abolition movement should have enlisted Whittier's sympathy was not strange. His Quaker heritage accounted partially for it; the Quakers, consistent with their belief in independence and democracy, had as early as 1784 freed whatever slaves they may have held. Whittier's own sympathy, his own experience of labor, quickened his insight into the distress of the oppressed. As a further cause was his association with Garrison. Garrison, interested in one reform or another, had finally given himself wholly to the cause of Abolition. In 1831 he had founded *The Liberator,* an Abolition journal which boasted for its motto "Our country is the world—our countrymen are mankind." Through the efforts of this zealous leader, Whittier was enrolled as a worker.

The progress of the Abolition movement in the United States was by no means a smooth and unimpeded one. In addition to the obvious antagonism of slave-holders and of those not in sympathy with its main purpose, there were dissensions within the ranks of the Abolitionists, themselves. Methods of procedure, secondary issues—such as the attitude towards churches, the Federal constitution, the participation of women—all these caused diversity of opinion, factions within the party, and, at times, the separation of various groups into other organizations. The history was indeed a stormy one.

But throughout it, Whittier held firmly to its prime purpose, the freeing of the slaves. Minor issues, however praiseworthy in themselves, did not swerve him. Always he looked at the problem from the sane practical point of view which was his. It was not the fanaticism of the reformer, but the conviction of the believer, that moved him. So, for example, although he himself had a liberal attitude toward women's activity in public affairs, he knew that others were prejudiced against it; therefore, since it aroused opposition of itself, he felt that in the cause of Abolition it should be restricted. So, too, though it finally meant a separation from Garrison, he favored authorized political means of freeing the slaves rather than the overthrow of the constitution itself.

It was with cool reasoning and statement of figures and facts that Whittier presented his first piece of Abolition writing in 1833: *Justice and Expediency: or, Slavery Considered with a View to Its Rightful and Effectual Remedy, Abolition.* In December 1833, he attended a meeting of the American Anti-Slavery Society in Philadelphia and helped draw up its statement of principles, of which he later said, "I set a higher value on my name as appended to the Anti-Slavery Declaration of 1833 than on the title-page of any book." From that time forth, he gave his effort and attention, in so far as his always troubling health permitted, to the work. He served as district organizer for the Anti-Slavery Society, traveling in New England and the Middle Atlantic states. He edited Abolition papers. He saw his offices in Philadelphia burned by an angry mob; he, himself, traveling with the English Abolitionist, George Thompson, was mobbed at Plymouth, New Hampshire. And he wrote— wrote anti-slavery poems that were published in *The Haverhill Gazette,* in *The Liberator, The Boston Courier,* and *The Pennsylvania Freeman.* They were published; they were widely copied; they were read aloud and declaimed; they served as rallying cries for the adherents and as propaganda for those to be converted. In 1837 these poems were, without Whittier's knowledge, gathered together and published under the title *Poems Written During the Progress of the Abolition Question in the United States Between the Years 1830 and 1838.* In 1838, appeared a volume of poems chosen by Whittier, himself. In this edition, the anti-slavery poems, by far the larger number of those included, formed the first part of the book, followed by a few religious, reform, and historical poems. These poems were, for the most part, rhymed anti-slavery tracts. But if they were transitory in their influence and if they have little significance for the present, for their own time they served as ringing and heartening calls.

In 1840, returning ill health made Whittier give up his active work. He retired to the home on Friend Street in Amesbury, which he had bought in 1836 for his mother and sister after selling the Haverhill farm. In 1836 there had been a six months' tenure of the editorship of *The Haverhill Gazette*. In 1844, he edited a weekly, *The Middlesex Standard*, of Lowell, Massachusetts. From 1847 to 1860 he was associated with *The National Era*, the Washington journal which published *Uncle Tom's Cabin*. But this was his only professional activity.

Though his life thereafter was a quiet one, it was not a secluded one. Whittier was never a recluse. His home was open to all who wished to call. Visiting Friends and visiting Abolitionists found there a warm and hospitable welcome. He had a large circle of dear friends, among whom were a number of women.

Yet in his life there was a sense of disappointment. He was poor. He was, at heart, lonely. There were rumors of his engagement to be married and in his poems allusions to love affairs; but he never did marry. His affection, his tenderness, his love were lavished upon his mother and his sister. "I know there has something very sweet and beautiful been missed," he said, "but I have no reason to complain."

However well he later adjusted himself to his existence, there was a brief period of inquietude and perplexity. His temperament he declared, "ill adapted to that quiet, submissive, introverted state of patient and passive waiting for direction and support under these trials and difficulties." His troubling doubts he voiced in a poem "My Soul and I," written in 1847:

> Stand still, my soul, in the silent dark
>   I would question thee
> Alone in the shadow drear and stark
>   With God and me.

His questions:

> I am; how little more I know!
> Wherever came I? Whither do I go?

never received for him complete or direct answers. But there came a return of the sincere faith of his childhood, a faith without doubt. In 1852, he was able to write in "Questions of Life":

> To Him, from wanderings long and wild,
> I come, an over-wearied child,
> In cool and shade His peace to find,
> Like dew-fall settling on my mind.

From that time forth that was the faith to which he held. From that time, too, one notes in his poetry an insistent return to boyhood themes, in such poems, for example, as "The Barefoot Boy," and "To My Old Schoolmaster."

Thereafter, his poetry became his main existence. There had been, apparently, a brief period when he felt it necessary to apologize for writing verse, a necessity which may have arisen from the early attitude of his Quaker father and from the general suspicious attitude of Americans toward poets. He presented his apology in his poem "To My Sister":

> And, knowing how my life hath been
> A weary work of tongue and pen,
> A long, harsh strife with strong-willed men,
>   Thou wilt not chide my turning
> To con, at times an idle rhyme,
> To pluck a flower from childhood's clime,

> Or listen, at Life's noonday chime,
> For the sweet bells of Morning.

But once that period had passed, he felt himself free to translate the active world of affairs, from which his poor health held him, into terms of poetry. Whatever affected him, whether some event in the political or literary world, whether some incident in his personal life, was reflected in his verse.

He wrote prolifically. *The National Era* of Washington and, with its establishment in 1857, the *Atlantic Monthly* became his chief organs of expression. Month after month his poems appeared. Simple, direct, representative of the manner and thought of the people about him, they were popularly and enthusiastically received. In 1857, the first complete edition of his verse was published. New poems were eagerly awaited. His royalties increased. The life of his household became one of greater comfort. He, himself, at last achieved recognition and success.

The great mass of his poetry, as the great activity of his life, centered about the freeing of the slaves. How significant this was to him is shown by the fact that long after the Civil War had ended, he still retained these poems in the complete edition of his writing, even though he recognized their literary defects. "They were written with no expectation that they would survive the occasions which called them forth: they were protests, alarm signals, trumpet-calls to action, words wrung from the writer's heart, forged at white heat, and of course lacking the finish and careful word-selection which reflection and patient brooding over them might have given."

Many of them have their place only in a history of the Abolition movement; but some of them are true poetry, having a present emotional appeal. Such are "The Kansas Emigrants," "Massachusetts to Virginia," and that most soul-moving poem, "The Farewell of a Virginia Slave Mother" with its haunting refrain:

> Gone, gone—sold and gone,
> To the rice-swamp dank and lone,
> From Virginia's hills and waters;
> Woe is me, my stolen daughters!

The recurring note in these poems of protestation is that of the physical suffering and anguish of the slaves. The black man's champion, Whittier becomes the laureate of the nation, signalizing each event in the long fight against slavery. In 1850, after Daniel Webster's Seventh of March speech in support of Clay's Compromise, a speech in which Whittier felt that Webster was deserting the great cause, the poet wrote "Ichabod," which for intensity of feeling and for force coming from restraint is a poem with few equals:

> So fallen! so lost! the light withdrawn
>   Which once he wore!
> The glory from his gray hairs gone
>   Forevermore!

A massacre of men in South Kansas evoked "Le Marais du Cygne"; the execution of John Brown, "Brown of Ossawatomie."

The inevitable culmination of the progress of events into war, Whittier early foresaw. In 1856 in "What of the Day," he wrote:

> I fain would thank Thee that my mortal life
>   Has reached the hour (albeit through care and pain)
> When Good and Evil, as for final strife,
>   Close dim and vast on Armageddon's plain.

As a Quaker, Whittier was naturally opposed to war. Yet in a war fighting for a principle which Quakers, themselves, believed fundamental to human existence, he and the Society had to take some positive position. In a circular letter to the Society of Friends, Whittier wrote:

"Steadily and faithfully maintaining our testimony against war, we owe it to the cause of truth to show that exalted heroism and generous self-sacrifice are not incompatible with our pacific principles." How could that best be done? By caring for the sick and wounded, by helping those impoverished by the war, as he suggested in "Anniversary Poem":

> The levelled gun, the battle-brand,
>   We may not take:
> But, calmly loyal, we can stand
> And suffer with our suffering land
>   For conscience' sake.
>
>   .   .   .   .   .
>
> And we may tread the sick-bed floors
>   Where strong men pine,
> And, down the groaning corridors,
> Pour freely from our liberal stores
>   The oil and wine.

But throughout the years of the conflict, there was ever the longing for peace, as he expressed it in "The Watchers" and in the very beautiful "What the Birds Said."

These poems seized immediately on the popular imagination and sympathy. Some were put to music and sung to the soldiers of the Union army. "Ein Feste Burg Ist Unser Gott":

> In vain the bells of war shall ring
>   Of triumphs and revenges,
> While still is spared the evil thing
>   That severs and estranges.

was read at a Cabinet meeting. "Barbara Frietchie," even though the incident on which it was based may not have been accurately reported to Whittier, still was so true to possibility and desire that it had a general appeal. So close was Whittier to the nation at large, that when the war was over and the Constitutional amendment abolishing slavery was finally ratified, Whittier could in "Laus Deo" speak for his country:

> Ring and swing,
> Bells of joy! On morning's wing
> Send the song of praise abroad!
> With a sound of broken chains
> Tell the nations that He reigns,
> Who alone is Lord and God!

While he was sharing the sorrows of a warring people and the joys of one again at peace, he had to bear his own very personal griefs. In 1857, his mother died. Shortly after he wrote "Telling the Bees":

> Just the same as a month before,—
> The house and the trees,
> The barn's brown gable, the vine by the door,—
> Nothing changed but the hives of bees.

In 1864 his dear sister Elizabeth died. "It is terrible—the great motive of life seems lost." Again he turned to his poetry for comfort. He wrote "The Vanishers," with its hope of immortality, and "Snow-Bound," which fixed permanently in his memory and in that of his readers his boyhood home before it had been scarred by death.

Whittier continued to live at Amesbury. "It is not as pretty there," he wrote, "but it is more like home, and I seem nearer to the dear ones who lived there with me." If his life was quiet, it was very pleasant. It was colored by a gentle humor, such as could enable him to write to a friend:

But I'm "snow-bound," and cold on cold like layers of an
    onion,
Have piled my back and weighed me down as with the pack
    of Bunyan.

He was popular; his friends were many. He enjoyed occasional brief visits to Boston, to the home of his publisher
and friend, James Fields. His summer vacations in the
mountains were happy interludes, in which he was the center
of a group of younger and older people. His interests were
wide. He, himself, might be restricted to the boundaries of
the New England states, but his mind was free to travel
widely. "I travel a great deal, however, by proxy," he
wrote; and his interest in the Orient, in particular, he manifested in such poems as "The Dead Feast of the Kol-Folk,"
and "The Palm Tree." Alert, calm, sympathetically tender,
he came to be loved both as poet and man. Thus was he
described by Lyman Abbott, the editor of *The Outlook,* in
the January 19, 1921, issue of that magazine:

"No one could call his face handsome; it was better, it
was beautiful. The features were homely, though the forehead was high and the eyes were luminous. Photographs
but illy represent him. For his face was a transparency; the
spirit within lighted it up; and photographs rarely, the older
photographs never, interpret the spirit."

On his seventieth birthday, in 1877, the beloved poet was
greatly honored. *The Literary World* of Boston issued a
special Whittier number; the *Atlantic Monthly* gave him a
dinner. His eightieth birthday was celebrated at Oak Knoll,
a large estate in Danvers, where Whittier was then living
with some distant relatives. On that occasion he was visited
by the governor of Massachusetts who served as the official
representative of the people of the state.

The fame which he had sought as a young man was now
his. The forces which then had driven him first in one direc-

tion and again in another now were at peace. Tranquilly, he awaited the end of life. In August 1891 he wrote to Oliver Wendell Holmes, "I wait the call with a calm trust in the Eternal Goodness." The winter following he was sick. The summer of 1892 he spent with friends at Hampton Falls, New Hampshire. There on September 7, he died. Almost his very last words were, "Love—love to all the world."

If Whittier's life had not been very full in external events, it still had been rich in inner meaning and significance. His whole rounded personality is revealed in his poetry. Essentially, Whittier was a New Englander and a Quaker. He was simple, unaffected; he saw plainly and with clear vision. There was a sane practicality about his life and his thought. "Discussion is doubtless good," he said; "but sometimes bread and meat are better."

There was, as a result, little place for philosophical theorizing about life. The simple faith of the Quakers, after his one period of questioning, satisfied him. As outward symbols of his creed, he wore throughout his life the Quaker coat and he retained in his speech the Quaker *thee* and *thou*. His religious beliefs he expressed again and again in his poetry.

In the generous sweep of his religious tolerance, there was no sympathy with narrow doctrine or with priestcraft:

> Whose mirror of the beautiful and true,
> In Man and Nature, was as yet undimmed
> By dust of theologic strife, or breath
> Of sect, or cobwebs of scholastic lore.

As he was opposed to religious prejudice, so was he opposed to religious fanaticism. His faith was simple, but it held a depth of passion and a strength of conviction that were the results of the overcoming of his early conflicts.

The one need he felt and one which his religion supplied, was the need for belief in immortality.

> I have friends in Spirit Land,
> Not shadows in a shadowy band,
> Not others, but themselves are they.

he wrote; and again:

> Yet Love will dream, and Faith will trust
> (Since He who knows our need is just),
> That somehow, somewhere, meet we must.

The God in whom Whittier believed, He who knew his needs, was essentially a God of goodness and of love. This he declared again and again, in "Expostulation," in "The Eternal Goodness," in "At Last," the poem which he called "the expression of my deepest religious feeling":

> Love Divine, O Helper ever present,
> Be Thou my strength and stay!

So acceptable is this faith of Whittier's, a faith unalloyed by theological and creedal wrangling, that his religious hymns are found in the hymnals of many and varying denominations.

Whittier's conviction was a conviction from within; his illumination, from the "Inner Light." Nature, as a result, taught nothing new; nature for him was simply a further revelation of God and of His goodness.

> The simple faith remains, that He
> Will do, whatever that may be,
> The best alike for man and tree.

The supreme expression of this revelation is in the eloquent poem, "The Last Walk in Autumn."

One other aspect besides its religious one nature had for

Whittier; its sheer beauty delighted him. He wrote poems extolling the frost, the arbutus, the sweet fern. For him, as for Emerson in his poem "Rhodora," "beauty, in and of itself, is good."

This more objective attitude toward nature he showed in his keen observation of the countryside about him. His own farm, the mountains and lakes he visited, the walks he took, are all described with such faithfulness that from his poems complete, detailed pictures of what he saw may be constructed.

The world he drew was never a man-less one. The warmth of Whittier's own personality colors his poems; his interest in men pervades them. In his poems, men and women live, and work, and dream. His interest in human problems leads him to be among the first of American poets to see poetry in labor. His "Songs of Labor" sing the glory of the shoemakers, fishermen, lumbermen, ship-builders, drovers and huskers:

> In labor, as in prayer, fulfilling the same law.

His sympathy for the worker led him in "The Problem" to express a belief in economic practice founded on divine law:

> And well for Gain if it ungrudging yields
> Labor its just demand.

In spite of a dignified reticence, Whittier was not chary of himself in poetry. Lightly, tenderly, he suggests his own personal and intimate desires. "Memories" refers to a romance of the poet's youth. "My Playmate" is a recalling of what was dear to him when he was young.

These references to his youth are many. If "Snow-Bound" is the fullest expression of this clinging to the past, no less suggestive are such lines as

The hills are dearest which our childish feet
Have climbed the earliest,

and

Oh for boyhood's time in June,
Crowding years in one brief moon,

from "The Barefoot Boy"; or such a poem as "In School Days."

Whatever has thus far been said has been rather the consideration of Whittier the man than of Whittier the poet. In what does his significance as a poet lie? Of chief importance is the fact that Whittier was at no time identified with a literary group, not even with that centering about the *Atlantic Monthly.* The source of his own power, therefore, was within him; there, too, was the source of his weakness.

He had formulated for himself a theory of American poetry. He wrote in an article in *The National Era:* "Our poetry is cold—abstract—imitative—the labor of overtasked and jaded intellects, rather than the spontaneous outgushing of hearts warm with love, and strongly sympathizing with human nature as it actually exists about us—with the joys and griefs, the good and even the ill of our common humanity." "We have no Yankee pastorals," he elsewhere wrote.

In his writing, writing which supplied this lack, Whittier contributed little technically. If spontaneity was present—and refreshingly welcome—carelessness also existed. Weak rhymes, like *fact—passed, shared—heard,* are frequent. Meter is often halting, as in a line like

Be she Papist or beggar who lies here, I know and God
knows.

There are several mannerisms which become insistently disturbing. Such is the frequent use of lines ending in *ing*. Such, too, is a habit of reversing the natural order of terms of a comparison:

> Than tyrant's law, or bigot's ban,
> More mighty is your simplest word.

or

> Than yours at Freedom's trumpet-call,
> No craftsmen rallied faster.

Whittier, himself, was not a craftsman of his art. In "The Wreck of Rivermouth," for example, is so highly alliterative a line as

> Their scythes to the swaths of salted grass.

Yet in a letter Whittier wrote, "I am glad to be able to tell thee that I never, in that, or any other poem, consciously sought alliteration, and indeed was not aware of it in 'The Wreck of Rivermouth,' until my attention was called to it by thy letter." He made frequent changes in his poems; but he seemed not to feel the necessity for precision or for perfection. He spoke of the rhymes and meters "which have so long annoyed my friends who have graduated at Harvard instead of a district country school." He wrote to his friend Fields: "I know that 'pearl' and 'mail' do not jingle together well—but the lines have a meaning in them and if the reader will roll his r's a little they will do."

However much Whittier may have lacked technical training and discipline, he possessed a rich native endowment. He presented vivid pictures of the world about him, employing the usual devices of figures of speech: "stag-horn sumach," "hulks of old sailors run aground," "the low hum of home-returning bees,"

Left by the stream whose waves are years
The stranded village seems.

Of as much significance as these flashing glimpses into
the objective world are the keen insights into the inner
world of thought and feeling. His lyrics have refreshing
spontaneity and depth of feeling. Their simplicity, in manner and in use of unaffected diction, adds to their effectiveness and widens their appeal. They are true and recogniz-
ably true.

It is, however, in the field of legend and ballad that Whit-
tier is conspicuous. He is preëminently the story-teller of
New England. There are memorable Oriental tales, "The
Two Rabbin" for example; but those which will doubtless
live longest are those derived from his own New England:
"The Witch of Wenham," "Cassandra," "Maud Muller,"
"Skipper Ireson's Ride," "The Prophecy of Samuel Sewall,"
"The Countess."

In thus recapturing for the future the stories and atmosphere of New England, Whittier was acting consciously as
an American poet. He felt—and felt strongly—that for an
American the source of poetry lay in his own country, not
in Europe. He thus enlarged the field of poetry for his countrymen.

The Indian in poetry had been presented before Whittier.
This tradition he continued. One of his earliest poems,
"Mogg Megone," which he greatly wished to suppress since
it suggested to him "a big Indian in his war-paint strutting
about in Sir Walter Scott's plaid," was essentially native in
its story of the strife between New England settlers and
their Indian neighbors. Other poems of Indian theme are
such poems as "The Truce of Piscataqua" and "Funeral
Tree of the Sokokis."

Besides the Indian, the Quaker becomes, with Whittier,
a figure of poetry. It is not simply that as projections of him-

self his poems are touched with the color of Quaker belief. It is more than that: Quaker individuals are presented as heroic figures, in "Barclay of Ury," for example, and in "Cassandra Southwick," and "The King's Missive."

The first of these three poems happens to be about a Scotch Quaker; the other two are set in the New World. The background of these latter poems is the persecution to which the Quakers in New England were subjected. Whittier, as a student and a lover of New England, recognized the defects as well as the virtues of his Puritan forebears. He refused, as he himself said, to "allow their claim of saint-ship without some degree of qualification." So his pictures of the New England past were as accurate as he could make them. For the New England of his own time, the New England which has now become part of the historical past, his poems can serve as social documents. The life, the spirit, the flavor are in them, reconstructing for the present

These Flemish pictures of old days.

The truth of these poems, their humanity, give them a universal appeal. In two other respects, Whittier, the poet of New England, is a poet for all. As one of the first to dignify labor in poetry, he has a wide appeal. And as the religious poet of simple and undogmatized faith, he speaks for a vast number of people less articulate than he.

It is true that Whittier's poetry is unequal in value. The force of much of his occasional verse died with the occasion for which it was written. Much of his poetry could well be omitted from a permanent collection. Obviously, Whittier is not one of the world's greatest poets. His more modest place, he, himself, suggests:

With not unglad surprise
I see my life-work through your partial eyes;

Assured, in giving to my home-taught songs
A higher value than of right belongs,
You do but read between the written lines
The finer grace of unfulfilled designs.

Yet it is for more than his "unfulfilled designs" that Whittier rightfully holds a place among the greater American poets. He is essentially an American poet and has expressed the thoughts and feelings of his own times. More than that, he has written lasting poems, ballads and legends that have a present interest, lyrics that voice emotions still felt today, and hymns that express a religious faith in which many today still believe.

EDGAR ALLAN POE

FEW AMERICAN writers have presented to biographers more mysteries than has Edgar Allan Poe. Some periods of his life remain a blank, to be made the subject of conjecture by research workers. Others are so beclouded by legends, some of them of Poe's own telling, that factual truth must ever be difficult of discovery. Yet for an understanding of Poe and of his poetry, it seems most unimportant that the time and place of each biographical detail be exactly determined. Poe's life, in so far as it affected his writing, was "a dream within a dream"; and his poetry, the expression of that life, was the stuff of dreams, wherein is little place for facts.

There are, however, some few dates, fairly well removed from doubt and dispute, around which it is convenient to build up the forces that went into the molding of the man. There are, too, facts that cannot be disregarded in attempting some understanding of him.

Some time at the very beginning of the nineteenth century, David Poe of Baltimore, the son of another David who had won the honorary title of General through his services in the Revolution, abandoned his study of the law to become an actor. In the company which he joined was a young actress, Elizabeth Arnold, who at the age of nine had come to America from England with her actress mother and since then had spent her life in the theatre. In 1804 she married a fellow actor, C. D. Hopkins. Their married life was brief, for in 1805 her husband died. In the following year she and David Poe were married.

The troupe of which the Poes were members traveled the eastern coast from Massachusetts to Virginia and South Carolina. When the company was in Boston in 1809, Edgar Poe, the second son of the couple, was born, on January 19. In July of the year, the father, who apparently played only minor rôles on the stage, either died or disappeared. The mother continued her professional career. With her young family, now composed of two sons and a daughter, she endured the hardships and poverty of the road. At the end of 1811, ill, without resources, she was in Richmond, Virginia. Benefit performances were played for her. Some money may possibly have been raised; at best it could have been but little. For, completely destitute, she died in December, leaving as sole material inheritance to her two-year-old son Edgar a miniature of herself and a small picture of Boston Harbor, on the back of which was the injunction to "love Boston, the place of his birth, and where his mother found her best and most sympathetic friends."

What was to become of the three orphans? The elder boy was taken care of by his paternal grandparents in Baltimore, with whom he was apparently visiting when the final tragedy overtook his mother. With the two others the citizens of Richmond concerned themselves. Finally, a family named MacKenzie undertook the care of the little girl Rosalie. Edgar was taken into the household of a merchant, John Allan, whose initial objections to the arrangement were overcome by his wife's pleadings. Mrs. Allan showed the boy the utmost tenderness and devotion. The name Allan was incorporated as a middle name into his own. But, significantly enough, there was never a legal adoption.

These events of his early years could not fail to affect the boy. He must have felt the loss of his own mother and realized that her place was only partially filled by Mrs. Allan. He must have felt, too, the insecurity of his position in the

Allan family. And in a Southern community where family and race counted for much, he must have felt some sense of inferiority to the children about him.

Yet such feelings could not have been always uppermost in his mind. For much of his life was pleasantly lived in the comfortable Allan atmosphere. There are stories of gay parties, at which the little boy, slender, graceful, large-eyed, was permitted to be present, to propose a toast to the guests, or to entertain them with some recitation. At all events, his education was not neglected. At six, attending private school, he was able to read and draw and dance.

In the summer of 1815 Mr. and Mrs. Allan and their foster son sailed for Europe. The trip was in part a business one for Mr. Allan and in part an opportunity for him to visit his family in Scotland. But even the sea trip was not permitted to interfere too severely with Edgar's education, for according to records he took with him a reader and two spelling books.

The European sojourn proved to be a long one. The Allans visited their relatives in Ayrshire, in the Burns country of Scotland. Edgar attended the local Academy. In 1816 they went to England; and Edgar became a pupil first at the Misses Dubourg's School in London, later at the Manor House School of the Reverend John Bransby at Stoke Newington, the school which doubtless was called upon to provide the setting when he came later to write his tale, "William Wilson."

"The house, I have said, was old and irregular. The grounds were extensive, and a high and solid brick wall, topped with a bed of mortar and broken glass, encompassed the whole. This prison-like rampart formed the limit of our domain; beyond it we saw but thrice a week—once every Saturday afternoon, when, attended by two ushers, we were permitted to take brief walks in a body through some of the neighboring fields—and twice during Sunday, when we were paraded in the same formal manner to the morning and evening service in the one church of the village. Of this church the principal of our school was pastor."

At the English school he learned mathematics, a little Latin, and some poor French. The head of his school considered him clever but spoilt.

In the summer of 1820, the American family returned home. Established once again in Richmond, the boy went to the school of one Joseph H. Clarke. He enjoyed the schoolboy sports of running and boxing. He was an excellent swimmer. He was a member of the school's Thespian society. He had some reputation for verse-writing; for when Mr. Clarke retired in 1823, it was Poe who wrote an original ode in his honor. He was lieutenant of the Richmond Junior Volunteers or Morgan Legion, a band of boys who were called upon for service in the celebration attending the visit of General Lafayette in 1824. Altogether, it should have been a rich and full life for the schoolboy who left the Academy in March 1825 to prepare more intensively for entrance into the University of Virginia.

But Poe was not happy. "Since the sad experience of my schoolboy days to this present writing," he wrote in 1840, "I have seen little to sustain the notion held by some folks, that schoolboys are the happiest of all mortals." He took long, lonesome tramps. He gazed through the telescope which his foster father had fixed on the upper portico of his home, searching space for some sort of comfort. He read books that were available to him through Mr. Allan's importing business, *Don Quixote*, *Gil Blas*, Byron, Moore, Coleridge, Wordsworth, Goldsmith and Scott. *Robinson Crusoe*, in particular, seemed to fascinate him.

"How fondly do we recur in memory to those enchanted days of our boyhood when we first learned to grow serious over Robinson Crusoe!—when we first found the spirit of wild adventure enkindling within us, as by the dim firelight we labored out, line by line, the marvelous import of those pages, and hung breathless and trembling with eagerness over their enchanting interest. Alas! the days of desolate islands are no more." [1]

It was the search for a "desolate island," removed from the demands and responsibilities of the world, that was to engross Poe during his life. The island never become a physical reality, but it had no less real an existence within his imagination. Even in his school days he seemed to touch it in his verse writing. The earliest of his known writing, dated 1824, suggests his groping, melancholy turn of mind, his longing for respite from sadness:

> Last night with many cares and toils oppress'd
> Weary . . . I laid me on a couch to rest.

One episode of the schoolboy period is significant, not only because it shows the manner in which his emotions colored his life, but because it is only the first of a number of more or less similar events. Somehow Poe became attracted by Mrs. Jane Stith Stanard, the mother of one of his schoolmates. At most, he could have seen her but several times; yet his feelings were deeply stirred. Possibly, he romantically put her in the place of the mother he had lost. At all events, her death in April 1824 plunged him into despair. His poem "To Helen" (Poe exercised the happy faculty of changing names to suit his purpose and of modifying poems to serve various occasions) is believed to commemorate this early attachment:

[1] Quoted from the *Southern Literary Messenger*, 1836, in *Israfel— The Life and Times of Edgar Allan Poe*, by Hervey Allen, Geo. H. Doran Co.

Helen, thy beauty is to me
Like those Nicéan barks of yore,
That gently, o'er a perfumed sea,
The weary, way-worn wanderer bore
To his own native shore.

It was, then, a sensitive, withdrawn boy of seventeen who in February 1826 entered the University of Virginia in Charlottesville, in the School of Ancient and Modern Languages. The University, only a year old, exemplified a number of interesting and, for America, novel principles. Courses were conducted in the Continental lecture manner; the elective system of work was followed; chapel and military training were optional; and discipline was removed from the hands of the college faculty and put in those of the civil authorities. In this atmosphere, Poe was able to maintain a high standing in class, doing well in Latin, Greek, French, Spanish, and Italian. Outside the classroom he cultivated his own talents, writing verses, and evolving long, fascinating tales to the delight of the students whom he gathered about him.

But even here his life was not secure. The allowance that Mr. Allan gave him was not sufficient for his needs, certainly not for his wants. The desire, evidently, to live the life of those around him, to appear the same as they, led him to gamble, as they did. He became deeply involved in debts. He drank with his companions; but unlike them, he was affected by a single glass.

In December 1826, disturbed by reports of his foster son's conduct, Mr. Allan appeared at the University. Poe was in debt for more than $2,000. Impatient with Poe's weaknesses, Mr. Allan removed him from college and brought him back to Richmond. There, one more blow was to strike Edgar Allan. He had left Richmond engaged to a young girl,

Sarah Elmira Royster. He returned to find that his correspondence with her had been interfered with and that she
was now engaged, with her family's consent, to marry a
Mr. Shelton.

There were several months of fretful disturbance. Mrs.
Allan, Edgar's true friend, was not well. Mr. Allan, with
whom Edgar never seemed in complete rapport, appeared to
have plans distasteful to his foster son. There was evidently
a brief interval spent in the counting-room of Mr. Allan's
business. There may have been a desire on Mr. Allan's part,
a desire unshared by Edgar, that the young man study law.
Whatever the reason, in March 1827, the young man ran
away from home, using the name of Henri Le Rennét.

A few months later found him in Boston, his birthplace.
There, under the name of Edgar A. Perry and pretending to
twenty-two instead of eighteen years of age, he enlisted in
the United States Army.

Early in his military career, in October 1827, appeared
his first book of poems, *Tamerlane and Other Poems by a
Bostonian,* a small volume of ten poems prefaced by this
statement:

"The greater part of the poems which compose this little
volume were written in the year 1821-2, when the author
had not completed his fourteenth year. They were of course
not intended for publication; why they are now published
concerns no one but himself. Of the smaller pieces very little
need be said, they perhaps savour too much of egotism; but
they were written by one too young to have any knowledge
of the world but from his own breast."

How much of this statement is true, one cannot know.
Poe rarely could be relied upon for accuracy of details. But
if they were not the work of a boy of fourteen, they were
that of a boy not more than eighteen.

According to Poe's custom, he was to revise these poems

again and again so that in somewhat altered form they were to appear in each new volume of his verse. It is sufficient here to note that they indicated a sensitivity to beauty and to melody that was to characterize all of Poe's writings.

Poe's writing, however, did not conflict with his career. In his company, which from Boston was transferred to Fort Moultrie, Charleston Harbor, he became company clerk and later Sergeant Major. His services appeared satisfactory to his superior officers so that he had their consent when he applied to Mr. Allan to furnish a substitute for him so that he in turn might go to West Point.

Mr. Allan was somewhat more difficult to convince. There were many complications, many involved incidents. In April 1829, Poe received his army discharge. In February, Mrs. Allan had died. As though released by her death from all claims his foster son may have hoped to have on him, Mr. Allan wrote a most grudging letter on his behalf by way of application for admission to West Point: "Frankly, sir, I do declare that he is no relation to me whatsoever." Finally in June 1830, again falsifying his age, but this time to appear younger than he actually was, Poe was admitted to the Academy.

The interval between his army discharge and his admission to West Point is one of the mysterious intervals of Poe's life. But of what is known, one fact is important: a second volume of verse, *Al Aaraaf, Tamerlane and Minor Poems*, was published under his name in Baltimore. A letter which he wrote at this time to a newspaper said, "I am young—not yet twenty—am a poet—if deep worship of all beauty can make me one—and wish to be so in the more common meaning of the word. I would give the world to embody one half the ideas afloat in my imagination."

It is quite possible, but not certain, that part of this period was spent in Baltimore with his father's family, with his aunt, Mrs. Maria Clemm, who was later to become so important a part of his life.

Removed from certainty and even from probability are the fascinating stories of this period, stories concerned with foreign travels, stories which must have originated somehow in Poe's own telling. They are interesting—as interesting as if they were true—since they reveal Poe's desire to cover with glamor what he wished to keep unknown.

In spite of Poe's own desire to enter West Point, his stay there was brief and terminated by his own efforts. A little more than a year after his entrance, his foster-father married again. Poe, who seemed always to have felt some reliance upon him, must have realized that this new relationship would sever what slender ties held the two. He must have realized that, with the possibility of Mr. Allan's having children of his own, Poe's own hopes for some share of the Allan fortune were groundless. He may have felt that it was the time for a devil-may-care attitude. At all events, quite deliberately Poe set about breaking the regulations of the Academy, absenting himself from classes and from drills, and disobeying officers. The result was court-martial and, in the spring of 1831, expulsion from West Point.

He left the Academy with his army cloak, twenty-four cents, and subscriptions from his former fellow students to a proposed volume of verse. This appeared in March 1831, *Poems,* dedicated to the United States Corps of Cadets.

It contained an introductory letter wherein Poe made clear that he had already formulated the theory of poetry, from which he was not to deviate:

"A poem, in my opinion, is opposed to a work of science by having, for its immediate object, pleasure, not truth; to romance, by having for its object, an indefinite instead of a definite pleasure, being a poem only so far as this object is attained; romance presenting perceptible images with definite, poetry with indefinite, sensations, to which end music is an essential, since the comprehension of sweet sound is our most indefinite conception. Music, when combined with a pleasurable idea, is poetry; music without the idea is simply music; the idea without the music is prose from its very definiteness."

Somehow, the young poet, having left West Point and having seen to the publication of his poems in New York, made his way to Baltimore. There he became part of the household, poor and crowded, of his aunt, Mrs. Clemm. She was the one efficient person on whom all depended, her mother, her children, Poe, and Poe's elder brother. As death claimed one, then another, of the family, it was Mrs. Clemm who kept up courage. When poverty denuded it, it was Mrs. Clemm who miraculously secured the necessities of existence. The group dwindled until it was composed of Mrs. Clemm, her very young daughter Virginia, and her nephew, Edgar Allan Poe. The ties uniting them became stronger. Upon Edgar, Mrs. Clemm lavished an unwavering devotion and loyalty. In her he found that protection and security he had always been seeking.

What were his contributions to the household? There were several attempts to find work, attempts, however, that failed. And there must have been, either as efforts to make money, or—more probably—as escapes from reality, much writing of tales and of poems; for when the *Baltimore Sunday Visiter* in 1833 announced a literary competition, Poe entered contributions of verse and of prose. His *Tales of the Folio Club* won the prize in the prose division, "Mss. Found in a Bottle" being the story chosen for publication. "The Coliseum" was chosen as the prize-winning poem; but when the anonymously submitted poem was found to be by the same author as the prize-winning story, the verse-prize was awarded elsewhere.

John P. Kennedy, one of the contest judges, became interested in Poe. He invited him to dine. The straits to which Poe was reduced are suggested by his answering note: "I cannot come—and for reasons of the most humiliating nature in my personal appearance." This admission was accompanied by a request for some money, a request which pride did not restrain Poe from making again and again to friends and acquaintances.

Kennedy proved a loyal friend. Through him, Poe's tales were published in the *Southern Literary Messenger* of Richmond, Virginia. As these and an occasional poem were published, Poe became more and more widely known.

Finally he was offered the position of assistant to the editor of the Richmond publication. One can imagine the eagerness with which the offer was accepted. Here was an opportunity to earn a living and to justify the time he had spent in writing. Here was an opportunity, furthermore, to return to Richmond, the city of his youth, the only place where he had felt at home—where he was ever to feel quite at home. Mr. Allan, it is true, had died without leaving anything to his foster son; but there were friends in Richmond ready to welcome him.

Poe left, held his job successfully for a short time, and then lost it through intemperance. Poe's drinking and, later, his use of drugs were scarcely indulgences for the sake of pleasure; they were, rather, acknowledgments of his inability to adjust to the world about him, efforts to find the "desolate island" where he might be at peace.

In this instance, the owner of the *Southern Literary Messenger* had a sincere belief in Poe's ability and shortly afterwards invited Poe to resume editorial charge. From now on, Poe's life was connected with various periodicals and newspapers in Richmond, in Philadelphia, in New York. An editorial position would be secured. A quarrel, pride too easily hurt, intemperance, or a misunderstanding would lose it. Plans would be made by Poe for a magazine of his own— and would never be put into effect. A new position would be obtained; and the process repeated.

There is, however, no question that Poe was a skillful editor. Under his guidance, magazines like the *Messenger* and *Burton's Gentleman's Magazine* and *Graham's Magazine* increased enormously in circulation. A new journalistic era was beginning, one in which periodical readers were sought among women and among the large average public; Poe sensed this and was able to meet the demands of his new subscribers. His success made him well known.

Another factor contributed to his prestige in the literary world. Much of Poe's writing consisted of literary criticism. In this he was bold, even defiant, and his caustic statements involved him in a number of controversies. In his criticism he revealed a pathetic pretense of recondite learning; a confidence in his own omniscience that occasionally led to woeful errors of judgment; an obsessive concern with evidences of what he considered plagiarism in others. But he did formulate certain literary canons, particularly for his own kind of poetry and for his form of short story; and he did encourage the literary independence of the growing number of American writers.

Still another aspect of Poe's literary work must be considered, that of his own creative writing. His short stories appeared in various periodicals, "The Gold Bug" winning a $100 prize and his "Balloon Hoax" proving a New York sensation for several days. After many trials with publishers, his tales were published in book form. But neither from individual nor from book publication was Poe's remuneration great.

In these tales the hero was always a projection of Poe, himself. In the stories of ratiocination, it was Poe the logical thinker he thought himself to be; in those of the supernatural, of the weird outpourings of a distorted mind, it was Poe seeking in his imagination an escape from poverty, sorrow, and bitterness.

Like these latter stories were his poems. Reworked completely, or changed word by word, they appeared now in one form, now in another. But always they were touched with melancholy, with an air not of this world. Some sang of the love of a dead woman; some, of a mystical, imagined land. All suggested the longing for the Eldorado of escape:

> And, as his strength
>   Failed him at length,
> He met a pilgrim shadow—
>   "Shadow," said he,
>   "Where can it be—
> This land of Eldorado?"
>
> "Over the Mountains
>   Of the Moon,
> Down the Valley of the Shadow,
>   Ride, boldly ride,"
>   The shade replied,—
> "If you seek for Eldorado."

What was there in Poe's life, in addition to a pursuing, unrelenting poverty, that might be a reason for this search by way of poetry, of drink, and of drugs?

In 1836, a rather amazing event had taken place. Poe was then in Richmond, editor of the *Southern Literary Messenger*. He sent for his aunt Mrs. Clemm and her daughter, Virginia. In May of that year he married his cousin, who was then not quite fourteen. There may even have been a secret marriage in Baltimore the year before. But the Richmond ceremony was an open and public one; and guests marveled at the youthfulness of the bride, whose age had been falsified for the ceremony. Thereafter the Poe household, until broken up by death, consisted of Edgar, Virginia, and of Mrs. Clemm, the stay of the household, the source of aid and of comfort for the poet.

Because I feel that, in the Heavens above,
    The angels, whispering to one another,
Can find, among their burning terms of love,
    None so devotional as that of "Mother,"
Therefore by that dear name I long have called you—
    You who are more than mother unto me.

The devotion which Poe, in turn, lavished upon his young wife was profound and unchanging. But there could scarcely have existed between them that mutuality of relationship which is the basis of most marriages. For in addition to the disparity in years, there was a vast difference between the two in intellect. Virginia mentally seemed never to mature completely.

Moreover, she was far from strong. While they were living in Philadelphia, one evening she began to sing and in her singing burst a blood vessel. Thereafter, the threat of death hung constantly over her. Its menace added to Poe's own insecurity. "This I can endure as becomes a man," Poe wrote after her death. "It was the horrible, never-ending oscillations between hope and despair which I could not longer have endured, without total loss of reason."

While in Philadelphia, Poe was fired with the desire to have a Government position, a clerkship in the customs house for example, which might bring in some steady source of income to his household. There seemed at one time some possibility of this being accomplished. But a trip to Washington to further the matter ended in intoxication and the proper contacts were not made. Although on his return Poe still had some hope of an appointment, none was forthcoming.

Finally, in 1843, Poe and Virginia left for New York, leaving Mrs. Clemm in Philadelphia to follow when she could. Poe's letter to his mother-in-law on his arrival gives intimate details of the boarding-house life in which they found themselves. It reveals, too, how very, very low were their resources. "We have now got four dollars and a half left. Tomorrow I am going to try and borrow three dollars, so that I may have a fortnight to go upon."

Mrs. Clemm soon arrived, and the household resumed its usual course. Poe did occasional work on New York newspapers. He had a few articles and stories published. But always poverty and illness haunted the family.

On January 29, 1845, about a year and a half after Poe's coming to New York, the *Evening Mirror* printed a long, strange poem, with a haunting refrain:

Quoth the Raven, "Nevermore."

The poem was "The Raven." Published at first anonymously, it soon became known as Poe's. Instantly, it sprang into popularity. Its insistent melody, its intricate rhythm, its sense of the unreal, its suggestion of possible profundity of meaning, all these caught the public imagination. Poe became famous. At the end of the year, *The Raven and Other Poems*, his collected verse, was published.

This fame, notoriety almost, made him a part of New York's literary circle. The group included a number of women, minor poets, dabblers in literary wares, or mere hangers-on to the literary fringe. Poe, who seemed always to need the affections of women, liked them and, in turn, was admired by them. Earlier poems were now changed so that they might be made to apply to these new acquaintances. Letters were written. Possibly mild flirtations indulged in.

But there was in all this no disloyalty to Virginia. Occasionally she attended with Poe one of the frequent literary soirées. More often, however, illness prevented her presence.

The family now was living in Fordham, a few miles outside of New York City, in a tiny house, bare but scrupulously clean. There some of the New York littérateurs were visitors, and devoted friends called and did what they could to help the family. There, in spite of care and devotion, Virginia died at the end of January, 1847.

Poe was plunged into grief, which is echoed in "Ulalume."

> Thus I pacified Psyche and kissed her,
>   And tempted her out of her gloom—
>   And conquered her scruples and gloom;
> And we passed to the end of the vista,
>   But were stopped by the door of a tomb—
>   By the door of a legended tomb;
> And I said—"What is written, sweet sister,
>   On the door of this legended tomb?"
>   She replied—"Ulalume—Ulalume—
>   'Tis the vault of thy lost Ulalume!"
>
> Then my heart it grew ashen and sober
>   As the leaves that were crisped and sere—
>   As the leaves that were withering and sere,
> And I cried—"It was surely October
>   On *this* very night of last year
>   That I journeyed—I journeyed down here—
>   That I brought a dread burden down here—
>   On this night of all nights in the year,
>   Ah, what demon has tempted me here?

Well I know, now, this dim lake of Auber—
This misty mid region of Weir—
Well I know, now, this dank tarn of Auber,
This ghoul-haunted woodland of Weir."

After his wife's death, Poe resumed his plans for a magazine of his own. In order to raise money for this project, he undertook a series of lectures. The subject for these lectures was based on a work then engaging Poe's efforts, a work indicative of his self-confidence, "Eureka," a prose poem. This aimed to supply a complete physical explanation of the universe. With assurance Poe declared, "What I have propounded will (in good time) revolutionize the world of Physical and Metaphysical science. I say this calmly, but I say it."

After his wife's death came, too, a renewed need for the affection of women. For a time, a Mrs. Shew, a woman with some medical ability who had befriended the Poes, was close to him. Indeed, from her is said to have come the initial creative impulse for his poem "The Bells." But she soon felt it wiser to end the relationship and did so.

There followed a curious set of romances. On one of his lecture trips to Boston, in passing through Providence, Poe saw a Mrs. Sarah Helen Whitman, one of the numerous minor women poets of the time. He was attracted by her. Poems were anonymously exchanged. A meeting was arranged. And then Poe paid open court. There was an acknowledged engagement, conditional upon Poe's abstinence from drink. The date for the marriage was fixed. But Poe, on this last visit to Providence, succumbed once more. He became drunk. Mrs. Whitman broke the engagement. This affair, thus briefly outlined, was punctuated by periods of infatuation and by one attempt at suicide. Yet throughout its course, Poe was writing warm, devoted letters to another woman, a Mrs. Annie Richmond, to whom he went for soothing, calming affection.

Lectures and plans for a magazine had taken Poe North, where one romance was begun and ended and another platonically pursued. Now they were to take him South, where he revived still another romance.

In the summer of 1849 he left for Richmond. On the way he stopped at Philadelphia, where he had a still unexplained misadventure which again involved intoxication. But arriving at last at Richmond, he was warmly welcomed and became a part of the social and literary life there. He lectured. He wrote. And he met once more his boyhood love, Sarah Elmira Royster, now the widowed Mrs. Shelton. The youthful love affair was renewed. There were quarrels and reconciliations, partings and meetings. But finally the date for the marriage was set for October 17.

It was necessary for Poe to arrange his affairs in New York. He bade farewell to Mrs. Shelton and early on September 27 sailed for Baltimore. After his arrival there, there followed a period of five days about which nothing is known. Guesses and possible explanations are many. The fact is, however, that on October 3, he was picked up from the street, unconscious and unquestionably suffering from alcoholism. He was taken to the Washington Hospital where he died on Sunday, October 7, murmuring, if one can believe the story, "Lord help my poor soul."

Mourning him, faithful in her insistence on her Eddy's gentleness, kindliness, and sobriety, was his aunt and mother-in-law, Mrs. Clemm.

It was a strange, conflicted life that passed away, a life that from the grave had power to stir up long discussions and bitter controversies. In an autobiographical letter to James Russell Lowell, Poe gave some clew to its strangeness: "I have been too deeply conscious of the mutability and evanescence of temporal things to give any continuous effort to anything—to be consistent in anything. My life has been *whim*—impulse—passion—a longing for solitude—a scorn of all things present, in an earnest desire for the future."

Yet even in this he was not completely honest. He did not always scorn "all things present." His agonized statement to a Fordham visitor, "I love fame—I dote on it—I idolize it—I would drink to the very dregs the glorious intoxication," belies that.

In his pretended scorn for his contemporaries, was there not a longing for superiority? "My whole nature," he wrote in "Eureka," "utterly *revolts* at the idea that there is any Being in the Universe superior to myself!" In the universe which he, himself, created, the universe of his imagination and of his poems, he was supreme.

The life of a person like Poe for some people inevitably raises the question of the relationship between morals and art. In one respect, the two are quite completely distinct. The quality of a work of art cannot be determined by the presence or absence of moral rectitude in its creator. That is the criterion for judging him as a man, not as an artist. So Poe's lack of moral stamina cannot of itself be used to condemn Poe's poetry.

Morals may enter the realm of esthetics, however, when art is used to reveal a moralistic philosophy. But then it becomes the subject matter of art, not art itself.

This aspect Poe definitely refused to admit to his poetry. "With the Intellect or with Conscience, it has only collateral relations. Unless incidentally, it has no concern whatever either with Duty or with Truth." Pleasure he considered the object of poetry; the search for truth, he declared, destroys pleasure and so destroys art.

SONNET—TO SCIENCE

Science! true daughter of Old Time thou art!
  Who alterest all things with thy peering eyes.
Why preyest thou thus upon the poet's heart,
  Vulture, whose wings are dull realities!
How should he love thee? or how deem thee wise,
  Who wouldst not leave him in his wandering
To seek for treasure in the jewelled skies,
  Albeit he soared with an undaunted wing?
Hast thou not dragged Diana from her car?
  And driven the Hamadryad from the wood
To seek a shelter in some happier star?
  Hast thou not torn the Naiad from her flood,
The Elfin from the green grass, and from me
The summer dream beneath the tamarind tree?

Whether his poems are illustrations of his philosophy of
poetry or whether that philosophy is an after-explanation of
the one kind of poetry he could write, makes little difference.
This is what he declared to be his philosophy of poetry;
these are the poems he wrote. Measuring the latter by the
former, are they successful?

In thus removing all moral implication from his work—
whether from true conviction or whether from his own inability to do otherwise—Poe set himself as one of the first
American poets to insist upon art for art's sake. In this insistence he maintained for many years a complete isolation.
In this country, he exerted no immediate or direct influence.
America was a morally righteous country and for a time
needed an art closely identified with its morals.

But there was something in Poe that did appeal to a large
number of people. In the narrow field to which he limited
himself, he did stir the emotions as few have stirred it.
Vague, haunting unrest—each one feels this at some time

and this Poe did express. But haunting unrest is not the only human emotion, and, in limiting himself to this, Poe limited his appeal and his greatness.

How did Poe thus restrict himself? He was a poet who revealed no broad human philosophy. He showed no conception of human character; and in his delineation of a single human emotion he revealed no saving sense of humor, no sense of proportion. He becomes, then, a poet simply of abstract beauty.

"The rhythmical creation of beauty" was Poe's object in writing poetry. The test of his poetry's success was the emotional response of the reader. "For a poem is not the Poetic faculty," he declared, "but the *means* of exciting it in mankind."

Poe worked out an elaborate theory of composition to achieve his desired effect. His explanation of the writing of "The Raven," for example, is a highly logical elucidation of his method. Again, it is open to question whether this explanation reveals the complete truth. But the importance of it, as the importance of all Poe's theories, is the revelation of Poe's consciousness of craftsmanship and of his consummate mastership of his art.

A poem, since it aims at emotional appeal and since no single emotion is long lasting, must, according to Poe, be brief. Most of his own poems are short; certainly, his most successful ones are. Such longer poems as "Tamerlane" and "Al Aaraaf," in their difficult confusion, justify Poe in his decision.

A poem, then, must be brief, and it must provoke an emotion. To Poe the greatest emotion, the purest pleasure, came from the contemplation of beauty. In its perfect form, some touch of strangeness and of sadness must be added. So to Poe the death of a beautiful woman seemed the highest expression of this emotion, the most poetical one. This would appear a pattern running through his life as in his poetry. Beauty never completely attained, love never quite fulfilled —the deaths of his own mother and of Mrs. Allan, the incomplete romances with Mrs. Shelton and Mrs. Whitman, the strange marriage with his cousin—separation of some sort from a beautiful woman, this is the theme of many of his poems. It is the theme of "The Sleeper," for example, of "Lenore," of "The Raven" and of "Ulalume." It is the burden of "Annabel Lee."

> But our love it was stronger by far than the love
>   Of those who were older than we—
>   Of many far wiser than we—
> And neither the angels in heaven above,
>   Nor the demons down under the sea,
> Can ever dissever my soul from the soul
>   Of the beautiful ANNABEL LEE:
>
> For the moon never beams, without bringing me dreams
>   Of the beautiful ANNABEL LEE;
> And the stars never rise, but I feel the bright eyes
>   Of the beautiful ANNABEL LEE:
> And so, all the night-tide, I lie down by the side
> Of my darling—my darling—my life and my bride,
>   In the sepulchre there by the sea—
>   In her tomb by the sounding sea.

One other pattern, carried over from Poe's life, is found in his poetry. His efforts to escape from this world are revealed in his creation of worlds of his own. If they are strange, morbid, shadowy ones, they must be the counterparts of his mind subjected to liquor and to drugs. His world he may call Eldorado or "distant Aidenn"; it may be a "City in the Sea" or a "Valley of Unrest." Whatever its name, whatever its location, it is

A wild weird clime that lieth, sublime
Out of SPACE—out of TIME.

It is a land where "huge moons there wax and wane," a land of darkness, of sullen waters, of strangely shaped buildings, of melancholy, and of ruin. "The City in the Sea" reveals a world typically Poesque in its sense of strangeness and of desolateness:

Lo! Death has reared himself a throne
In a strange city lying alone
Far down within the dim West,
Where the good and the bad and the worst and the best
Have gone to their eternal rest.
There shrines and palaces and towers
(Time-eaten towers that tremble not!)
Resemble nothing that is ours.
Around, by lifting winds forgot,
Resignedly beneath the sky
The melancholy waters lie.

The epitome of desolation and of futility is reached in the poem "The Conqueror Worm." All human activity, all efforts of those made "in the form of God on high" come to nothing. The angels, themselves, are made to declare

That the play is the tragedy, "Man,"
And its hero the Conqueror Worm.

The sense of climax in these two lines, the closing ones of the poem, a sense of climax shown again and again, noticeably in "The Raven," suggests the ability with which Poe was able to handle his material.

His methods were conscious and deliberate. Occasionally, they appear too conscious, too elaborate. But for the most part they are successful in their accomplishment.

One of these methods is the use of symbols. Frequently suggestion is more effective than expatiation. Poe was well aware of this. The bird in "The Raven" becomes the symbol of unremitting sorrow and despair. "The Haunted Palace" in its entirety is the symbol of a disintegrating mind.

Almost like symbols in their associative quality are the names Poe uses. This, in itself, is a manifestation of Poe's ability to produce effect simply through sound; for many of these names are manufactured: Nesace, Ligeia, Ulalume. The music of sound appealed to Poe. Consider, for example, the adroit use of the letter *s* in his poem, "The Sleeper":

> Strange is thy pallor! strange thy dress!
> Strange, above all, thy length of tress,
> And this all solemn silentness!

Or the use of *l* in these lines from "Dream-Land":

> Their lone waters—lone and dead,—
> Their still waters—still and chilly
> With the snows of the lolling lily.

The supreme examples of Poe's use of word-tones to create effect is, of course, that tour-de-force of onomatopœia, "The Bells."

The two ordinary poetic devices, those of rhyme and of meter, Poe held in complete control. Poe's rhyme schemes are never obvious. Sometimes, as in "A Dream Within a Dream," a third rhyming-line is found where one might, otherwise, expect couplets. The pattern is rarely fixed. In "Israfel," for example, two successive five-line stanzas have different schemes. Double rhymes are frequent; almost any poem, chosen at random, reveals this. His use of internal rhyme is shown in the lines from "Lenore":

Ah, broken is the golden bowl! the spirit flown forever!
Let the bell toll!—a saintly soul floats on the Stygian river.

Somewhat allied to rhyme, in its creation of a sense of
recognition and in its effectiveness, is Poe's use of parallel-
ism and of repetition, a characteristic and frequently used
device. The poem, "I Saw Thee on Thy Bridal Day" repeats
with a change of only three words a whole stanza. "The
Raven" uses "Nevermore" as a haunting refrain. But much
more subtle and infinitely more effective are repetition of
lines and of phrases within the stanza itself. These lines
from "Lenore" suggest the method:

An anthem for the queenliest dead that ever died so young—
A dirge for her the doubly dead in that she died so young.

The lines from "Dream-Land":

> Their lone waters, lone and dead,—
> Their sad waters, sad and chilly,

reveal still another variation of this device. "The Raven" is
replete with it. So, too, is "Ulalume."

> And now, as the night was senescent
> And star-dials pointed to morn—
> As the star-dials hinted of morn—
> At the end of our path a liquescent
> And nebulous lustre was born,
> Out of which a miraculous crescent
> Arose with a duplicate horn—
> Astarte's bediamonded crescent
> Distinct with its duplicate horn.

If Poe was able to use sound in surprising, in effective
ways, he was equally successful in the use of meter and the
introduction of metrical changes. He was less happy in fixed

forms like the sonnet, or like blank verse, as in his poem
"To Helen," beginning

> I saw thee once—once only—years ago.

But in his lyric meters, he could ring whatever changes he
wished. The lines of "Ulalume," for example, provide a noticeable contrast with those of "The Raven." "The City in
the Sea" reveals a wide variation in feet. In "Israfel," the
short last line of each stanza is most effective; the stanza
form, itself, defies outlining. Short lines are introduced, un-
expectedly, in "The Haunted Palace." Underneath these
variations, however, is a basic flow of music; behind Poe's
flexibility is a canny understanding of the tremendous
power of repetition combined with change.

There can be no question of Poe's technical skill. His
place as a poet cannot be so definitely fixed. Depth of feeling, variety of experience, broad philosophy—these his
poems lack. Frequently, they lack even meaning. But if one
can admit the standard which Poe set for himself, the creation of an emotional effect, one must acknowledge the un-
dying success of some few of his poems. "The City in the
Sea," "The Sleeper," "Ulalume," these seem destined to be
a permanent part of American literature. So, too, does
"Israfel" with its bold, challenging last stanza:

> If I could dwell
> Where Israfel
>   Hath dwelt, and he where I,
> He might not sing so wildly well
>   A mortal melody,
> While a bolder note than this might swell
>   From my lyre within the sky.

Those simple lyrics, "To Helen," "For Annie," and "Annabel Lee," must surely endure.

But what of Poe as an American poet? His Americanism was the mere accident of birth. So far as his poetry is concerned, Poe is outside space and outside time. He does not stimulate. He answers no human questioning. He offers no solace. He was the "weary, way-worn wanderer," whose songs reflect his restlessness and will continue to reflect it through the years. Love, Beauty, and Death—with these only is Poe concerned; of these is he the limited, but triumphant singer.

OLIVER WENDELL HOLMES

O N AUGUST 29, 1809, Abiel Holmes, the pastor of the
First Congregational Church of Cambridge, Massachusetts, made a marginal notation in his almanac: "—29
son b." The son whose birth was thus recorded was Oliver
Wendell Holmes. The eighty-five years of his life were to
be surprisingly free of external incidents worthy of almanac
dates and recording; but rich in interests and in feelings,
they were to make him a beloved person and a beloved poet.
Definitely circumscribing his activities by the limits of Boston, which he facetiously termed the Hub of the Universe,
Holmes was to have a general appeal wherever the qualities
of breeding, urbanity, kindliness, and zest for life were appreciated.

To whatever extent America has traditions of aristocracy,
Holmes inherited them and, in his turn, passed them on. In
his book, *The Autocrat of the Breakfast Table,* he wrote:
"I go for the man with the family portraits against the
one with the twenty-cent daguerreotype, *unless* I find that
the latter is the better of the two. I go for the man who in-
herits family traditions, and the cumulative traditions of at
least four or five generations." One whose ancestors had for
several generations the advantages of a college education
and had been members of one of the three professions, law,
medicine, or theology, one who, through this very inheritance, had an air of breeding and an ease with books be-
longed to what Holmes called "the Brahmin caste of New
England."

Through both his father and his mother Holmes was

rightfully one of that caste. The Holmes family, tracing its history back to 1686, when one John Holmes arrived in Woodstock, Connecticut, from England, had its share of the lawyers, ministers, and doctors whom Holmes considered necessary for family dignity. The poet's grandfather, David, a doctor, fought in the French and Indian Wars and was a surgeon in the Revolution. Abiel, the poet's father, was a graduate of Yale; he combined with his pastoral duties an antiquarian interest and a sound scholarship that resulted in his book, *Annals of America*. The poet's mother, Sarah Wendell, bright, vivacious, and sprightly, was the daughter of Oliver Wendell, a graduate of Harvard and a judge. Through her the poet traced his descent from Ann Bradstreet, the first American woman poet; and through his mother came the slight Dutch dilution of an otherwise purely English heritage:

Mynheers, you both are welcome! Fair cousin Wendell P.,
Our ancestors were dwellers beside the Zuyder Zee;
Both Grotius and Erasmus were countrymen of we,
And Vondel was our namesake, though he spelt it with a V.

Because of his firm belief in the influence of heredity upon the individual, his belief that "our life is half underground," the double line of distinguished ancestors meant much to Holmes.

His boyhood, in a family of two sons and three daughters, was spent in Cambridge, a center of learning and culture as the seat of Harvard University. His home was a gambrel-roofed house, "an unpretending mansion, such as very possibly you were born in yourself, or at any rate such a place of residence as your minister or some of your well-to-do country cousins find good enough, but not at all too grand for them."

The boy began his formal education with women teachers

in what were called Dame's Schools. After a few years he became a pupil of William Biglow; still later, at the age of ten, he went to the "Port School," at Cambridgeport, a mile from the college.

But with him, as with so many other writers, it was the life lived outside of school hours that apparently provided the more lasting impressions and the stronger influences. One of his chief joys he found in the books at his disposal, those in his father's large library—English classics, sermons, and other theological works—and those which changing tastes had relegated to the attic. He admitted later to having read few of the books through; but there began in those early days that characteristic of his life, his profound love of books for their subject matter and for their physical form. His favorite reading was Pope's Homer. "To the present time the grand couplets ring in my ears and stimulate my imagination, in spite of their formal symmetry, which makes them hateful to the lawless versificators who find anthems in the clash of blacksmiths' hammers, and fugues in the jangle of the sleigh bells." Moved by the poetry he read, he began to make verses in imitation of Pope or Goldsmith; to the influence of these poets can unquestionably be traced something of Holmes's own nicety and precision in verse form.

Not only with books, but with people too, Holmes early grew familiar and friendly. The poet's father was a man of importance in the community; his home was a gracious and hospitable one. To it came visitors who widened the boy's horizon, particularly the various clergymen who at times filled the pulpit of Dr. Holmes's church. Their influence on young Oliver was great. In *The Poet at the Breakfast Table* he names some of these clerical visitors and then goes on to say:

"It was a real delight to have one of those good, hearty,

happy, benignant old clergymen pass the Sunday with us, and I can remember some whose advent made the day feel almost like 'Thanksgiving.' But now and then would come along a clerical visitor with a sad face and a wailing voice, which sounded exactly as if somebody must be lying dead upstairs, who took no interest in us children, except a painful one, as being in a bad way with our cheery looks, and did more to unchristianize us with his woebegone ways than all his sermons were like to accomplish in the other direction. I remember one in particular, who twitted me so with my blessings as a Christian child, and whined so to me about the naked black children who, like the 'Vulgar Little Boy,' 'hadn't got no supper and hadn't got no ma,' and hadn't got no Catechism, (how I wished for the moment I was a little black boy!) that he did more in that one day to make me a heathen than he had ever done in a month to make a Christian out of an infant Hottentot. . . . I might have been a minister myself, for aught I know, if this clergyman had not looked and talked so like an undertaker."

Although he was thus to be saved from a ministerial career, his childhood was still to be filled with questions and puzzles of a theological flavor. He speculated upon the problem of existence and reached the solution of considering himself "afloat like a balloonist in the atmosphere of life." God became for him "an Old Man." Taught the Westminster Catechism, he revolted against the idea that men are fallen wretches.

But even in the liberalized atmosphere of a Congregational home, he could not shake off completely the Puritan heritage of a sense of sin and of evil. He was tormented by a fear of evil spirits which were embodied for him in the "Devil's Footsteps," barren spots in the fields near his home and breaks in the walls of the college buildings. "Two spectres haunted my earliest years," he afterwards said, "the dread of midnight visitors and the visits of the doctor."

It is particularly interesting in the case of Holmes to see the modification of these childish fears and their effect upon the development of the man. His innate kindliness and sympathy struggled with these dreads and overcame them. As a result Holmes, himself, became a doctor and, more important, his whole mature philosophy was heartened by a hopeful trust in the goodness of God and by an unwavering charitableness toward mankind which ignored completely the possibility of sin and guilt.

However serious some of the young boy's thoughts may have been, philosophical speculation did not engross him completely.

"Exceptional boys of fourteen or fifteen make home a heaven, it is true," Holmes writes in his autobiographical article "Cinders from the Ashes," "but I have suspected, late in life, that I was not one of the exceptional kind. I had tendencies in the direction of flageolets and octave flutes. I had a pistol and a gun, and popped at everything that stirred, pretty nearly, except the house-cat. Worse than this, I would buy a cigar and smoke it by installments, putting it meantime in the barrel of my pistol, by a stroke of ingenuity which it gives me a grim pleasure to recall; for no maternal or other female eyes would explore the cavity of that dread implement in search of contraband commodities."

It was, then, a very real and active boy who, at the age of fifteen, was about ready to enter college. For the year of preparatory study which was thought necessary he went to Phillips Academy at Andover, Massachusetts, in the fall of 1824. The twenty-mile trip from Cambridge to Andover was made by horse and wagon, his parents accompanying the "slightly nostalgic boy."

How like a dagger to my sinking heart
Came the dry summons, "It is time to part;
Good-by!" "Goo-ood-by!" one fond maternal kiss—
Homesick as death! Was ever pang like this?
Too young as yet with willing feet to stray
From the tame fireside, glad to get away,—
Too old to let my watery grief appear,—
And what so bitter as a swallowed tear!

His new schoolmates at the Academy, his new teachers, the family with whom he lived, the residents of Andover, all these widened Holmes's circle of acquaintances and deepened his capacity for human relationships. From the Andover period, too, came Holmes's "First Verses," his earliest available poetry, a translation from the first book of *The Æneid:*

The god looked out upon the troubled deep
Waked into tumult from its placid sleep;
The flame of anger kindles in his eye
As the wild waves ascend the lowering sky.

In these verses Holmes was still carrying out the classical tradition.

After a year at Phillips, Holmes entered Harvard, a member of the famous class of 1829, made famous, indeed, because he became its poet laureate. He was a fair student, interested particularly in modern languages and in chemistry and mineralogy. From the scientific approach to problems with which he thus became acquainted he apparently derived much satisfaction; for it later influenced his choice of profession and it indubitably affected his general attitude toward life.

The Harvard years were years of joyous living. His social life was full. He was a member of Medical Faculty, a college mock society. His poetic ability was recognized both by his fellow students, who made him class poet, and by the faculty, who assigned him poems as his share in college exhibitions. With characteristic lightness and gayety, which did not hesitate at choosing himself as a subject for humorous comment, he presented his own pen portrait to Phineas Barnes, who had been a Phillips classmate.

"When you come here you must not expect to see in me a strapping grenadier or a bearded son of Anak, but a youth of low stature and an exceeding smooth face. To be sure I have altered a little, since I was at Andover. I wear my gills erect, and do not talk sentiment. I court my hair a little more carefully, and button my coat a little tighter; my treble has broken down into a bass, but still, I have very little of the look of manhood. I smoke most devoutly, and sing most unmusically, have written poetry for an Annual, and seen my literary bantlings swathed in green silk and reposing in the drawing-room. I am totally undecided what to study; it will be law or physick, for I cannot say that I think the trade of authorship quite adapted to this meridian." [1]

Among the writings to which Holmes referred in this letter was a series of satirical poems, *Poetical Illustrations of the Athenæum Gallery of Paintings,* on which he collaborated with two college mates, John Osborne Sargent and Park Benjamin. Although this work strengthened Holmes's reputation, he had reached the same conclusion that other American poets reached: writing could not be made a vocation. The Brahmin tradition, so strong in Holmes, pointed to one of the three recognized professions. The church he had rejected long before. Of the remaining, his first choice was law.

[1] *Life and Letters of Oliver Wendell Holmes,* John T. Morse, Jr., Sampson Low, Marston and Co.

For one year after his graduation from Harvard he studied law at home at the Dana Law School. But as early as January 1830, he had grown discontented, failing to find in his studies the satisfaction he sought: "I know not what the temple of the law may be to those who have entered it, but to me it seems very cold and cheerless about the threshold." Before the year had ended, he abandoned his first choice to take up the study of medicine, a preference which his college scientific interests might have suggested to him earlier.

Not only for his final decision concerning his profession was the year 1830 important; that same year marked the real beginning of his avocation of poetry. His friend John Sargent was editor of *The Collegian,* a college magazine which eagerly accepted verse. To this Holmes contributed some twenty-five poems, among them "Evening, by a Tailor," "The Dorchester Giant," and "The Height of the Ridiculous," humorous poems which almost justified the lines of the last:

> And since, I never dare to write
> As funny as I can.

The publication of these verses gave Holmes his "first attack of author's lead poisoning" and something of a local reputation. It was a single poem, however, published in that same year, which made Holmes known throughout the country. In the *Boston Daily Advertiser* of September 14, 1830, he had read a reference to the recommendation of the Secretary of the Navy that the frigate *Constitution* should be disposed of. Public opinion was not in sympathy with such treatment of the historic boat of the War of 1812. Holmes shared the nation-wide disapproval. His patriotic feelings were stirred. In a fervent outburst of indignation he rapidly wrote "Old Ironsides," a protest against the Secretary's decision:

> Oh, better that her shattered hulk
> Should sink beneath the wave;
> Her thunders shook the mighty deep,
> And there should be her grave;
> Nail to the mast her holy flag,
> Set every threadbare sail,
> And give her to the god of storms,
> The lightning and the gale!

On September 16 the *Advertiser* published the poem. It apparently crystallized the general feeling of the country. It was widely copied and published. It saved the ship.

Whatever writing Holmes was doing was not permitted to interfere with his medical studies, which he was following at the private school of Doctor James Jackson. It was decided that his work in this country should be supplemented by study in European hospitals; so in the autumn of 1833 he sailed for Europe. He arrived in France, went to Paris, where he very rapidly felt himself at home and most assiduously applied himself to his work. His day began at half-past seven in the morning with attendance at La Pitié Hospital and with hospital practice and study continued until five. Dinner was eaten with his fellow students. The theatres, the social and cultural opportunities that Paris offered, were not neglected; nor was the opportunity to travel in England and in countries on the continent other than France. But Holmes's chief purpose in being in Europe was not forgotten: he was a most serious student. That his ability was recognized was shown by the fact that M. Louis, the idolized instructor of so many medical students, gave him free access to his hospital wards, "a favor which he has granted only to a few." Indeed, so whole-heartedly was the student devoting himself to medicine that he had done no writing, even refusing a request for material from Sargent, who had bought the *New England Magazine:* "No, John, a heavier burden from my own science, if you will, but not another hair from the locks of Poesy, or it will be indeed an ass's back that is broken."

In December 1835 Holmes returned to America. He brought back with him as external symbols of his European studies a library, a set of instruments, and a skeleton. More important, if less obvious, he brought back two characteristics. The one was a scientific attitude which was indicated by what he wrote in a letter: "However, I have more fully learned at least three principles since I have been in Paris: not to take authority when I can have facts; not to guess when I can know; not to think a man must take physic because he is sick." The other was a strengthening of a natural predilection for delicacy, lightness of touch, perfection of form, qualities that are characteristically French and which Holmes was to manifest later in his poetry.

In 1836 he received his M.D. from Harvard and was made a member of the Massachusetts Medical Society. He set up practice in Boston, allowing his sense of humor to preface his professional career with the statement "Smallest fevers thankfully received." If he permitted an occasional smile where smiles are usually absent, he still was serious about his work. Of four medals offered for medical dissertations in 1836 and 1837, Holmes won three.

Curiously enough, the beginning of his professional work inaugurated renewed interest in writing. He was invited to write the 1836 Phi Beta Kappa poem for Harvard and chose for his subject "Poetry: A Metrical Essay." In this he suggested the purpose of the poet and traced the development of various kinds of poetry, pastoral, epic, legend, and drama. The publication of this poem was made the occasion for his gathering together his early verses and their appearance in his first volume of poetry in 1836.

From this time on, Holmes's life pleasantly combined his scientific and his literary interests. There were periods when his writing was less prolific than at others; but there was never any question of his joyous delight in it. His medical interest, too, underwent modifications. Keenly sensitive to the suffering of others, Holmes found himself better adjusted to the teaching of his profession than to general practice.

In 1839 he was appointed Professor of Anatomy and Physiology at Dartmouth. In the following year, after his marriage to Amelia Lee Jackson of Boston, the daughter of an Associate Judge of the Supreme Judicial Court, he resigned his professorship to devote himself wholly to his practice in Boston. But in 1847, the Harvard Medical School made him Parkman Professor of Anatomy and Physiology. In 1849 he gave up his general practice, limiting himself thereafter to his college work, which was continued until 1882, when he was made Professor Emeritus. As a professor he was not only popular, but able. His lectures were well planned, informative, and interesting.

While he was engaged in his scientific work, lecturing, inventing a hand stereoscope, making a noteworthy contribution to the checking of fever among new mothers, his pen was far from idle. His facility with verse and his graciousness in complying with requests made him in active demand as poet of any and every public or semi-public occasion—dinners, receptions, dedications. In 1851 began the first of his poems for his Harvard class reunions which, with scarcely a break, he was to provide each year until the sixtieth anniversary, when he wrote his tender farewell, "After the Curfew." In these poems he was at his best because in them he could best reveal his personal qualities. He was addressing those whom he knew, those who to some extent shared his background and interests, those who sympathized with his joyousness, his alertness, his zest for life, and his determined clinging to a youthful temper. One must not misunderstand his attitude; it was not one of maudlin sentimentality, but one of tenderness and of rich memories.

Holmes's reputation as a wit and as a graceful presence on the speaker's platform increased. In 1852, he gave a series of lectures on the English Poets of the Nineteenth Century, and included in each lecture a poem on the author discussed. Thereafter there were occasional isolated lectures; but the man's own preferences kept him at home instead of letting him become a familiar platform figure to a country eagerly welcoming the lecture and lyceum systems as means of culture.

It was a periodical rather than a platform that introduced Holmes to his widest circle of acquaintances and friends. In 1857 a magazine was founded in Boston. James Russell Lowell became editor on the condition that Holmes be the first contributor to be engaged. The condition was accepted. Holmes not only became a contributor but gave the magazine its name, *Atlantic Monthly*. The first number of the magazine contained a paper, "The Autocrat of the Breakfast Table," beginning, "I was just going to say, when I was interrupted." The interruption to which the speaker referred was one of a quarter of a century. Twenty-five years before, Holmes had contributed to the *New England Magazine* two papers with the title which he had chosen for his newest literary work. The Autocrat papers and, in their turn, *The Professor at the Breakfast Table, The Poet at the Breakfast Table,* and *Over the Teacups* instantly caught the imagination of the public and cemented between the readers and the writer a strong bond of intimacy and of devotion. The papers did sketch characters and did tell a slight, a very slight story; but they were neither fiction nor pure essays. They were primarily extensions of Holmes's own personality; they were the vehicle for Holmes to talk each month, as he alone could talk, charmingly, gracefully, wittily on any subject that came into his mind, enriching his observations by the vast fund of his information. In these papers either as the writing of one or another of his characters or as something they thought worthy of notice, he included a number of his poems, among them some of his best known: "The Chambered Nautilus," for example, and "Latter-Day Warnings," "The Deacon's Masterpiece: Or the Wonderful One-Hoss Shay," "Homesick in Heaven."

So closely identified are the ideas of his poems with those of his prose works that it might be well here to mention his three works of fiction, his "medicated novels" or novels of purpose: *Elsie Venner*, 1861; *The Guardian Angel*, 1867; and *A Mortal Antipathy*, 1885. In these books he manifested his scientific preoccupation with the question of the effect of heredity and environment upon the life and character of the individual. He reached and propounded the conclusion that so influential are they that one cannot unhesitatingly assign moral responsibility to the individual. If moral responsibility goes, sin must go, and so too must go eternal damnation,—a view completely opposed to the orthodox religious views of the times. These novels made Holmes the object of critical attack; they were his boldly flung challenge to the besetting problems of his youth.

The three novels, his biographies of Motley and of Emerson, and his various volumes of verse provide the outstanding, almost the only, date-marks of the later years of Holmes's life. Just as there were few external events to mark his years, so were there few occasions to break the routine of his cordial, friendly, intimate Boston existence. His friends were, for the most part, residents of Boston or of near-by places; his manifold interests could be, and were, indulged in in Boston; his life was bound up with Boston.

One break, however, came with the Civil War. Holmes was opposed to slavery; but in the early days of the anti-slavery agitation he felt that though slavery could not be prevented, dis-union could be. One of his most moving poems, "Brother Jonathan's Lament for Sister Caroline," was a remonstrance against secession:

She has gone,—she has left us in passion and pride,—
Our stormy-browed sister, so long at our side!
She has torn her own star from our firmament's glow,
And turned on her brother the face of a foe!

coupled with the promise of a welcoming return to the union:

But when your heart aches and your feet have grown sore,
Remember the pathway that leads to our door!

With the outbreak of hostilities, Holmes's sympathy was thrown whole-heartedly on the Northern side. His son, Oliver Wendell Holmes, Jr., served in the War and was wounded at the battle of Antietam. The poet's journey to find his wounded son took him south to Baltimore, Frederick, and Middletown and resulted in his vivid article, "My Hunt After the 'Captain.'"

In 1886 came another break with a trip to Europe, spent mostly in England. The poet, then almost eighty years old, enjoyed to the full the celebrities he met and the attentions that were showered upon him. Oxford, Cambridge, and the University of Edinburgh gave him honorary degrees, as Harvard had already done in 1880. He met Browning, Gladstone, Pasteur. He was received by royalty. He attended receptions and went to races. He made a zestful record of his trip in his book, *Our Hundred Days in Europe*.

Two years before his European journey, his younger son had died. After his return, death entered his family twice again. In the winter of 1887-1888 his wife died; the following year he lost his only daughter. His one surviving son, the Captain of the hunt and the present Ex-Justice Holmes of the United States Supreme Court, now made his home with him.

Dr. Holmes was now well advanced in what he, mindful of the Biblical computation, called the "superfluous decade." He was beginning to feel like the subject of his own "The Last Leaf." Thus he could write in thanks for a gift for his eightieth birthday:

> "For whom this gift?" For one who all too long
> Clings to his bough among the groves of song;
> Autumn's last leaf, that spreads its faded wing
> To greet a second spring.

He suffered from the infirmities of age. Cataracts formed on his eyes. But the possibility of blindness he faced cheerfully. "The dismantling of the human organism," he wrote to Whittier, "is a gentle process, more obvious to those who look on than to those who are the subject of it." At the age of eighty-four he wrote this buoyant—and unforcedly buoyant—letter to his friend, the Philadelphia doctor and novelist, S. Weir Mitchell:

"My birthday found me very well in body and I think in mind. If I am in the twilight of dementia I have not found it out. I am only reasonably deaf; my two promising cataracts are so slow about their work that I begin to laugh at them. I discovered one and studied it, as it was reflected in my microscope, more than a dozen years ago, and I can see with both eyes and read with one; and my writer's cramp is very considerate, and is letting me write without any interference, as you can see."

A year after writing this letter, on October 7, 1894, he

died as he had lived, calmly and peacefully. A liberalist beyond creeds, he was buried from King's Chapel of which
he had been a lifelong member. Clergymen paid living
tribute to him whose opinions they had earlier condemned.
The world had gradually begun to approach his point of
view.

When Holmes on his European voyage had received some
farewell verses, he had asked that they be considered his
Envoi.

> May all good thoughts go with you from this shore,
> All kindly greetings meet thee on the other;
> Bring all they can they will not give thee more
> Than we send with thee, Poet, Friend, and Brother.

What sort of man was he who evoked so tender a tribute?
One can find his revelation in his poetry, for his poetry was
himself. Although it was about his Breakfast-Table series
that he wrote the following lines, they apply equally well
to his poetry.

> What have I rescued from the shelf?
> A Boswell, writing out himself!
> For though he changes dress and name,
> The man beneath is still the same,
> Laughing or sad, by fits and starts,
> One actor in a dozen parts,
> And whatsoe'er the mask may be,
> The voice assures us, *This is he.*

His temperament, his preferences, his ideas—all these, if not
definitely stated, are suggested in his verse.

The force of his family tradition was great. Through his
family, because of its training and its position in the community, he was a conservative—a conservative in political
and in social life. But this natural conservatism was modi-

fied by his scientific attitude and by his innate great-hearted-
ness, a modification that resulted in his generous views toward theological problems. There was a further modification
of the stern New England type through the grace and delicacy of his manner, results possibly of his early French
sojourn. Above all, Holmes was a gentleman and a "gentleman of the world." His care for the niceties of social de-
meanor is suggested, humorously but none the less strongly,
in "A Rhymed Lesson":

> Some words on LANGUAGE may be well applied,
> And take them kindly, though they touch your pride.
> Words lead to things; a scale is more precise,—
> Coarse speech, bad grammar, swearing, drinking, vice.
>
>   .   .   .   .
>
> Once more: speak clearly, if you speak at all;
> Carve every word before you let it fall;
> Don't, like a lecturer or dramatic star,
> Try over-hard to roll the British R;
> Do put your accents in the proper spot;
> Don't—let me beg you—don't say "How?" for "What?"
> And when you stick on conversation's burs,
> Don't strew your pathway with those dreadful *urs*.
>
> From little matters let us pass to less,
> And lightly touch the mysteries of DRESS;
> The outward forms the inner man reveal,—
> We guess the pulp before we cut the peel.

Such admonitions suggested to Holmes the observance of
something more than transient styles; to him they were the
reflection of years of breeding, of standards rooted in the
past.

> I love the memory of the past,—its pressed yet fragrant
>   flowers.

This sense of the past had as one of its manifestations an intensely patriotic devotion. Something of its fervor was suggested in the reference to "Old Ironsides." Just as notably is it present in such poems as "Lexington," "Never or Now," "Parting Hymn," and the more lightly told "Grandmother's Story of Bunker-Hill Battle" with its intermingled romantic and historical tales.

That—in short, that's why I'm grandma, and you children all are here!

The matter of family heritage, of the forces that enter into the making of an individual, suggested in these lines, was with Holmes so inextricably woven with his sense of the past that one cannot completely disentangle cause from effect. This mystery of identity is suggested again in "Dorothy Q." If Dorothy had not married the man she did—

> Should I be I, or would it be
> One tenth another, to nine tenths me?
>
> .   .   .   .   .   .
>
> O lady and lover, how faint and far
> Your images hover,—and here we are,
> Solid and stirring in flesh and bone,—
> Edward's and Dorothy's—all their own,—
> A goodly record for Time to show
> Of a syllable spoken so long ago!—
> Shall I bless you, Dorothy, or forgive
> For the tender whisper that bade me live?

If the individual is so undeniably the creature of forces beyond his control, Holmes pursued his reasoning, how can he be considered a person of free will and so morally responsible for his acts? This question and its implied answer that sin and punishment must be examined in the light of human causes threw Holmes in conflict with orthodox organized religion. He was opposed to formal creeds that strengthened themselves by unalterable dogma:

> "Ye go to bear the saving word
> To tribes unnamed and shores untrod;
> Heed well the lessons ye have heard
> From those old teachers taught of God.

> "Yet think not unto them was lent
> All light for all the coming days,
> And Heaven's eternal wisdom spent
> In making straight the ancient ways."

Holmes's religion was a religion of compassion for mankind and of trust in God. Tolerance and broad-mindedness are urged:

> Deal meekly, gently, with the hopes that guide
> The lowliest brother straying from thy side;
> If right, they bid thee tremble for thine own;
> If wrong, the verdict is for God alone!

The more certainly can one trust in God because, for Holmes, God was a God of love, of love that transcends creedal worship. This idea one finds again and again in Holmes's poems, in "What We All Think," for example, in "A Sun-Day Hymn," "The Living Temple," and in "Tartarus":

> While in my simple gospel creed
> That "God is Love" so plain I read,
> Shall dreams of heathen birth affright
> My pathway through the coming night?

This feeling that Holmes manifested is all the more significant because it was the outcome of questioning, of doubt, and of resulting hope rather than the sustaining conviction of faith.

"I should prefer," he wrote in a letter in 1867, "to say that I trust there will be a righting of this world's evils for each and all of us in a future state, than say that I share the unquestioning certainty of many of those about me." In the face of uncertainty, courage gave him the strength to question.

> This is my homage to the mightier powers,
> To ask my boldest question, undismayed
> By muttered threats that some hysteric sense
> Of wrong or insult will convulse the throne
> Where wisdom reigns supreme.

Although religion could not with any absolute certainty offer Holmes the unchanging truth, although faith failed to present it to him in convincing form, he still urged its search. In "Our Limitations" he suggests the incapacity of the human mind to reach it:

> Each truth we conquer spreads the realm of our doubt;

and in his statement "Truth is often very uncomfortable," he suggests the suffering that the search may entail. But he follows up that statement with another, "I can't help it whether I gain or lose by a truth, I *must* accept it."

Where was it to be found? In goodness consistent with man's highest possibilities, was Holmes's answer.

> Seek thine own welfare, true to man and God!

And again, as in the poem "Idols":

> Let us be true to our most subtle selves.

In "Manhood," Holmes is still more explicit:

> This is the new world's gospel: Be ye men!

In thus shifting the motive power of man's conduct from the external dictates of dogma to the inner demands of man's own nature, Holmes was showing but one of the many ways in which he was in sympathy with the ideas of a developing civilization. The glories of the physical world, suggested in the poems making up the "Wind-Cloud and Star-Drifts" series of the Young Astronomer, are celebrated in "The Living Temple." It is, however, the celebration not of a materialist, but of a religious scientist, of one who found no conflict between religion and science. For Holmes was, above all, a scientist; he looked upon the steadfastness of science as a lighthouse—the figure he uses in his poem "The Stability of Science"—which, "all unconscious of the mischief done" when feeble birds dash themselves against its weight, still flashes its guiding light.

It was not simply the abstract principles of science in which Holmes was interested; his was an active interest in its application, in the world of things. So one finds poems like "The Steamboat," or like "The Broomstick Train," or "The Return of the Witches," the delightfully humorous poem about electric trolley cars. Naturally enough, the science of medicine, his own profession, was a frequent subject for his poetry. Sometimes it is humorously treated as in "The Morning Visit," "The Stethoscope Song," or "Rip Van Winkle, M.D." At other times, it becomes the subject for serious treatment, as in "The Two Armies," or "Poem at the Centennial Anniversary Dinner of the Massachusetts Medical Society, June 8, 1881":

> Our lesson learned, we reached the peaceful shore
> Where the pale sufferer asks our aid no more,—
> These gracious words our welcome, our reward!
> Ye served your brothers; ye have served your Lord!

In his concept of the doctor's function—

> Of all the ills that suffering man endures,
> The largest fraction liberal Nature cures.

and in his evaluation of medicine as a preventive science

> To guard is better than to heal,

his point of view was altogether modern.

With a keen eye and a receptive mind, Holmes made his contact with men and with things. Nothing was ever too trivial to be worthy of his attention; but always his interest had mankind as its center:

> I love all sights of earth and skies,
> From flowers that glow to stars that shine;
> The comet and the penny show,
> All curious things, above, below,
> Hold each in turn my wandering eyes:
> I claim the Christian Pagan's line,
> *Humani nihil*—even so,—
> And is not human life divine?

His affection for the things of this earth was very great. It prompted the confession in *Our Hundred Days in Europe:*

"I have sometimes thought that I love so well the accidents of this temporary terrestrial residence, its endeared localities, its precious affections, its pleasing variety of occupation, its alternations of excited and gratified curiosity, and whatever else comes nearest to the longings of the natural man, that I might be wickedly homesick in a far-off spiritual realm where such toys are done with." This was his attitude as an old man, drawing near to the end of life. Some sixteen years before he had expressed a similar idea, more tenderly, more delicately, in his very moving poem, "Homesick in Heaven."

In that poem the homesick dwellers in heaven miss most

the people they have left behind. One feels the same would have been equally true of Holmes. However much things meant to him—and they did mean much—people meant still more. Humanity was his essential characteristic and it was, naturally, in his contact with people, particularly in brilliant and witty conversation, that that quality shone at its best. The same ease and flow that characterized his conversation are present in his verse. In fact some of his poems have the colloquial rhythm and diction of a speaker rather than the literary form of a writer. "The Archbishop and Gil Blas" is an example of this, as are "A Poem for the Meeting of the American Medical Association at New York, May 5, 1883," and "Once More." Holmes's conscious use of this particular medium is suggested by the line in "Rip Van Winkle, M.D.," when with a humorous self-consciousness he recalls himself to poetic dignity:

He tumbl—dismounted, slightly in a heap.

Holmes's humor was irresistible. He seemed to delight particularly in playing with words and indulged—even in his poems—in the use of puns, a form of humor which he pretended to disdain.

Hard is the job to launch the desperate pun,
A pun-job dangerous as the Indian one.

More generally, his humor is the reflection of a geniality of temperament and of an appreciation of the incongruous in human affairs, as in "The Parting Word" and in "Cacoethes Scribendi." Sometimes it is sheer farce, as in "The Stethoscope Song," and "The Ballad of the Oyster Man." One might also include in this latter group "The Deacon's Masterpiece or, The Wonderful One-Hoss Shay," were it not for its implied criticism of too much dependence upon logic; and "Parson Turell's Legacy or, The President's Old Arm-

Chair," except for this latter poem's criticism of a dead past's restricting the present.

To a noteworthy degree Holmes possessed the ability thus to coat a serious thought with pleasant jesting. Some of his most pleasing poems have a satiric strain that make them social criticisms. "My Aunt" is delicate satire against old maids and the conditions that produced them; "Aunt Tabitha" is a modification of the same idea. "Latter-Day Warnings," based on the fear of many people that the world was to be destroyed by the comet of 1857, is prefaced by the statement, "If certain things, which seem to me essential to a millennium, had come to pass, I should have been frightened; but they haven't." The list of imperfections and frailties ranges from dishonesty in legislators to adulteration in coffee. Until these are corrected, says Holmes:

> *Till* then let Cumming blaze away,
>   And Miller's saints blow up the globe;
> But when you see that blessed day,
>   *Then* order your ascension robe.

Only once did Holmes's humor become bitter. That was in "The Sweet Little Man," written in 1861 and hurled against those who failed to do their share in the Civil War:

> First in the field that is farthest from danger,
>   Take your white-feather plume, sweet little man!

It has been suggested that these qualities of Holmes which shine in his poems flashed most highly in his contact with people. Meetings with friends, public gatherings, seemed to kindle the spark. An ability to say the gracious thing and to say it gracefully made Holmes a person in demand on such occasions:

> I'm a florist in verse, and what *would* people say
> If I came to a banquet without my bouquet?

The opening of a theatre, the dedication of a monument to Halleck, the completion of an organ for the Boston Music Hall, the coming of the Russian Grand Duke Alexis to Boston, the birthday of Whittier—these and many other occasions like them called for appropriate stanzas. Often enough such occasional verse does not outlive the event for which it was written. Much of Holmes's occasional verse, however, escaped this fate; because he could see beneath the surface of the event to the underlying emotions, and because he could express these emotions aptly and gracefully, he was able to write for the future as well as for his immediate present. "At a Meeting of Friends," for example, written for his own fiftieth birthday, describes the general human tendency to resist old age. "International Odes," written for the visit of the Prince of Wales to Boston, hymns international peace. But of all the occasional poems that Holmes wrote, few will outlast those forty-odd that make up the "Poems of the Class of '29." From the first one, "Bill and Joe," through those of the middle years, "The Boys," "The Girdle of Friendship," and "The Broken Circle," to the pathetic, yet brave farewell, "After the Curfew":

> In every pulse of Friendship's heart
> There breeds unfelt a throb of pain,—
> One hour must rend its links apart,
> Though years on years have forged the chain.

they breathe of friendship, of youthful buoyancy, and of the treasure of memories held in common.

These views Holmes could—and frequently did—express in prose. That he also used poetry as a medium of expression was due to his theory of the poet's function. For him a poet needed more than mere ability to handle meters and rhymes. He needed more than sensitivity to impression; this latter quality many may share who can never be poets, as Holmes suggests in "To the Poets Who Only Read and Listen." The true quality of the poet was for Holmes "the power of transfiguring the experiences and shows of life into an aspect which comes from the imagination and kindles that of others." He is the poet

> In whom the unreal is the real world.

The imaginative transfiguration of impressions which was for Holmes the essence of poetry he, himself, manifested.

In addition he possessed to a remarkable degree that control of poetic technique which he rated the less important element of poetry. So far as his own poetic methods were concerned, he acknowledged his allegiance to the older classic poets:

> I smile to listen while the critic's scorn
> Flouts the proud purple kings have nobly worn.

As a result of his meticulous attention to the technical requirements of verse, there is nothing slovenly in his meter or rhyme. It is not that they seem stilted or forced; they are simple and free, but exact. For the most part, the metrical scheme of his poems follows traditional patterns; but there is an occasional experiment in verse form, as in "The Last Leaf" and "The Chambered Nautilus."

The poems of Holmes are, however, something more than neat examples of the rules of prosody. They are crowded with telling phrases, with pointed figures, that give evidence of his wide interests and his keen observation. "Spendthrift Crocus," "the varnished buds of Spring," "plume-bound fleur-de-lis," show his ability to see accurately and transmit beautifully objects of nature.

But it is in the variety and richness of his analogies that Holmes is most noteworthy. To point his comment, no human activity lies outside his poetic province. The simplest method of illustrating this characteristic is to choose at random some of the figures with which his verse is enriched, as a necklace, so he himself might say, is starred with jewels. Humorous or serious, whatever its mood, the figure is invariably apt.

> And silence, like a poultice, comes
> To heal the blows of sound.

> Stick to your aim: the mongrel's hold will slip,
> But only crowbars loose the bulldog's grip.

> Who cares that his verse is a beggar in art
> If you see through its rags the full throb of his heart?

> The text of our lives may get wiser with age,
> But the print was so fair on its twentieth page!

> To you the words are ashes, but to me they're burning coals.

> No life worth naming ever comes to good
> If always nourished on the selfsame food;
> The creeping mite may live so if he please,
> And feed on Stilton till he turns to cheese,
> But cool Magendie proves beyond a doubt,
> If mammals try it, that their eyes drop out.

Frequently the comparison that Holmes makes is sustained throughout the poem—the figure, and thought, and poem being built up together. This is the method in "The Old Cruiser," wherein the Class of '29 and a younger Harvard class are compared to boats; in "Our Banker," a comparison between Time and a banker; in "The Girdle of Friendship," wherein the gradual loss of friends is likened to a shortening chain. Possibly the poem best showing this method, the poem which is most popularly known and which, incidentally, was one of Holmes's own favorites, is "The Chambered Nautilus."

> Build thee more stately mansions, O my soul,
>> As the swift seasons roll!
>> Leave thy low-vaulted past!
> Let each new temple nobler than the last,
> Shut thee from heaven with a dome more vast,
>> Till thou at length are free,
> Leaving thine outgrown shell by life's unresting sea!

In a number of poems the reverse of this method is used. Instead of the elaboration of a single figure, one finds allusion crowding allusion, a variety of references bound up in a single poem, a lightning play of intellect which, however, does not strain unity of effect.

> My verse is but the curtain's fold
>> That hides the painted scene,
> The mist by morning's ray unrolled
>> That veils the meadow-green,
> The cloud that needs must drift away
> To show the roses of opening day.

Obviously, the manner of Holmes's writing was important. Ease and felicity of method, it is true, were indulged in often at the expense of profundity of thought and of feeling. But Holmes was writing for an educated and sophisticated audience who might prefer to have their emotions but lightly touched and ideas suggested rather than explored. In this method of treating lightly some serious theme or, perchance, treating seriously some humorous one, in the nice blending of pathos and humor, Holmes is a preëminent writer of *vers de société*. "Bill and Joe," "Homesick in Heaven"—these are examples of Holmes at his best. But beyond all other poems that distinguish Holmes as a writer of "society verse," is "The Last Leaf." "It was with a smile on my lips that I wrote it," Holmes wrote; "I cannot read it without a sigh of tender remembrance."

> I know it is a sin
> For me to sit and grin
>   At him here;
> But the old three-cornered hat,
> And the breeches, and all that,
>   Are so queer!
>
> And if I should live to be
> The last leaf upon the tree
>   In the spring,
> Let them smile, as I do now,
> At the old forsaken bough
>   Where I cling.

For the most part Holmes used a smile to conceal some of his inmost feelings. But occasionally, as in "The Silent Melody," he wrote almost sentimentally. And frequently he wrote with a purity and depth of feeling that did not aim at a jauntiness of manner, as he did in such poems, for example, as "Martha," "The Turn of the Road," or "Under the Violets."

It is a rich picture of himself that Holmes transmitted through his poetry. In clear light he presented himself a Brahmin of New England, educated, cultured, a gentleman of the world with a nice regard for dignity and decorum. His intellectual capacity was made to serve his profession and to keep him alertly interested in the affairs of this world. His broad and tender sympathies made him tolerant and merciful. The warmth and kindliness of his personality colored all his relationships. He lived with a love for God and for his fellowmen.

I come not here your morning hour to sadden,
  A limping pilgrim, leaning on his staff,—
I, who have never deemed it sin to gladden
  This vale of sorrows with a wholesome laugh.

If word of mine another's gloom has brightened,
  Through my dumb lips the heaven-sent message came;
If hand of mine another's task has lightened,
  It felt the guidance that it dares not claim.
      .   .   .   .
And now with grateful smile and accents cheerful,
  And warmer heart than look or word can tell,
In simple phrase—these traitorous eyes are tearful—
  Thanks, Brothers, Sisters,—Children,—and farewell!

JAMES RUSSELL LOWELL

IN 1818, the Reverend Charles Lowell, pastor of the West Congregational Church of Boston, purchased Elmwood, a stately three story house set in ten acres of ground. Built in 1767, it was one of Tory Row, a group of houses about a mile from Harvard College in Cambridge, Massachusetts. There he brought his wife and his family of three sons and two daughters; and there, on February 22, 1819, a sixth child was born, a son, James Russell Lowell.

Into the make-up of the boy entered two distinct strains: the one, through his father, that of the Puritan Brahmin New England; the other, through his mother, the more imaginative, mystic one of the Scotch Highlands. The father traced his ancestry to Perceval Lowle, who had come to Massachusetts in 1639. He had carried on the double family tradition, that of education at Harvard, and, after a short diverging period of study of law, that of the ministry as a profession. Lowell's mother, Harriet Traill Spence, was said to be a descendant of the ballad hero, Sir Patrick Spens. Of great beauty, herself, she was a lover of beauty, fanciful, mystic, interested in the occult, and possessed by a languorous dreaminess called "the Spence negligence."

But in addition to the inheritance from his parents, as a molding influence in the boy's life was Elmwood. The close and affectionate ties that bound him to his family seemed all the stronger because they were associated with the physical home, itself. "It is what my eye first looked on," he wrote in later years, "and I trust will look on last." His wish was to be granted. Except for a number of more or less brief intervals, Elmwood was his home throughout his life. "I often wish I had not grown into it so," he wrote in 1873. "I am not happy anywhere else." Elmwood became for him the solace to which he turned always for comfort, the symbol of all he held most dear. In it centered all his family associations, those of the boy and of the man; from love of it developed his representative New Englandism and, more embracing, his patriotic devotion to his country.

> Kindlier to me the place of birth
> That first my tottering footsteps trod;
> There may be fairer spots of earth,
> But all their glories are not worth
> The virtues in the native sod.

For the boy growing up two worlds of beauty and adventure were open. The outdoor world, the world of Elmwood grounds and of the countryside, called forth his love. This was the world of his poem, "An Indian-Summer Reverie," a world wherein "birds and flowers and I were happy peers."

> I learned all weather-signs of day or night;
> No bird but I could name him by his flight,
> No distant tree but by his shape was known,
> Or, near at hand, by leaf or bark alone.
> This learning won by loving looks I hived
> As sweeter lore than all from books derived.
> I know the charm of hillside, field, and wood,
> Of lake and stream, and the sky's downy brood,
> Of roads sequestered rimmed with sallow sod,
> But friends with hardhack, aster, goldenrod,
> Or succory keeping summer long its trust
> Of heaven-blue fleckless from the eddying dust;
> These were my earliest friends, and latest too,
> Still unestranged, whatever fate may do.

The other enticing world was the world of literature. His father's library was a large one and was open to him. His mother and his sister Mary, to whom he was especially devoted, recited poems and sang old songs to him. He was read to sleep with passages from Spenser's *Faërie Queene.* His imagination was stirred. He had strange, whimsical visions, queer, fantastic dreams, particularly a frequently recurring one of the world being put into his hands "like an orange."

The rich experiences of his youth, nature, books, a visit to Portsmouth when he was seven, short trips with his father into neighboring parishes and a longer one with him to Washington and Alexandria, remained prized possessions for him always. "I believe it is one of the most happy things in the world, as we grow older," he wrote from his mature observations, "to have as many ties as possible with whatever is best in our own past, and to be pledged as deeply as may be to our own youth."

The variety of his interests is suggested by a letter written to his brother, when he was not yet nine.[1]

"Jan. 25, 1827

My dear brother The dog and the colt went down today with our boy for me and the colt went before and then the horse and slay [sleigh] and dog—I went to a party and I danced a great deal and was very happy—I read french stories—The colt plays very much—and follows the horse when it is out.

Your affectionate brother

JAMES R. LOWELL.

I forgot to tell you that sister Mary has not given me any present but I have got three books."

[1] *Letters of James Russell Lowell,* edited by Charles Eliot Norton, Harper and Brothers.

Shortly after this letter had been written, Lowell entered the boarding and day school kept by an Englishman, a Mr. William Wells. He had previously attended a Dame's School,

> Propped on the marsh, a dwelling now, I see
> The humble school-house of my A, B, C,
> Where well-drilled urchins, each behind his tire,
> Waited in ranks the wished command to fire,
> Then all together, when the signal came,
> Discharged their *a-b abs* against the dame.

Now, in the more advanced school, the elementary training of the Dame's School was supplemented by other studies, Latin being particularly stressed. At school, the boy's creative ability found expression in the stories that he told to delighted school-mates.

At fifteen, Lowell had finished his preparatory schooling. Cambridge, as the seat of Harvard, was steeped in the college atmosphere. The Lowell tradition demanded college and Harvard. So there was no question in the Lowell household of the course to be chosen by the youngest son. Naturally, he was to go to college; naturally, that college was to be Harvard.

In 1834, he entered the Freshman class. The emphasis of the curriculum was placed upon Greek, Latin, and Mathematics. But in addition to his college studies, he continued the habit formed in his father's library. He read Butler, Southey, Cowper, Dante, Coleridge, Carlyle, Landor, Hume, the Greek Anthology, Milton, who "has excited my ambition to read all the Greek and Latin classics which he did"; Byron, of whom he wrote, "Discovered two points of very striking resemblance between myself and Lord Byron"; Keats, who was to furnish him the inspiration for much of his own poetry and particularly for his sonnet, "To the Spirit of Keats":

> Thy clear, strong tones will oft bring sudden bloom
> Of hope secure, to him who lonely cries,
> Wrestling with the young poet's agonies,
> Neglect and scorn, which seem a certain doom;

and Burns, who was to become the subject of the centennial poem, "At the Burns Centennial," and of "An Incident in a Railroad Car":

> But better far it is to speak
> One simple word, which now and then
> Shall waken their free nature in the weak
> And friendless sons of men.

More immediately, Burns provided him with a model for much of the lighter jingles and verses that he was then writing.

Letters to his friends were studded with verses. One contains the following plea for subscriptions to *Harvardiana,* the college magazine: [2]

> Now if ye do your vera best
> In this maist glorious behest,
> By gettin' names and a' the rest
> I need na tell
> Yese thus fulfil the airn'st request
> O' J. R. L.

For Lowell, because of his literary interests, had been made an editor of *Harvardiana.* He was, moreover, a member and secretary of the Hasty Pudding Club. Indeed, classroom assignments absorbed neither all his time nor all his

[2] Quoted in *James Russell Lowell, a Biography,* by Horace Elisha Scudder, Houghton Mifflin and Co.

interests. His letters suggest that at this time he was experiencing a youthful love affair. "Shack, pity me!" he wrote to a friend, "I am in love—and have been so for some time, hopelessly in love."

To his father it seemed that Lowell was not accomplishing his scholastic work with the proper amount of success. Before sailing for Europe in 1837, the elder Lowell wrote his son a letter of advice, offering him a variety of rewards scaled according to his scholastic standing and holding out this final promise for attendance in the classroom: "If you do not miss any exercise unexcused, you shall have Bryant's 'Mythology' or any book of equal value, unless it is one I may specially want."

Evidently the father's proffered rewards were not sufficient incentive. In his Senior year, Lowell absented himself frequently from class and from chapel. There were, apparently, other lapses from college discipline. For on June 25, 1838, the faculty "voted that Lowell, senior, on account of continued neglect of his college duties be suspended till the Saturday before Commencement, to pursue his studies with Mr. Frost of Concord, to recite to him twice a day, reviewing the whole of Locke's 'Essay,' and studying also Mackintosh's 'Review of Ethical Philosophy,' to be examined in both on his return, and not to visit Cambridge during the period of his suspension."

The suspension from college and the consequent Concord banishment an aunt of Lowell's attributed to "indolence, to be sure; indolence and the Spence negligence." But the period of exile was not spent in idleness. Studies were pursued and reported upon to the Reverend Barzillai Frost. Acquaintances were made. Emerson, in particular, took a kindly interest in the young man; but Lowell was not yet ready to accept the older thinker's point of view and dismissed him with a "He is a good-natured man, in spite of his doctrines." There was, moreover, steady application to the class poem which Lowell had been chosen to write but which the faculty decree prevented his delivering at the Class Day exercises. The poem, which was privately printed after its Class Day presentation, reflecting an inherent conservatism in Lowell, satirized all the current movements for social reform: Transcendentalism, Abolitionism, vegetarianism, the temperance movement.

The years immediately following graduation were troubled, disturbing ones for Lowell. He felt ill at ease, unadjusted to the world about him. "I go out sometimes," he wrote, "with my heart so full of yearning toward my fellows that the indifferent look with which even entire strangers pass me brings tears to my ears." His love affair pursued an unhappy course. He was confronted with the puzzling question of his future career. He decided against the ministry because he felt himself unable to subscribe to all the necessary religious tenets of his church. Literature as a profession was not wholly acceptable to the current American point of view; nor did it offer adequate financial returns, and the loss of some of the elder Lowell's fortune made this an important consideration. Finally, he decided to study law and began reading Blackstone "with as good a grace and as few wry faces as I may." But he was not sure of his decision. Possibly business might offer better opportunities. He went to Boston to seek "a place in a store." In Boston, he heard Webster try a case and was moved by that lawyer's eloquence and ability to resume his own legal studies. But in February 1839 he announced, "I have quitted the law forever." A lecture at Concord that paid him $4 and a brief period as a substitute for his brother in a coal-dealer's office suggested that neither the lecture platform nor the clerical desk offered him a bright future. "At all events, I was never made for a merchant, and I even begin to doubt whether I was made for anything in particular but to loiter through life." The day after writing this, in May 1839, Lowell entered the Dane Law School. Two months later, he wrote again: "If I live, I don't believe I shall ever (*between you and me*) practice law. I intend, however, to study it and prepare myself for practicing. But a blind presentiment of becoming independent in some other way is always hovering round me." In August 1840, he received the degree of Bachelor of Laws and shortly after entered the law office of Charles Greely Loring in Boston.

Meanwhile, however, Lowell's interests were shifting and changing. The emotional stress, which at one time had led him to contemplate suicide, now found an outlet in his writings. His poem "Threnodia" was published in the *Southern Literary Messenger*. Losing some of his youthful complacency, he was becoming interested in the wave of humanitarianism sweeping the country. His sympathies were enlisted on the side of the Abolitionists.

An influence still more significant for Lowell arose out of a visit which, late in 1839, he paid to a classmate's home in Watertown, an influence which helped to fuse his emotions and activities into some sort of unity, one which encouraged him in his desires and aided him in their accomplishment. On this visit he met his friend's sister, whom he thus described: "His sister is a very pleasant and pleasing young lady, and knows more poetry than any one I am acquainted with. I mean, she is able to repeat more. She is more familiar, however, with modern poets than with the pure wellspring of English poesy."

Within a year, the "pleasant and pleasing young lady," Maria White, and James Russell Lowell were engaged to be married. There was no immediate prospect of marriage, for Lowell was still far from able to take care of a wife and family. The years of the long engagement, however, the intimate relationship with Miss White, were momentous in molding Lowell's temperament and character.

Lowell felt in himself always two distinct and, sometimes, conflicting strains. "I find myself very curiously compounded of two utterly distinct characters," he wrote in 1847. "One half of me is clear mystic and enthusiast, and the other humorist." The habit of self-analysis here called into play led him at times into a strange objective attitude toward himself. "It is curious, when I am in company I watch myself as if I were a third person, and *hear the sound of my own voice,* which I never do in a natural mood." And again, "I remember the ugly fancy I had sometimes that I was another person, and used to hesitate at the door when I came back from my late night walks, lest I should find the real owner of the room sitting in my chair before the fire." Tormented by these queer fancies, visited by visions and mystic experiences in which he thought he had "a personal revelation from God himself," he found himself unable to meet people on the basis which he preferred. Always, in his thoughts he was prodded by a desire for fame. "If I don't die, George," he wrote to a friend, "you will be proud of me. I *will* DO somewhat." But always—until his last days—what he most wanted was affection, approval of himself rather than of his accomplishments. "For my own part, I would give all the praise I ever received for the right to be valued simply for my personal good qualities alone." "For I would rather be loved than anything else in the world. I always thirst after affection, and depend more on the expression of it than is altogether wise."

If he was never to be completely satisfied with his relationship to other people, still some of the difficulties arising from unrest were smoothed out for him by the complete understanding and sympathy of his fiancée and wife. "I believe," he wrote in 1845, "Maria only knows how loving I am truly. Brought up in a very reserved and conventional family, I cannot in society appear what I really am." Miss White was, herself, a remarkable character. She was beautiful. She was a poet of some ability. She possessed deep feelings and great thoughts. But more than that, she was touched with a serene and calming goodness, a capacity for active good-doing. Her praise Lowell sang in "My Love" and in "Irené":

> Yet sets she not her soul so steadily
> Above, that she forgets her ties to earth,
> But her whole thought would always seem to be
> How to make glad one lowly human hearth.

Through Miss White, Lowell met a group of young people from Cambridge, Boston, Watertown, and Salem, with whom he felt at ease, who liked him and appreciated him. It is of no diffident, repressed young man that he presents the portrait in his letter to his future brother-in-law: [3]

"I have just come from spending the evening at ——'s (where Maria is making sunshine just now), and have been exceedingly funny. I have, in the course of the evening, recited near upon five hundred extempore macaronic verses; composed and executed an oratorio and opera (entirely unassisted and, *à la* Beethoven, on a piano without any strings, to wit: the centre-table); besides drawing an entirely original view of Nantasket Beach, with the different groups from Worrick's disporting themselves thereon, and a distant view of the shipping in the harbor, compiled from the ship-news of our indefatigable friend Ballard, of the *Daily*, and making a temperance address; giving vent moreover, to innumerable jests, jokes, puns, oddities, quiddities, and nothings, interrupted by mine own laughter and that of my hearers;

[3] *Letters of James Russell Lowell,* edited by Charles Eliot Norton, Harper and Brothers.

and eating an indefinite number of raisins, chesnuts (I advisedly omit the 't'), etc., etc., etc., etc."

But more important than adding to his parlor graces, this group of young people deepened further his interest in social causes. Known as "The Band," they participated actively in the current efforts to ameliorate social conditions. Lowell, fired by their enthusiasm, himself became an ardent worker. He gave a lecture before a temperance society; he allied himself with the cause of woman's rights; he identified himself with the Abolitionists. Those very principles which had been the object of his derision in his Class Day poem were now the principles for which he whole-heartedly stood. As evidence of his change of heart, he now wrote on the cover of a copy of his early poem, this retraction and apology:

> Behold, the baby arrows of that wit
> Wherewith I dared assail the woundless Truth!
> Love hath refilled the quiver, and with it
> The man shall win atonement for the youth.

More and more, too, was he writing poetry. In tribute to his fiancée, he finally printed late in 1840, but bearing the date of 1841, a volume of verse, *A Year's Life*. With the publication of this volume, Lowell began to feel the possibility of making literature his life work. The warm reception given to his essays on Old English Dramatists, published in *The Boston Miscellany* in 1842, pleased him and increased his "hope of being able one day to support myself by my pen, and to leave a calling which I hate, and for which I am not *well* fitted, to say the least."

In the autumn of 1842, he decided definitely to abandon the law. With an associate, he made plans for the publication of a magazine, *The Pioneer*, which was to be essentially American in spirit, and which in its prospectus made the challenging announcement of independence from tradition. "Let us learn that romance is not married to the past." The first number appeared in January 1843. But at this time Lowell developed an eye malady that necessitated treatments in New York. In consequence of his absence from Boston, he was unable to keep in closest touch with his magazine. Affairs became tangled. Agreements were not adhered to. Finally, the contract which had been made with the publishers was broken and, after a few issues, the magazine was suspended.

Lowell had meanwhile made Elmwood his home once more. From there he issued in December 1843, dated 1844, his second volume of verse, *Poems*. This book gave evidence of the crystallization of Lowell's temperament. In it he included a sonnet which he had written for his twenty-fourth birthday, a sonnet which declared that his youthful fears and doubts had been overcome:

> Now, have I quite passed by that cloudy If
> That darkened the wild hope of boyish days.

The tone of the volume, unlike that of the intensely personal one of his first book, was marked by an interest in moral and political issues. It contained the elaborate and not wholly successful "A Legend of Brittany." But more typical of the volume's content and of its author's attitude of mind were "Rhœcus" with its plea for love in its humblest form; "Prometheus" with its love for justice:

> Wrong ever builds on quicksands, but the Right
> To the firm centre lays its moveless base;

and "Stanzas on Freedom":

> Is true Freedom but to break
> Fetters for our own dear sake,

And, with leathern hearts, forget
That we owe mankind a debt?
No! true freedom is to share
All the chains our brothers wear,
And, with heart and hand, to be
Earnest to make others free!

They are slaves who fear to speak
For the fallen and the weak;
They are slaves who will not choose
Hatred, scoffing, and abuse,
Rather than in silence shrink
From the truth they needs must think;
They are slaves who dare not be
In the right with two or three.

Lowell had accepted the battle standard of the Abolitionists and had allied himself with them. He was now to be
one of their accepted spokesmen. For after his marriage to
Miss White on December 26, 1844, the young couple moved
to Philadelphia where, for $10 a month, Lowell was to write
for *The Pennsylvania Freeman,* an organ of the Abolition
party. This connection lasted but a short time. In the late
spring, the poet and his bride returned to Elmwood. Lowell,
however, continued his Abolition activities, contributing articles on "Anti-Slavery in the United States" to the London
Daily News and arranging to contribute to *The National
Anti-Slavery Standard* and later, in 1848, to become its corresponding editor.

With this return to Cambridge, Elmwood once more resumed its position, which it was never to lose, of center for
all Lowell's tenderest and deepest feelings. It was the scene
of many joys and many sorrows. The elder Mrs. Lowell,
about whom the poet wrote "The Darkened Mind," suffered
a mental derangement; an older sister was similarly afflicted.

The poet's first daughter, Blanche, whose birth at the end of 1845, brought great joy, died when she was but little more than a year old. "She Came and Went" and "The Changeling" express Lowell's sense of loss. "The First Snow Fall," written after the birth of a second daughter, reopens his sorrow. Always, from this time on, in addition to the grief from the death of dear ones, Lowell was haunted by the threat of poverty. His finances were never adequate; he sold off much of the land about Elmwood. Yet in spite of his every effort, "as usual, my income is never so large as my auguries."

But out of these besetting troubles rose a year which was most remarkable for Lowell, the creative artist. The year 1848 saw the publication of his three longest and best-known works. "The Vision of Sir Launfal," mystic in tone and, it must be admitted, somewhat confused in form, illustrated Lowell's insistent belief in democracy and in humanity as the service of divinity:

> The Holy Supper is kept, indeed,
> In whatso we share with another's need;
> Not what we give, but what we share,
> For the gift without the giver is bare;
> Who gives himself with his alms feeds three,
> Himself, his hungering neighbor, and me.

In addition to this glorification of man's service to man, the poem presented Lowell's intense love of nature. The Prelude to Part First contains that pæan in praise of June, the poet's favorite month:

> And what is so rare as a day in June?
> Then, if ever, come perfect days.

In "A Fable for Critics," the second of the long poems, Lowell manifested another facet of his ability. Humorously, but with a great measure of understanding and of justice, he drew in that poem pictures of his literary contemporaries, Emerson, Bryant, Whittier, Hawthorne, Cooper, Poe, Longfellow, Dana, Holmes. Nor is he less sparing in his self-delineation:

> There is Lowell, who's striving Parnassus to climb
> With a whole bale of *isms* tied together with rhyme,
> He might get on alone, spite of brambles and boulders,
> But he can't with that bundle he has on his shoulders,
> The top of the hill he will ne'er come nigh reaching
> Till he learns the distinction 'twixt singing and preaching;
> His lyre has some chords that would ring pretty well,
> But he'd rather by half make a drum of the shell,
> And rattle away till he's old as Methusalem,
> At the head of a march to the last new Jerusalem.

The third of the 1848 works was the first series of the "Biglow Papers." These were made up of nine poems written in the Yankee dialect, supposedly by one Hosea Biglow, a native of Jaalam, and bound together by exaggeratedly serious and erudite notes by the young man's pastor, the Reverend Homer Wilbur. One of the poems had appeared in *The Boston Courier* as early as 1846; the others were published in that paper and in *The National Anti-Slavery Standard*. Brought together in book form, they made a ringing denunciation of the Mexican War and a satiric picture of the political condition of the country. The characters of Biglow and of Wilbur suggested the two strains, that of humor and that of seriousness, in Lowell; Lowell, as their composite, became the accepted spokesman for the New Englanders, the enunciator of their attitude toward national problems.

The straddling candidate for office:

Ez to my princerples, I glory
In havin' nothin' o' the sort;
I ain't a Whig, I ain't a Tory,
I'm jest a candidate, in short;

the pusillanimous editor, whose creed includes the tenet:

In short, I firmly du believe
In Humbug generally—;

the inglorious adventures of Birdofredum Sawin; the pronouncements of

John P.
Robinson he;

the denunciation of the war

Ez fer war, I call it murder,—
There you have it plain an' flat—

all these were widely quoted. Lowell had become a national figure.

The year following the appearance of these works, 1849, Lowell brought out a two volume edition of his poems. By this time he had shown the lines of his greatest poetical interests: the sentiments attached to his home, the love of nature, devotion to books and studies, humanitarianism, and patriotism.

By now he had shown, too, that he might write in one of several moods, in burning seriousness, in tenderness, or in lighter humorousness. But whatever the mood might be, always was there an undercurrent of unquestionable sincerity.

After the publication of his collected verse, Lowell apparently dedicated himself more exclusively to his poetical work. His contact with the Cambridge circle of literary men may have had some influence in his determination. At all events, his political writing became less frequent and, in 1850, he was able to give a résumé of his past and a program for his future poetry:

"My poems have thus far had a regular and natural sequence. First, Love and the mere happiness of existence beginning to be conscious of itself, then Freedom—both being the sides which Beauty presented to me—and now I am going to try more *wholly* after Beauty herself. Next, if I live, I shall present Life as I have seen it."

The Cambridge existence made up of writing, studying, and friendly contact with neighbors, was, in 1851, interrupted by a trip to Europe. Lowell's family had, meanwhile, undergone further changes. His mother had died. A third daughter had been born and had died; a son had been born. Mrs. Lowell's father, too, had died; but his death had left them a small inheritance which made the European trip a possibility. In July, Lowell, his wife, their daughter Mabel, their son Walter, a nurse, and a goat sailed for the Mediterranean. For a little more than a year they traveled. During the months away, their son died and news reached them of the elder Lowell's being stricken by paralysis. The return home to Cambridge, in October 1852, sufficiently sad, was still further saddened for Lowell by the realization that his beloved wife was becoming ill and growing weaker and weaker. The following year she died. Lowell was overwhelmed with grief. "I am afraid of myself." Years later in "After the Burial," Lowell recurred to his inconsolable sorrow at the loss of his wife and children:

> Console if you will, I can bear it;
> 'Tis a well-meant alms of breath;
> But not all the preaching since Adam
> Has made Death other than Death.

> It is pagan; but wait till you feel it,—
> That jar of our earth, that dull shock
> When the ploughshare of deeper passion
> Tears down to our primitive rock.

Lowell, however, gave himself to his studies and to writing. A course of lectures on the English poets given at the Lowell Institute in Boston in 1854-55 was most enthusiastically received. Shortly thereafter, Lowell himself was offered the Smith Professor of French and Spanish Languages and Literatures and Belles-Lettres at Harvard, as successor to Longfellow. To prepare himself he went to Europe for a year's study in modern languages.

On his return he took up his professorial duties. As a professor, he brought to bear his wide and loving interest in literature and its creators. He evidenced, too, a keen interest in philology. If he did not have a learned background or a store of scholarly information, he nevertheless had and showed appreciation and imagination in his judgments; and he was able to arouse enthusiasm in his students. For himself, his college work had little permanent effect either on his point of view or on his poetical writing.

With the inauguration of his professorial duties, Lowell's life fell once more into a happier course. In September 1857, he married Miss Frances Dunlop who, as the sister of a dear friend of his first wife, had undertaken the care of his daughter Mabel. His literary activities, too, were broadened. In May there had been held the famous dinner at the Parker House in Boston at which was born the *Atlantic Monthly*. Lowell was chosen editor and saw its first number appear in November 1857. "Free without being fanatical," the magazine provided him a hospitable medium for his political articles and for his poems. But chiefly did he make his influence felt in the reviews and book notices which he contributed to each issue, articles which were marked by his sympathetic appreciation, his imaginative criticism, and his devotion to an original and what he called a natural American literature.

The *Atlantic Monthly*, which he edited until 1861, and *The North American Review*, which he began to edit in 1864, were two of the periodicals that welcomed his contributions. His writings for the next few years showed his attitude and, in reflection, that of his New England fellow citizens toward the Civil War. The April 1861 number of the *Atlantic Monthly* carried his statement: "We have no desire for dissolution of our confederacy, though it is not for us to fear it." In the November number appeared "The Washers of the Shroud," a moving call for combat on the side of right:

> "Tears may be ours, but proud, for those who win
> Death's royal purple in the foeman's lines;
> Peace, too, brings tears; and mid the battle-din,
> The wiser ear some text of God divines,
> For the sheathed blade may rust with darker sin.

> "God, give us peace! not such as lulls to sleep,
> But sword on thigh, and brow with purpose knit!
> And let our Ship of State to harbor sweep,
> Her ports all up, her battle-lanterns lit,
> And her leashed thunders gathering for their leap!"

He resumed his device of the "Biglow Papers" and in their second series drew satiric pictures of the South and indignant criticism of England's attitude toward the war.

Lowell's feelings engendered by the war were not the result of detached thought alone. He knew the sorrow of the death in battle of dear nephews and cousins. His feelings he was able to universalize and his grief included within it the grief of Southerners who had experienced similar losses:

My eyes cloud up for rain; my mouth
  Will take to twitchin' roun' the corners;
I pity mothers, too, down South,
  For all they sot among the scorners.

 . . . . .

Come, while our country feels the lift
  Of a great instinct shoutin' forwards,
An' knows that freedom ain't a gift
  That tarries long in han's o' cowards!
Come, sech ez mothers prayed for, when
  They kissed their cross with lips that quivered,
An' bring fair wages for brave men,
  A nation saved, a race delivered!

Joyfully Lowell welcomed the end of the war. "I wanted
to laugh and I wanted to cry, and ended by holding my
peace and feeling devoutly thankful." When in July 1865,
Harvard held services to commemorate her men, dead in
the war, Lowell was asked to write and recite the Ode. He
seized the opportunity, "not in anger, not in pride," to
glorify those who had fought for an ideal and to pour out
his own love for his country and for his fellow man.

No poorest in thy borders but may now
Lift to the juster skies a man's enfranchised brow.
O Beautiful! my Country! ours once more!
Smoothing thy gold of war-dishevelled hair
O'er such sweet brows as never other wore,
 And letting thy set lips,
  Freed from wrath's pale eclipse
The rosy edges of their smile lay bare,
What words divine of lover or of poet
Could tell our love and make thee know it,
Among the Nations bright beyond compare?

What were our lives without thee?
What all our lives to save thee?
We reck not what we gave thee;
We will not dare to doubt thee,
But ask whatever else, and we will dare!

In its revised form the Ode contained, too, the glowing tribute to Lincoln:

New birth of our new soil, the first American.

After the war, Lowell returned to his books, his writing, and his lecturing. Another volume of poems, *Under the Willows*, appeared. In 1872, he resigned his professorship and left for another sojourn in England. During the years he was away, he wrote only a few poems, but among them was one which he felt to be among his best verse, the poem in memory of Agassiz:

He that was friends with earth, and all her sweet
Took with both hands unsparingly.

His time, though not given to writing, was spent with the literary and political leaders of Europe. Honors were given him. Oxford gave him the degree of D.C.L. Cambridge made him Doctor of Laws. His pleasure at these honors was almost that of a child. "How it would please my father!" he wrote.

Absence from America did not prevent, however, his keeping in touch with the American scene. The political corruption that followed the Civil War moved him to indignation. His criticism in "Tempora Mutantur":

Add national disgrace to private crime,
Confront mankind with brazen front sublime,
Steal but enough, the world is unsevere,—

criticism repeated later in "The World's Fair, 1876," was resented on the part of some Americans, who felt that Lowell had been pampered and spoiled for a democracy by the attentions of aristocratic England.

But another faction in America hailed the evidence of Lowell's renewed interest in politics. Lowell, on his return from Europe in 1874, had reconsidered his resignation from Harvard. Back again in Cambridge, once more giving his lectures at the college, he was looked upon as a leader by the young men of Cambridge. His services were enlisted for political meetings. In the presidential campaign of 1876, he was a delegate to the Republican nominating convention and, in time, a presidential elector on the Republican ticket chosen to cast his vote for Hayes.

In the spring of 1879 there were rumors of Lowell's being appointed to a diplomatic post. These rumors were substantiated when, after refusing an appointment to Austria, he was made minister to Spain. Lowell felt a sympathetic understanding of the Spanish people; he knew their language; his favorite poet was their poet, Calderon; he was popular at the Spanish Court. The one unhappiness of his stay was Mrs. Lowell's illness.

In 1880, Lowell was suddenly transferred to London. Mrs. Lowell's increasingly bad health prevented the American minister from playing the official host. But he was able nevertheless to enter into the capital's social life and, through the warmth of his personality, he instantly became popular. His judicious handling of the question of the citizenship of some naturalized Americans born in Ireland who were implicated in Irish disturbances won him general approval. He was made Doctor of Laws at Edinburgh University. He was asked to deliver an address at the Birmingham and Midland Institute; and, speaking on Democracy, recurred once more to his fundamental belief: "Our healing . . . will be revealed by the still small voice that speaks to the conscience and the heart, prompting us to a wider and wiser humanity." So great, indeed, was his hold on the English people, so much at home did he feel with them that, when Mrs. Lowell died in 1885 and there seemed every possibility that Lowell might feel it necessary to return to America, an effort was made to keep him in England by offering him a professorship at Oxford. This Lowell refused. In June 1885, he sailed for America to make his home with his daughter; but for several summers he visited England to resume his old friendships there.

Lowell, on his return to his native land, felt himself old. He had for a number of years struggled against the thought of old age. Now he confessed that he consented "to grow old only because I can't decently help it." Politically never a strict party-man, he felt himself outside the Republican party. Made professor emeritus at Harvard, his active professorial duties were ended. The last years of his life were spent in writing those letters to his friends, which reveal him as the most charming of correspondents; in reading and reflecting on his books; in writing poems. In 1888 his volume of verse, *Heartsease and Rue,* appeared. In 1889, *The Critic* of New York issued a special Lowell number in honor of his seventieth birthday. In the following years, he prepared all his writing, his poems and his many prose articles, for a ten-volume edition of his collected works.

Lowell was once more at Elmwood. He had moved there with his daughter and his grandchildren after brief interludes at his daughter's home in Southborough, Massachusetts, and at his sister's home in Boston. In the spring of 1890, he became ill, suffering most intensely. In spite of this, he tried to devote himself to his reading, to planning further work and to keeping up the treasured contact with friends. But he steadily grew worse and on August 12, 1891, he died. In Lowell's poetry one finds no single predominating theme. In it are represented those various subjects that moved the other New England poets of his time to write: the emotions of domestic life, patriotism, freedom, humanity, nature.

"The older I grow," Lowell wrote, "the more I am convinced that there are no satisfactions so deep and so permanent as our sympathies with outward nature." His attitude toward nature included no tenuous or subtle philosophy; rather was it one of pure enjoyment. "An Indian-Summer Reverie," "Under the Willows," "The West," the description of June in "The Vision of Sir Launfal," the opening stanzas of "Sunthin' in the Pastoral Line":

> Then all comes crowdin' in; afore you think,
> Young oak-leaves mist the side-hill woods with pink;
> The catbird in the laylock-bush is loud;
> The orchards turn to heaps o' rosy cloud;
> Red-cedars blossom tu, though few folks know it,
> An' look all dipt in sunshine like a poet;

these show his observing, tender affection for the world of the countryside.

There is perhaps less of feeling and more of intellect in his attitude toward social problems. If his devotion was of the mind rather than of the heart, it was none the less dedicated whole-heartedly to the ideas of democracy and of the brotherhood of man. The principles of justice and of right were the foundation of his philosophy:

> Once to every man and nation comes the moment to decide,
> In the strife of Truth with Falsehood, for the good or evil
>   side.

In each challenge that arises from a moral issue lies, Lowell felt, an opportunity to serve Deity:

> the eternal law
> That who can saddle Opportunity
> Is God's elect.

A challenge to moral action is always present; the opportunity for service is immediate. So Lowell felt an unwillingness to be restricted by the past:

> Therefore think not the Past is wise alone.

Still further did he develop his belief. If God is served in the present, so too does He make Himself felt in the present.

> God is not dumb, that he should speak no more;
> If thou hast wanderings in the wilderness
> And find'st not Sinai, 'tis thy soul is poor.

So Lowell's religion is a religion that transcends creeds fixed by the past; his God is a God above dogma.

> God is in all that liberates and lifts,
> In all that humbles, sweetens, and consoles.

In startling contrast to the modernity of his religious attitude is Lowell's reactionary attitude toward science. Far from being able to include it in the poetic, he looked upon science with suspicion; he felt it to be a potential undermining of his belief. "Not that I like science any better than I ever did," he wrote. "I hate it as a savage does writing, because he fears it will hurt him somehow." In science Lowell could see only a force that gloried in its exultant overthrowing of orthodox beliefs; with test-tube and formulæ it was destroying

> The Heaven, so neighborly with man of old.

He was unable to see the necessary unity of science and
religion, the common search for truth carried on by both.
So he

> frankly must confess
> A secret unforgivingness
> And shudder at the saving chrism
> Whose best New Birth is Pessimism;
> My soul—I mean the bit of phosphorus,
> That fills the place of what that was for us—
> Can't bid its inward bores defiance
> With the new nursery-tales of science.

Just as this confession seems strange to modern ears, so
do some of Lowell's poetic mannerisms appear outdated.
He had not, even in his desire to be independent of the
canons of the past, completely rejected "poetic diction."
In his poetry, one finds expressions like "enshield" and
"dazéd eyes." One finds elaborate and confusedly wrought
figures:

> A new-made star that swims the lonely gloom,
> Unwedded yet and longing for the sun,
> Whose beams, the bride-gifts of the lavish groom,
> Blithely to crown the virgin planet run,
> Her being was, watching to see the bloom
> Of love's fresh sunrise roofing one by one
> Its clouds with gold, a triumph-arch to be
> For him who came to hold her heart in fee.

Lowell, it must be admitted, did not show the most careful craftsmanship in his art. He is guilty of gauche expressions like

> Which souls of a half-greatness are beset with,

or

> Beyond the hillock's house-bespotted swell;

and of purely prosaic statements, like

We sit in the warm shade and feel right well.

He is frequently careless in rhyme:

> And, though I'm not averse to
> A quiet shade, even they are folks
> One cares not to speak first to.

In meter, too, he occasionally halts:

> Which, having colonized its rift i' th' wall

and

> May is a pious fraud of the almanac,
> A ghastly parody of real Spring,
> Shaped out of snow and breathed with eastern wind.

One feels that Lowell's poems suffer from hasty composition and from lack of careful revision.

From such criticism of Lowell's technical skill and of his inability to meet completely the modern point of view, it might indeed seem that Lowell meant more for his own day than he means for the present. To a great extent this is true. There are from all Lowell's verse but few memorable, telling lines, inevitably right; there are but a few poems which, in their entirety, are to be permanently treasured: "The Fountain," perhaps, the sonnet "I would not have this perfect love of ours," "The First Snow Fall," "The Courtin'."

This last poem and the other poems of the "Biglow Papers" are those most likely to continue Lowell's fame and to save him from the dusty obscurity destined for "classics." It was in these poems that Lowell was best able to fuse his many-sided personality, to blend humor and seriousness of purpose. These were the first poems to bring him general popularity; they were the first to emphasize his Americanism, his New Englandism.

This, in fact, is the importance of Lowell: he was essentially of his time and of his place—an American of the nineteenth century. His interests were those of his time: humanitarian movements, the Civil War, politics. From these he did not hold himself aloof; of them he made his poems.

The details of his poems, too, came from the world about him. The birch tree and the dandelion, the chipmunk, the crow, the features of the New England landscape he fondly painted. No lovelier picture could be presented than those of "An Indian Summer Reverie" and "Sunthin' in the Pastoral Line." In the latter and the other poems of the "Biglow Papers" and in "Fitz Adam's Story" are captured forever the speech and personality of the nineteenth century Yankee.

The Yankee, for all his high moral purpose, possessed a sense of humor. This quality Lowell had in abundance and expressed in his poems. A man who could write of his religion, "I take great comfort in God. I think he is considerably amused with us sometimes, but that he likes us, on the whole, and would not let us get at the match-box as carelessly as he does, unless he knew that the frame of his Universe was fireproof," could make his humor felt incisively in lines like

Fer where's a Christian's privilege an' his rewards ensuin'?
Ef 't ain't perfessin' right on eend 'thout nary need o' doin'?

He could use it to draw an apt picture:

The defect in his brain was just absence of mind,

typical of the portraits in "A Fable for Critics," or of summer tourists in "Fitz Adam's Story":

The summer idlers take their yearly stare,
Dress to see Nature in a well-bred way,
As 't were Italian opera, or play.

Encore the sunrise (if they're out of bed),
And pat the Mighty Mother on the head.

Or he can use it to give him the subject and color of a whole poem, as in "The Origin of Didactic Poetry."

In this delineation of the American spirit, Lowell was carrying out one of his principles for American Literature:

To your own New-World instincts continue to be true,
Keep your ears open wide to the Future's first call,
Be whatever you will, but yourselves first of all.

Lowell had, indeed, a theory of poetry and of poetic technique. "I don't believe in these modern antiques," he wrote of the classic myths. "It's like writing Latin verse—the material you work in is dead." He was just as critical of method, writing of the meter Longfellow had used in "The Courtship of Miles Standish," "It is too deceitfully easy."

One might begin at dawn nor end till the purple twilight,
Stringing verses at will, nor know it was verse he was stringing.
This is the modern way, the way of steamer and railroad
Where all the work is done, you scarcely know how, by the Engine.

Lowell had his conception of the function of the poet. "The poet is he who can best see and best say what is ideal —what belongs to the world of soul and of beauty." These for Lowell were the things of eternity. "The lives of the great poets teach us that they were the men of their generation who felt most deeply the meaning of the present."

Beauty, wonder, idealism, sincerity—these Lowell's poems possess. Wherein, then, did he fall short of his own ideal conception? The great paradox, the pitiful paradox, of Lowell lay in the fact that he was too many-sided a personality to be a great poet. "My being a professor wasn't good for me," he admitted. And again, "I suppose I should have been a more poetical poet if I had not been a professor. A poet should feed on nothing but poetry, as they used to say a drone could be turned into a queen-bee by a diet of bee-bread. However, my poems have mostly written themselves and I cannot account for them."

Lowell's life interfered with his poetry. However great was his desire for fame as a poet, poetry played only one part in his existence. As a result, Lowell's poems lack, on the one hand, the fervid glow and heat of inspiration and, on the other, the steady certainty that comes from reflection. Lowell's personality precluded the former; his many, varied interests were, conceivably, obstacles to the latter. Possibly no fairer judgment of him can be made than one he, himself, expressed: "A poet shouldn't be, nay, he can't be, anything else without loss to him as poet, however much he may gain as man."

WALT WHITMAN

A FAITHFUL and doubtless self-willed record," Walt Whit‑
man called his *Leaves of Grass*. A record of his emotional life, of his thoughts, his hopes, and his ideals, it is
filled with seeming inconsistencies and contradictions. These
are reflections of contrasts in Whitman's personality, of his
fervid intensity and his reticence, of his humility and his
proud self-confidence, of his power and his tenderness.

> Do I contradict myself?
> Very well then I contradict myself,
> (I am large, I contain multitudes.)

These very contradictions enter into his philosophy, which
is an attempt to accept light and dark, good and evil, as
essential parts in a complete and benevolent whole.

However great the contrasting elements in Whitman's life
and in his poetry, no less varied, no less contrasted are the
attitudes with which he and his work have been received.
He has been hailed as a messiah and has been denounced as
a libertine and reprobate. *Leaves of Grass* has been glorified
as inspired revelation and has been reviled as indecent and
immoral writing. Somewhere between these extremes the
truth must lie. What it may be each reader must find for
himself.

What sort of person, then, was this Walt Whitman, who
was able to stir up so much controversy, and who, untouched by arguments and dissensions, became a powerful
influence in thought and in literature? What elements entered into him so that he could feel himself the exponent

and champion of the average man, even though—and this
must be admitted from the very outset—he, himself, was
not average?

There was little in his ancestry to explain the phenome-
non of Walt Whitman; there was, however, a sufficiently
rich and varied inheritance to make him representative of
a large number of Americans of his time. An early Whitman,
of English stock, journeyed in the middle seventeenth century from Connecticut to Long Island, New York, across the
Sound. There he settled on the northern shore, in pleasant,
rich farming country. His great-grandson Jesse Whitman,
a farmer, married in 1775 Hannah Brush, a teacher. Their
son, Walter, a carpenter and builder, married in 1816
Louisa Van Velsor, of a Dutch and Welsh family. Quakers,
with a seafaring tradition derived, perhaps, from

Dutch Kossabone, Old Salt, related on my mother's side, far
    back.

To them a son was born on May 31, 1819, their second
child, Walter, called Walt to distinguish him from his father.

Through his parents, the boy became the inheritor of
Anglo-Saxon and of Dutch characteristics.

You liberty-lover of the Netherlands!
(You stock whence I myself have descended;)

His religious inheritance was that of Whitman independence
in faith with little regard for religious observance, modified
by his mother's Quakerism. His immediate family were not
members of any church, but always manifested an interest
in the Quaker doctrines; and Walt, himself, so far as he
was influenced by any religious sect, was influenced by the
Quakers. He inherited, too, from his family a love of the
land and a love of the sea, both later to show themselves
intensely in his poetry. There were, it is true, deficiencies in

his inheritance. A weak mental strain entered somewhere, so that one brother died a lunatic and another brother lived his life an imbecile. There was lacking, too, a tradition of learning and of formal education. But though the families presented no outstanding individuals, they did provide, for the most part, sturdy, dependable citizens.

Other sons and daughters were born to the Whitman family. One child died in infancy; but Walt had seven brothers and sisters with whom he grew up and from whom he learned those lessons that can be learned only in large families. The household was marked by freedom and spontaneity. There was little restraint of any sort, little discipline imposed from without. Affection and love were present; but the father seemed less able than the mother to hold the family with sympathy. For Walt, particularly, his mother became the center of his deepest emotions. Of this family, the poet presents a brief but suggestive picture in his poem, "There Was a Child Went Forth":

The mother at home quietly placing the dishes on the supper-table,
The mother with mild words, clean her cap and gown, a wholesome odor falling off her person and clothes as she walks by,
The father, strong, self-sufficient, manly, mean, anger'd, unjust,
The blow, the quick loud word, the tight bargain, the crafty lure,
The family usages, the language, the company, the furniture, the yearning and swelling heart,
Affection that will not be gainsay'd, the sense of what is real . . .

For a few years the Whitman family lived in West Hills, a little settlement near the village of Huntington on Long

Island. Then, when Walt was about four, the family moved to Brooklyn "of ample hills," a rapidly growing community across the river from New York. It was in Brooklyn that Walt went to school for a few brief years, receiving the only formal education he ever did receive. But more important for him than organized instruction was the education to be derived from the life about him. He became aware of the public events of the city and of the great men who lived there and visited it. He cherished the memory of having seen Lafayette at the dedication of a Brooklyn library and of having been kissed by him. The elder Whitman's trade of building put him in contact with work and workmen and made him conscious of social growth and activity. He met people, many people of many kinds. He absorbed the city; there became part of him

. . . all the changes of city and country wherever he went.

For the country entered no less into his experience. He made many visits to the family homes on Long Island. The Van Velsor household provided him with rich memories: "the vast kitchen and ample fireplace and the sitting-room adjoining, the plain furniture, the meals, the house full of merry people, my grandmother Amy's sweet old face in its Quaker cap, my grandfather 'The Major,' jovial, red, stout, with sonorous voice and characteristic physiognomy." He explored the countryside, the coves of Long Island Sound and the hills of the northern shore, the plains in the middle of the island, the bays and beaches of the south. To the water he felt himself irresistibly drawn. He went sailing on Great South Bay, swimming, fishing and eeling through the ice. "The shores of this bay, winter and summer, and my doings there in early life," he wrote later in *Specimen Days,* "are woven through L. of G." Woven through it, too, are the rhythm and pulse of the Atlantic, on whose beaches he spent many happy, gloriously filled hours.

A new note soon entered into the life of the little boy. Not yet in his teens, he left school and acted as office boy for some Brooklyn lawyers and for a Brooklyn doctor. The lawyers, a father and two sons, named Clarke, took an interest in the boy; "Edward C. kindly help'd me at my handwriting and composition, and (the signal event of my life up to that time) subscribed for me to a big circulating library. For a time I now revel'd in romance—reading of all kinds; first, the "Arabian Nights," all the volumes, an amazing treat. Then, with sorties in very many other directions, took in Walter Scott's novels, one after another, and his poetry (and continue to enjoy novels and poetry to this day)." Books and the printed word now became a part of his life.

Shortly their influence became even more immediate. When he was about fourteen, Whitman began to work in newspaper printing offices, first in that of the *Long Island Patriot,* then in that of the *Star.* An apprentice in the composing room, he learned to set type. In time he began to write various, tentative newspaper "pieces."

Apparently, it never occurred to Whitman to rebel at a fate that took him out of school and put him to work when he was scarcely more than a child. For one thing, his work did not interrupt his hours and days of rest and recreation; even this early newspaper period was interspersed with visits to the country and to near-by beaches. Furthermore, he seemed always to feel himself free to leave one position for another, to change his occupation as preference dictated.

So, at eighteen, Whitman left Brooklyn and returned to Long Island. For a few years, poorly equipped though he was, he taught school in a number of country settlements. From Huntington, he wrote and printed a newspaper, the

Long Islander. He undertook its distribution himself, riding long rides on horseback to deliver copies to subscribers.

In 1841, he was back again in Brooklyn and in New York, now as editor of the *Daily Aurora.* With this editorship began a period of varied activity. He wrote more and more, contributing to the *Tatler* and to the *Democratic Review.* He was asked to write a temperance novel which was published in 1842, *Franklin Evans; or the Inebriate: a Tale of the Times.* He wrote a few poems. He took part in the city's life. His newspaper connection gave him entrée to the city theatres. He saw plays at The Park and at The Bowery theatres. He went to the opera and to concerts. He visited the exhibit of Egyptian antiquities and Fowler's Phrenological Cabinet. He heard the leading orators of the time, Henry Ward Beecher, Wendell Phillips, William Lloyd Garrison. Something of a dandy and a fop, he became a familiar figure on Broadway, the city's busiest avenue. He felt himself part of the life about him, curiously identified with the crowds of people who walked along Broadway or rode in the omnibuses in which he, himself, loved to ride or sailed on the ferries, on which he loved to sail.

But even this period presented the Whitman of contrasts. For while the life and bustle of the city delighted him, he felt at times the need for retreat and for solitude. So he spent long hours at the beaches or in the woods. He withdrew from the current, active world to the world of books; he read the Bible, Shakespeare, Ossian, and, in translation, the Greek classics.

The editorship of the *Aurora* was followed by that of the *Brooklyn Daily Eagle.* No consuming ambition drove him to long hours of labor. His afternoons he spent away from his office in walking or in ocean bathing. His editorial position did not make him a leader of men. His editorials were marked by local pride, by patriotism, and by sympathy for the rights of the common people. But mediocre in style and, for the most part, uninspired in subject, they did not challenge his readers or summon them to a cause.

In 1848 he left the *Eagle;* possibly he was asked to leave because of some difference in political opinion from that of the owner. But shortly a new position opened. One night at the theatre he met a man who was starting a newspaper in New Orleans. In the time permitted by an intermission, the plan was outlined, Whitman was offered the editorship, and the offer was accepted. Two days later, with his favorite brother, Jeff, fourteen years his junior, Whitman left for the South. A long journey, chiefly by boat, brought him to New Orleans, where he began his duties as editor of the *Crescent.* After three months, that connection was terminated. Walt and Jeff left the Southern city and, by way of Chicago, returned to New York.

Why did Whitman leave? A number of reasons—all of them guesses—have been given: Jeff's health was being undermined by the Southern climate; Whitman was disappointed in the financial arrangements that had been made; an affair with some woman made his departure advisable. With the reticence with which he occasionally shrouded his acts, Whitman never explained why the New Orleans episode was so brief a one.

In spite of the mystery surrounding it, it was an important one for the poet's development. His silence makes it impossible to know whether or not he loved some New Orleans woman whom, for one reason or another, he could not or would not marry; and whether it was this unhappy love affair that released his emotions and turned them in a new direction. But it is quite apparent that something significant did occur to Whitman in New Orleans. His court reporting for the newspaper threw him in contact with all manner of unfortunates and wrong-doers, toward whom his sympathy went out. His new surroundings increased his sensitivity to beauty. His journey to the South and through the near West enlarged his vision. He was no longer a Northerner, a provincial New Yorker; he was now an American.

The Whitman who returned to his family in Brooklyn was a different one from the Whitman who had left. His interests were different. He became for a short time editor of the *Brooklyn Daily Freeman,* identifying himself with Abolition, a cause in which he had heretofore been only mildly interested. He was impelled by a desire to lead men; he made plans, never completely realized, for a series of lectures. He engaged for brief periods in his father's business of building; but the opportunities offered by it to make a satisfying fortune he completely disregarded. His very appearance was changed. By 1850, then only 30 years old, his hair was quite streaked with gray. His former meticulously chosen wardrobe was abandoned; he adopted the clothing of an ordinary workman, a costume to which he ever afterwards clung. More and more he made his closest relationship with workmen, with the drivers of the New York omnibuses, with the hands on the ferry boats.

His interests were modifying and developing, were becoming socialized. Sometime in the early 1850's, he became, he suggests in "Song of Myself," the subject of a mystic experience.

I mind how once we lay such a transparent summer morning,

. . . .

Swiftly arose and spread around me the peace and knowledge that pass all the argument of the earth,
And I know that the hand of God is the promise of my own,
And I know that the spirit of God is the brother of my own,
And that all the men ever born are also my brothers, and the women my sisters and lovers,

And that a kelson of the creation is love,
And limitless are leaves stiff or drooping in the fields,
And brown ants in the little wells beneath them,
And mossy scabs of the worm fence, heap'd stones, elder,
    mullein and poke-weed.

Mystically, then, Whitman experienced the essential one-
ness of the universe. All men are one. Mankind, nature, God
are one. The universe embraces everything: the body and
the soul; good and bad. In such a scheme, nothing can be
greater or more important than another; all have their
place and all are needed. More than this, the individual
becomes typical of the whole, representative of all. He, Walt
Whitman, made up of various qualities, with tendencies
toward evil and toward good, aware of beauty and of ugli-
ness, he was in small what the universe was in large! The
force of his vision overwhelmed him, inspired him with an
enthusiastic mission. He must proclaim his message to mankind, lead them to an eventual sharing of his faith and his
belief.

How could this be done? The printing experience of the
past now had its effect. The lecture platform had suggested
itself and been rejected. But there remained the power of
print! Slowly, carefully, he planned a book that would carry
his glowing message to the world.

In 1855, a short time after the death of the elder Whitman, appeared *Leaves of Grass,* unsponsored by any publisher, and carrying its author's name only in the copyright
notice and in a reference in one poem. In place of signature
was a frontispiece portrait, a picture of Walt Whitman in
his garb of a workman.

The book issued thus strangely contained, moreover, a
challenging preface. "America does not repel the past," it
began; and then went on to say that "the United States
themselves are essentially the greatest poem. . . . The

American poets are to enclose old and new for America is the race of races. Of them a bard is to be commensurate with a people. . . . The messages of the great poets to each man and woman are: Come to us on equal terms. Only then can you understand us. We are no better than you, what we enclose you enclose, what we enjoy you may enjoy. Did you suppose there could be only one Supreme? . . . The great poets are to be known by the absence in them of tricks and by the justification of perfect personal candor. . . . The great trial of him who would be the greatest poet is today. . . . A great poem is no finish to a man or woman but rather a beginning." Obviously, here was some one not content to trill pleasant lyrics, but some one imbued with a deep purpose to express the soul of America in song.

Yet the pages of the book did not look as if they carried song. Very strange they were in appearance. They most distinctly were not prose. Nor, according to the canons of the day, were they poetry. They were printed in uneven lines, but without an obvious pattern, without rhyme, and without a regular meter.

This verse form, through a process of rejection, Whitman had created for himself. He was familiar with conventional poetic forms and had used them for some of his earlier poems, as in "Sailing the Mississippi at Midnight":

> Vast and starless, the pall of heaven
> Laps on the trailing pall below;
> And forward, forward, in solemn darkness,
> As if to the sea of the lost we go.

But the exigencies of fixed rhyme and meter irked him, hindered him. He could not be thus restrained; he must seek a freer form. As early as 1843, he had found something more suited to his purpose, and used it in a poem "Blood Money":

Of olden time, when it came to pass
That the beautiful God, Jesus, should finish his work on
    earth,
Then went Judas, and sold the divine youth,
And took pay for his body.

This form, enlarged and developed, carrying the rhythmic flow of the Bible which he had absorbed completely or of the ocean which he loved, became the vehicle for his message. It had a freedom consonant with the freedom and democracy of America.

The strange form of his verse alone was sufficient to repel many. Those who were not deterred by broken lines from reading on in the slender book found a strange, bewildering theme, one unfamiliar to poetry. The poet's subject was human personality and he chose his own as representative of all:

I celebrate myself, and sing myself,
And what I assume you shall assume,
For every atom belonging to me as good belongs to you.[1]

He suggested his theory of the singleness of the universe, as in "Who Learns My Lesson Complete":

And that my soul embraces you this hour, and we affect each
    other without ever seeing each other, and never perhaps
    to see each other, is every bit as wonderful.

And that I can think such thoughts as these is just as won-
    derful,
And that I can remind you, and you think them and know
    them to be true, is just as wonderful.

[1] The 1855 versions of this and the three following quotations differ slightly from the forms quoted, which are from the definitive edition of *Leaves of Grass*, Doubleday, Page and Company, 1919.

And that the moon spins round the earth and on with the
earth, is equally wonderful,
And that they balance themselves with the sun and stars is
equally wonderful.

He elaborated his theory so that the universe included not
simply abstractions and ideals, but concrete, physical things,
the body as well as the soul. His poem, "I Sing the Body
Electric," glorified the body:

The love of the body of man or woman balks account, the
body itself balks account,
That of the male is perfect, and that of the female is perfect.

It drew pictures of men and of women, vivid because of
their physical strength and beauty; it described the human
body boldly, in detail, and called it beautiful. Surely, his
age criticized, that was worse than simply unpoetic, that
was indecent! Then as climax to his audacity, he announced himself in "Song of the Answerer" as the poet who
was to lead mankind:

And I answer for his brother and for men, and I answer him
that answers for all, and send these signs.

It is small wonder that the book with its peculiar form,
its harsh phrasing, its crude and sometimes coarse expressions, and its theme upsetting to the taste of the times, had
a very small sale. It is no less strange that among those
whom it did reach it should provoke harsh criticism, such
reaction as is reflected in one reviewer's judgment that it
"deserves nothing so richly as the public executioner's
whip." His own family, if not disgusted, was bewildered.
"Mother thought as I did," said his brother George, "did

not know what to make of it. . . . Mother said that if Hiawatha was poetry, perhaps Walt's was."

Whitman doubtless was more disappointed at the indifference to his book than he was disturbed at the disapproval of it. With characteristic unconcern for the niceties of conduct, for the amenities of a situation, he wrote for publication laudatory reviews of his own work. "An American bard at last!" he wrote in one. "He is the largest lover and sympathizer that has appeared in literature." In another review, insisting upon the close relationship between a man and his work, he drew his own portrait:

"He never offers others; what he continually offers is the man whom our Brooklynites know so well. Of pure American breed, large and lusty—age thirty-six years, (1855,)—never once using medicine—never dressed in black, always dressed freely and clean in strong clothes—neck open, shirt collar flat and broad, countenance tawny transparent red, beard well-mottled with white, hair like hay after it has been mowed in the field and lies tossed and streaked—his physiology corroborating a rugged phrenology—a person singularly beloved and looked toward, especially by young men and the illiterate—one who has firm attachments there, and associates there—one who does not associate with literary people."

The first edition of *Leaves of Grass* was, however, not wholly without readers and even admirers. Among the first who acclaimed it was Emerson, who found in it an echo, modified but real, of his own doctrines. On July 21, 1855, he wrote to Whitman: "I am not blind to the worth of the wonderful gift of *Leaves of Grass*. I find it the most extraordinary piece of wit and wisdom that America has yet contributed. . . . I greet you at the beginning of a great career, which yet must have had a long foreground somewhere, for such a start."

Such approval was pleasant to Whitman, but it was not needed to confirm him in his determination. It was his inner zeal, the fire and drive of his mission, the strength of his vision that made him determined to go on with his work. He must make his message clear. He must preach his gospel to mankind. So he continued to write his poems; and because of his belief that human personality was the all-important theme and that all his work must express his own single personality, he revised and revised and rearranged his earlier poems, added new poems, and printed new editions, combining old and new in single collections and using always the symbolic title *Leaves of Grass*. His second edition, appearing in 1856, bore across its cover, stamped in gilt, Emerson's message with his name, "I greet you at the beginning of a great career." This was done entirely without Emerson's permission. Its use was distasteful to the Concord philosopher. Particularly was this so, because the book contained some poems to which he objected on the ground of propriety.

Continuing the message of the physical of the earlier edition, Whitman had written some poems now included in the "Children of Adam" section. They were poems of the body, poems of sex, of the love between man and woman. They were not lewd. But they were frank and stark in their expression and because of that they did offend many.

By this time Whitman was becoming known, if not to the vast public to which he wished to appeal, at least to thinking individuals. He was visited by people who found him, as well as his writing, stimulating, by Alcott, by Bryant, by Thoreau.

In 1860, Whitman was preparing a third edition of his work and had gone to Boston to supervise its publication. There he saw Emerson, who sought to persuade him to modify some of the earlier poems. The two went for a walk. The elder argued, gave reasons. "What have you to say to such things?" he asked. And Whitman answered, with steady, sure self-confidence, "Only that while I can't answer them at all, I feel more settled than ever to adhere to my own theory and exemplify it."

In Boston, Whitman met William D. O'Connor, a young writer, who was to prove a loyal and devoted friend. Whitman's capacity for friendship was large; almost unbounded was his ability to stir the emotions of others and to answer them with the flow of his own feelings. He was drawn to young men, particularly to those of the working classes and the illiterate. He lavished upon them his affection, his tender devotions, his sympathy which seemed a mixture of the maternal and paternal. From these feelings developed a modification of his earlier belief. Love was the basis of the universe; but there was something more than the love between man and woman. There was the love of man for man, a socialized love. So the 1860 edition included a group of poems called "Calamus," preaching a religion of affectionate and democratic comradeship.

To one believing, as Whitman did, in democracy and in the brotherhood of man, the Civil War must have seemed shockingly cruel. But here again, one sees a Whitman of contrasts. War he deplored; but with his philosophy of acceptance, he accepted it as part of the inevitable plan. He had prophesied its coming. In "To the States, *To Identify the 16th, 17th or 18th Presentiad,*" he had written:

Are those really Congressmen? are those the great Judges?
 is that the President?
Then I will sleep awhile yet, for I see that these States
 sleep, for reasons;
(With gathering murk, with muttering thunder and lambent
 shoots we all duly awake,
South, North, East, West, inland and seaboard, we will
 surely awake.)

The war broke. A few days later, on April 18, 1861, Whitman recorded a vow: "I have this hour, this day resolved to inaugurate a sweet, clean-blooded body by ignoring all drinks but water and pure milk—and all fat meats, late suppers—a great body—a purged, cleansed, spiritualized, invigorated body." [2] What was his purpose? Was it to strengthen his body for a physical ordeal which he felt might come? Was it to perform some sacrifice to equal the sacrifices made by others? One does not know. Nor does one know his thoughts or his actions during the following year and a half.

Whitman did not rush with the volunteers for military service. He never entered the army. He saw the young men of his city depart for war and he exulted in their going and voiced his martial patriotism:

Mannahatta a-march—and it's O to sing it well!
It's O for a manly life in the camp.

And the sturdy artillery,
The guns bright as gold, the work for giants, to serve well
    the guns,
Unlimber them! (no more as the past forty years for salutes
    for courtesies merely,
Put in something now besides powder and wadding.)
And you lady of ships, you Mannahatta,
Old matron of this proud, friendly, turbulent city,
Often in peace and wealth you were pensive or covertly
    frown'd amid all your children,
But now you smile with joy exulting old Mannahatta.

He saw his own brother George enlist. As for himself, he withdrew, contemplated events, and sought to fit them into his philosophy of the universe.

[2] Quoted in *Whitman*, by Emory Holloway, Alfred A. Knopf.

In the middle of December 1862, news arrived that George had been wounded at the battle of Fredericksburg. Immediately Whitman was stirred to action. He left for Falmouth, Virginia, where he found his brother quite out of danger and not so badly hurt as his family had feared. There he spent several days with the wounded men. And there a great purpose was born in him. He would go to Washington and in the hospitals of that city help take care of the sick and wounded.

For the rest of the war, with but few and brief intervals of rest, Whitman stayed at Washington, giving himself without stint to the men in the hospitals. "Mother," he wrote in a letter, "one's heart grows sick of war, after all, when you see what it really is." The political and social issues of the war moved him less than did the personal suffering of the soldiers both Northern and Southern. What he could do to ease them he did. Day after day he visited the hospitals, leaving some small gift purchased out of his own slender income or from the funds which he was able to raise, talking, writing letters, assisting at operations, heartening the dying.

I onward go, I stop,
With hinged knees and steady hands to dress wounds,
I am firm with each, the pangs are sharp yet unavoidable,
One turns to me his appealing eyes—poor boy! I never
    knew you,
Yet I think I could not refuse this moment to die for you,
    if that would save you.

Throughout all his devoted ministrations—he, himself, estimated at eighty to a hundred thousand the number of those he helped—he clung steadfastly to what he considered his greater purpose in life. "I feel," he wrote to a friend in

1863, "to devote myself more and more to the work of my life which is making poems."

During the war years at Washington, Whitman lived first with his friend O'Connor and the latter's wife, and then in rooms of his own. He did some writing for newspapers that awakened interest in his hospital work. The money received from his writing was little. To provide himself with the bare necessities of his own existence and to get money to spend on his soldiers, he took a job as clerk in the army paymaster's office. Soon he was transferred to the Indian Bureau of the Department of the Interior. His tenure there was short. Secretary Harlan was told that among the men in his department was Walt Whitman, the author of the obscene *Leaves of Grass*. The Secretary went to the clerk's desk, found there a copy of the book which Whitman was then revising, and instantly ordered his dismissal. In the indignation that followed, no cry was louder than that of O'Connor. He rushed to his friend's defense in a fervid, glowing pamphlet, *The Good Gray Poet,* thereby bestowing upon Whitman a name which never left him. A post was then secured for Whitman in the Attorney-General's Office.

Meanwhile, Whitman had been writing. His war experiences had been transmuted into poems which he published under the title of *Drum-Taps*. Scarcely had the book come off the press, when Lincoln was assassinated. Whitman was horrified, grief-stricken. His grief poured forth in poems: "When Lilacs Last in the Dooryard Bloom'd," "O Captain! My Captain!", "Hush'd be the Camps Today," "This Dust Was Once the Man." As *Memories of President Lincoln* he grouped the poems and issued them as a sequel to *Drum-Taps*.

With each new edition of his work, Whitman's fame spread. His verse was translated into foreign languages. He was accepted in England as the poet of democracy; he was hailed by Symonds, by Swinburne, and by William Rossetti. In 1868, Rossetti made a selection of his poems and gave them an English publication. Through Rossetti, Mrs. Anne Gilchrist, a woman of intellect and breeding, became interested in the poetry and grew to admire it. In 1870, the *Boston Radical* printed her opinion of the American in "An Englishwoman's Estimate of Walt Whitman." Her article did much to modify the harsh opinion people still retained of Whitman and his work. The poet's point of view she could accept completely. Its expression she criticized on the score of good taste, not of morals: "Perhaps Walt Whitman has forgotten—or, through some theory in his head, has overridden—the truth that our instincts are beautiful facts of nature, as well as our bodies; and that we have a strong instinct of silence about some things."

In his own country, too, Whitman was receiving a wider hearing. Among the friends he had made in Washington was John Burroughs, the naturalist, who, in 1867, wrote *Notes on Walt Whitman as Poet and Person.* With increased knowledge of the man, came a wider interest in him and a greater demand for his writing. In 1871, Whitman published *Democratic Vistas,* a prose pronouncement not of praise for America's past but of faith in its future. In the same year he published his new poems as *Passage to India.* The opening of the Suez Canal and of the transcontinental railroad in the United States had stirred his imagination. With the breaking down of geographical barriers, other barriers, too, seemed broken. The past and future became mystically fused in the present; the soul voyaged unhampered to God. In 1872 Whitman was asked to give the Commencement poem at Dartmouth College. The invitation to so radical a person was issued as a prank by the students. But his poem "As a Strong Bird on Pinions Free" was well received; and jest or no jest, the invitation was evidence of Whitman's spreading fame.

Through 1872 and until the spring of 1873, Whitman lived in Washington. His strenuous activity during the war had not been without physical effect upon him. In January 1864, he had been seriously ill, the result of an infection caught while assisting at an operation. His health was slowly undermined. The heat of Washington summers was enervating. He made several visits to Brooklyn, hopeful always that rest and relaxation would help him to regain his health. But in January 1873, he could stand the strain no longer; he suffered a paralytic stroke. Slowly he recovered; bravely in his letters home he made much of each improvement. But he never again was completely well.

In May of 1873, he left Washington for Camden, New Jersey, where his mother was then living with one of his brothers. On the twenty-third, but a few days after he reached her, his mother died. The loss was one from which he never completely recovered. To a friend, Peter Doyle, he wrote, "I cannot be reconciled to that yet; it is the great cloud of my life; nothing that ever happened before has had such an effect on me."

Whitman's failing health necessitated his remaining in Camden. In midsummer of 1874, he was discharged from his Washington bureau. His Washington associations were broken. Henceforth he was to be the poet of Camden.

His years at Camden were a vain pursuit of health. For a time he gained some relief by days spent outdoors at Timber Creek, a few miles from the city. Nature, his teacher and friend, for a time acted as his doctor too. But there was no real improvement. His move from his brother's home to his own home in Mickle Street was marked by an increasing invalidism.

If there was a diminution of his physical strength, there

was no corresponding lessening of the force of his personality. He seemed to possess some psychic power of attracting people; he was able to evoke life-long devotions. Peter Doyle was a young stage driver of Washington days with whom he established a deep abiding relationship. He had won the loyalty of O'Connor and of Burroughs. Mrs. Gilchrist journeyed to America to offer him her affection and her love, a love which he gently refused. Elsewhere also in England, the force of his personality was felt. The English heard stories of American neglect and offered, in generous measure, financial aid. Dr. Richard Maurice Bucke of Canada visited him and from simply being charmed by him became an admirer and a loyal friend. In Camden, itself, Horace Traubel and Thomas B. Harned lavished upon him tireless attention. On all with whom he came in contact Whitman exerted a tremendous personal magnetism. His Mickle Street house became the mecca for many visitors. He sat in his room, crowded with books and clippings and unassorted odds and ends, receiving with dignity and composure all manner of guests. There was something gigantic, almost non-human, about him.

There were a few brief excursions from Camden, visits to New York, a few trips on which he delivered his lecture on Lincoln, a visit to Burroughs, to Dr. Bucke in Canada, and a longer trip to the Rocky Mountains.

There were, too, during these years excursions of his soul. He still clung to his philosophy of life and to his poetry as its expression. He continued his writing. In 1876 appeared *Two Rivulets,* a collection of prose and of verse; and a new edition, the centennial edition, of *Leaves of Grass.* In 1881, there promised to be for the first time a recognized publisher for the book. In that year James R. Osgood and Company published it; but because of complaints to the Massachusetts State's Attorney-General condemning the book as indecent, the issue was threatened with suppression. The publishers abandoned their project, turning their plates over to the author. In 1882, appeared *Specimen Days and Collect*, a collection of Whitman's notes and articles. *November Boughs*, 1888, a collection of prose and verse, and *Good-Bye My Fancy*, 1891, were published when the poet was failing steadily, when his literary work could never have seen print without the help of the devoted Horace Traubel. As each collection of verse appeared, it took its place in Whitman's monument, his volume *Leaves of Grass*.

With his friends about him, with his mind still actively alert, Whitman knew his life to be ebbing. The prospect of death did not appall him; what happens to all must be for the good of all.

Not summer's zones alone—not chants of youth, or south's
    warm tides alone,
But held by sluggish floes, pack'd in the northern ice, the
    cumulus of years,
These with gay heart I also sing.

More and more the burden of his poems was death.

In July 1885, he suffered a sunstroke. A few days after his sixty-ninth birthday, in 1888, he had a chill. His convalescence was slow; but his attitude was one of cheerful acceptance: "This will pass soon, and if it does not—all is well." But complications arose. There was another paralytic stroke. His activities were more and more confined within the four walls of his room. There was in October 1890 a last public appearance; and in 1891 there was a visit to the cemetery where Whitman chose his burial plot and made plans for the building of a family tomb. In December 1891, pneumonia set in. In January 1892, he wrote to his sister, with calm faith, "It is all right whichever way." On March 17, he wrote again, "Unable to write much—5 enc'd—y'r good letter rec'd—God bless you. W. W." On March 26, he died.

Four days later he was buried in Harleigh Cemetery, in Camden. It was a strange funeral. Crowds of people pressed into the cemetery, crowding close to the tent under which the services were held. No fixed religion dictated the form of these services. Friends spoke, eulogizing their lost friend and poet, reading from his poems, explaining his beliefs.

Whitman's death by no means terminated the controversy aroused during his life; nor did it in any way diminish the influence he exerted. As a matter of fact, while the battles continued to rage over his art and his morality, more and more people came to acclaim and accept the freedom of his thought and of his expression.

The very characteristic which, from the point of view of artistry, was for so many a stumbling block has become part of the accepted technique of modern poetry. The unrhymed, rhythmic lines of *Leaves of Grass,* puzzling his contemporaries by being neither prose nor verse, liberated poetry for a new place in a modern world. Whitman had in his early poems used conventional rhyme and meter. The former he soon abandoned completely, although there is a slight suggestion of it in the opening stanza of the "Song of the Broad-Axe." As for the latter, he was able to use a definite metric stanza scheme, as he did in "Pioneers! O Pioneers!", "Dirge for Two Veterans," "O Captain! My Captain!" But this apparently restricted him in his purpose. He wished to sing the songs of a new country, of a broad, sweeping, free America and he sought a medium appropriate to it.

As a strong bird on pinions free,
Joyous, the amplest spaces heavenward cleaving,
Such be the thought I'd think of thee America,
Such be the recitative I'd bring for thee.

The conceits of the poets of other lands I'd bring thee not,
Nor the compliments that have served their turn so long,
Nor rhyme, nor the classics, nor perfume of foreign court
    or indoor library;
But an odor I'd bring as from forests of pine in Maine, or
    breath of an Illinois prairie,
With open airs of Virginia or Georgia or Tennessee, or from
    Texas uplands, or Florida's glades,
Or the Saguenay's black stream, or the wide blue spread of
    Huron,
With presentment of Yellowstone's scenes, or Yosemite,
And murmuring under, pervading all, I'd bring the rustling
    sea-sound,
That endlessly sounds from the two Great Seas of the world.

Rhyme and old verse forms were not consistent with a new
America.

Can your performance face the open fields and the seaside?

That was the test. So he made his poems of lines of varying
length, each line containing a complete suggestion. The pattern of his verse, a rhythmic flow rather than a fixed meter,
he found in the sweeping rhythm of the ocean or of the
city's crowded streets. That rhythm carries the reader with
it when it is used at its best, as it is, for example, in "With
Husky-Haughty Lips, O Sea!":

    With husky-haughty lips, O sea!
    Where day and night I wend thy surf-beat shore,
    Imagining to my sense thy varied strange suggestions,

or in "Tears":

Tears! tears! tears!
In the night, in solitude, tears,

On the white shore dripping, dripping, suck'd in by the
    sand,
Tears, not a star shining, all dark and desolate,
Moist tears from the eyes of a muffled head;
O who is that ghost? that form in the dark, with tears?

or in "When Lilacs Last in the Dooryard Bloom'd":

When lilacs last in the dooryard bloom'd,
And the great star early droop'd in the western sky in the
    night,
I mourn'd, and yet shall mourn with ever-returning spring.
Ever-returning spring, trinity sure to me you bring,
Lilac blooming perennial and drooping star in the west,
And thought of him I love.

Whitman's theory of a technique of poetry suitable for
America included tenets of simplicity and of a free and flexible vocabulary. But in these respects, Whitman frequently
fell far short of the generally accepted standards of the poetic. He introduced into his poetry words which grate even
upon modern ears no longer insisting upon conventionalized
"poetic diction"—slang, words derived from other languages, and queer hybrid words of his own devising: *exalté,
libertad, philosophs, ma femme, eleve, blab,* "dainty dolce
affettuoso," "how plenteous, how spiritual, how résumé."
Sometimes he uses expressions that cannot conceivably be
considered poetic:

Cross out please those immensely overpaid accounts.

Sometimes, he even goes so far as to use phrases that are
not only not poetical, but are neither grammatical nor English:

City of orgies, walks and joys,
City whom that I have lived and sung in your midst will
one day make you illustrious.

or

O you whom I often and silently come where you are that
I may be with you.

Whitman's belief in an all-inclusive philosophy led him to
his peculiar mannerism of long catalogues. These fill many
of his poems; examples of them may be found in the fourteenth section of "Starting from Paumanok," in "The
Sleepers," in the anatomical list in section nine of "I Sing
the Body Electric," in the geographical one in section four
of "Salut au Monde." That these fail to move the reader as
Whitman wished them to may be due to the fact that for
him his phrases held certain connotations unknown to the
reader. Possibly, too, the long enumerations of items produced upon the poet an almost hypnotic effect leading him
to a state of mystic consciousness, an hypnotic effect to
which few readers are equally susceptible.

Occasionally, however, the catalogues flash poetic suggestions.

I hear of the Italian boat-sculler the musical recitative of
old poems,
I hear the locusts in Syria as they strike the grain and grass
with the showers of their terrible clouds,
I hear the Coptic refrain toward sundown, pensively falling
on the breast of the black venerable vast mother the
Nile,
I hear the chirp of the Mexican muleteer, and the bells of
the mule,
I hear the Arab muezzin calling from the top of the mosque.

It is quite obvious that this occurs when the list instead of being merely an enumeration, presents vivid, terse pictures. Whitman has the ability to choose a few specific, essential details and thus to draw glowing pictures within a small compass.

Where the humming-bird shimmers, where the neck of the
     long-lived swan is curving and winding,
Where the laughing-gull scoots by the shore, where she
     laughs her near-human laugh.

Observing the spiral flight of two little yellow butterflies
     shuffling between each other, ascending high in the air.

Through the ample open door of the peaceful country barn,
A sunlit pasture field with cattle and horses feeding,
And haze and vista, and the far horizon fading away.

The same ability shows itself in Whitman's use of exact, unerring epithet: "Mast-hemmed Manhattan," "husky-haughty lips," "white-maned racers."

Some few of Whitman's poems in their totality are perfect in form, completely poetic; such poems as "Good-Bye My Fancy!", "When Lilacs Last in the Dooryard Bloom'd," "When I Heard the Learn'd Philosophers," "Reconciliation," "Twilight":

The soft voluptuous opiate shades,
The sun just gone, the eager light dispell'd—(I too will soon
     be gone, dispell'd,)
A haze-nirwana—rest and night—oblivion.

The few poems that are thus completely satisfying technically are, however, but a very small part of Whitman's work. His significance scarcely lies in his craftsmanship.

The words of my book nothing, the drift of it every thing.

Yet Whitman's weak craftsmanship was no evidence that he lacked a very definite conception of the function of a poet. As a matter of fact he had a clear conception, one in keeping with ·his viewpoint that message was more important than method, one that motivated all his work.

Throughout his poems, particularly in "Song of the Answerer," "When the Full-Grown Poet Came," and in "By Blue Ontario's Shore," that poem reworked from the prose preface to the first edition of *Leaves of Grass*, one finds explained his theory of the poet.

All this time and at all times wait the words of true poems,
The words of true poems do not merely please,
The true poets are not followers of beauty but the august
    masters of beauty.

For Whitman the poet was a seer. And what was his own poetic vision that he felt compelled to give the world? It was a vision of a wide, generous, new America that permitted the complete and independent development of the individual; a vision of his own identity with all mankind; a vision of the unity of creation, of the continuity of time, of the mystic union of mankind, nature, and God. The one purpose of his life was to voice this vision in *Leaves of Grass*, to expound that philosophy of his which reconciled all contradictions, to express in his poems his own complete personality as the embodiment of that philosophy.

L. OF G'S. PURPORT

Not to exclude or demarcate, or pick out evils from their
    formidable masses (even to expose them,)
But add, fuse, complete, extend—and celebrate the immor-
    tal and the good.

Haughty this song, its words and scope,
To span vast realms of space and time,
Evolution—the cumulative—growths and generations.

Begun in ripen'd youth and steadily pursued,
Wandering, peering, dallying with all—war, peace, day and
    night absorbing,
Never even for one brief hour abandoning my task,
I end it here in sickness, poverty, and old age.
I sing of life, yet mind me well of death:
Today shadowy Death dogs my steps, my seated shape, and
    has for years—
Draws sometimes close to me, as face to face.

Loyalty to that purpose made him feel that anything—
everything—was fit subject for poetry.

I am not the poet of goodness alone, I do not decline to be
    the poet of wickedness also.

I am the poet of the Body and I am the poet of the Soul.

At a time when the human body was something to be draped
in secrecy, it was these poems of the body, particularly the
poems of sex, that brought against Whitman the charges of
indecency and obscenity. It is well here to realize that these
poems have been—and still are—unduly stressed; that they
form but a small part of all his poetry and should be judged
in proportion to the whole. Immoral they are not, when
viewed in the light of his philosophy. But that they do occasionally violate the canons of good taste, ignore the "instinct
of silence," and fail to be poetic cannot be denied.

They are, however, indisputably part of Whitman's inclusive philosophy, the vision that merged all time and all
things into a single whole.

I do not call one greater and one smaller,
That which fills its period and place is equal to any.

Such a doctrine is preëminently a democratic doctrine,
one in which women and men are equal, in which each man
or woman is the equal of every other man or woman.

Each of us inevitable,
Each of us limitless—each of us with his or her right upon
    the earth,
Each of us allow'd the eternal purports of the earth,
Each of us here as divinely as any is here.

Such a doctrine, Whitman felt, could best be expounded
in a country like America, founded on principles of democracy. Throughout his poems one finds a passionate love for
his country:

Chants of the prairies,
Chants of the long-running Mississippi, and down to the
    Mexican sea,
Chants of Ohio, Indiana, Illinois, Iowa, Wisconsin and
    Minnesota,
Chants going forth from the centre from Kansas, and thence
    equidistant,
Shooting in pulses of fire ceaseless to vivify all,

a firm purpose to "make a song for these States." Out of his
patriotism and his faith in the mission of America grew a
desire for world unity, for internationalism:

The ocean to be cross'd, the distance brought near,
The lands to be welded together.

Such a state of peace and democracy was to be desired so
that there might be permitted the freest development of the

individual. "The purpose of democracy . . . is . . . to illustrate this doctrine or theory that man, properly train'd in sanest, highest freedom, may and must become a law, and series of laws, unto himself, surrounding and providing for, not only his own personal control, but all his relations to other individuals, and to the State." For, always, it was the human personality, the individual, the average man or woman that was the center of Whitman's thought.

I swear I begin to see the meaning of these things,
It is not the earth, it is not America who is so great,
It is I who am great or to be great, it is You up there, or
    any one.

The individual, conscious of his significance in the universe, must cultivate sturdy self-reliance and independence. He must be dauntless in his purpose:

O the joy of a manly self-hood!
To be servile to none, to defer to none, nor to any tyrant
    known or unknown,
    .   .   .   .
To confront with your personality all the other personalities
    of the earth.

So it was something more than mere egotism that made Whitman write himself in *Leaves of Grass,* that made him hail himself as the poet and seer for all mankind.

I am an acme of things accomplish'd, and I an encloser of
    things to be.
I exist as I am, that is enough,
If no other in the world be aware I sit content,
And if each and all be aware I sit content.

And who but I should be the poet of comrades?

These are not simply self-laudations. Nor was there mere bravado in his calls to courage:

Sail forth—steer for the deep waters only,
Reckless O soul, exploring, I with thee, and thou with me.

My call is the call of battle, I nourish active rebellion,

For I am the sworn poet of every dauntless rebel the world
    over,
And he going with me leaves peace and routine behind him,
And stakes his life to be lost at any moment.

Whitman was in such lines using himself symbolically, as he used other symbols; he typified all mankind. What he saw in others, with humility he admitted in himself, the bad as well as the good:

Full of wickedness, I—of many a smutch'd deed reminiscent
    —of worse deed capable.

What he demanded for himself, he demanded for others:

Not I. Not any one else can travel that road for you,
You must travel it for yourself.

And no man understands any greatness or goodness but his
    own, or the indication of his own.

A world of individuals might easily be a world of conflict and of disorder. But there existed for Whitman a binding force, a constructive one. Love was the foundation of the universe:

Blow again trumpeter! and for thy theme,
Take now the enclosing theme of all, the solvent and the
    setting,
Love, that is pulse of all, the sustenance and the pang,

The heart of man and woman all for love,
No other theme but love—knitting, enclosing, all-diffusing
love.

The love that had its origin in the love between man and woman would develop with religious fervor into a love among fellow men. Whitman's poems were for "comrades and lovers." His purpose was "to infuse myself among you till I see it common for you to walk home in hand." It was this broader aspect of love that Whitman preached. Some very few of his poems, it is true, were based on personal, intimate feelings; but much more than the poet of personal emotions is Whitman the poet of sweeping, cosmic emotions.

Similarly, too, it is of the larger rather than the smaller aspects of nature that Whitman is the poet. With rare fidelity, he could catch the sight, or smell, or sound of some of nature's objects:

The smell of apples, aromas from crush'd sage-plant, mint, birch bark.

Occasionally he could write a nature poem of pure description, as in "The First Dandelion." Or he could paint the broad canvas of the sea as in "With Husky-Haughty Lips, O Sea!", or that of the prairies, as in "Night on the Prairies." But nature was for Whitman something more than objective beauty: it was the inspiration for his poetry, the test of its validity:

I think heroic deeds were all conceiv'd in the open air, and all free poems also.

Between nature and man, both essential to the scheme of things, existed a basic unity:

Nature and Man shall be disjoin'd and diffused no more,
The true son of God shall absolutely fuse them.

It were futile to look for creed and dogma in Whitman's poetry. All his beliefs, however, he felt to be expressions of religion.

I say the whole earth and all the stars in the sky are for religion's sake.

All the purpose of existence was a striving toward fusion, unity, identity with the deity. That is the essence of the moving poem, "Passage to India":

> Bathe me O God in thee, mounting to thee,
> I and my soul to range in range of thee.

This deity was not the God of the orthodox. He was not a removed, omnipotent ruler. He was present; He dwelt within all:

Why should I wish to see God better than this day?
I see something of God each hour of the twenty-four, and
    each moment then,
In the faces of men and women I see God, and in my own
    face in the glass,
I find letters from God dropt in the street, and every one is
    sign'd by God's name,
And I leave them where they are, for I know that where-
    so'er I go,
Others will punctually come for ever and ever.

But more than that, He was, according to Whitman's democratic religion, of no greater significance to the individual than the individual himself:

And nothing, not God, is greater to one than one's self is.

However startling and unorthodox such a statement was, there was a still more daring idea in "Chanting the Square Deific." For therein the ultimate basis of the universe included evil as well as good. It was a "square deific" composed equally of God Jehovah, the Saviour, Satan, and the individual:

Including all life on earth, touching, including God, including Saviour and Satan,
Ethereal, pervading all, (for without me what were all what were God?)
Essence of forms, life of the real identities, permanent, positive, (namely the unseen,)
Life of the great round world, the sun and stars, and of man, I, the general soul,
Here the square finishing, the solid, I the most solid,
Breathe my breath also through these songs.

The strength of religion shows itself in daily living and in the face of death. For the latter, Whitman had no fear. Since death came to all, it must be good. It was the ultimate answer to the questions of life:

O I see now that life cannot exhibit all to me, as the day cannot,
I see that I am to wait for what will be exhibited by death.

Supreme was his faith; for to him death implied immortality:

Do you suspect death? if I were to suspect death I should die now,
Do you think I could walk pleasantly and well-suited toward annihilation?

Pleasantly and well-suited I walk,
Whither I walk I cannot define, but I know it is good,
The whole universe indicates that it is good,
The past and the present indicate that it is good.

His confidence in the future was so supreme that he could with equanimity accept the present.

Have you fear'd the future would be nothing to you?
Is today nothing? is the beginningless past nothing?
If the future is nothing they are just as surely nothing.

Yet that present was important because of what was to come. Just as it was the result of the experience of the past, so, too, it was the producer of the future. It was a forward-looking philosophy to which Whitman subscribed; it was an optimistic one, developing, not static. More than it praised the past did it look to the future.

It was because of this optimistic faith, this sense of the continuity of time, that Whitman stressed so the individual. For only through the individual could the race—and the future—continue.

This is not only one man, this the father of those who shall be fathers in their turns.

This sense of continuity, merely another aspect of the philosophy of identity, is the basis of Whitman's thought. It is the quality that carries him into our present, that makes him a message-bearer for today. He saw and joyfully accepted the implications of his time. Industry, science—these he greeted and praised. "The Song of the Exposition" is a glorification of mechanical inventions and of industrial progress. "Passage to India" sees a symbolic prophecy in engineering achievements. "To a Locomotive in Winter," by its praise of the inventions of man, in its time opened a new field for poetry. Man became the center from which poetry sprang; so cities, the result of man's labors, became a fitting subject for poetry, as in "Mannahatta" and "Crossing Brooklyn Ferry."

Epitome of all Whitman's thought, fusion of his belief in man, his love for America, his faith in the future, are the closing lines of "Song of the Redwood Tree":

The new society at last, proportionate to Nature,
In man of you, more than your mountain peaks or stalwart
    trees imperial,
In woman more, far more, than all your gold or vines, or
    even vital air.

Fresh come, to a new world indeed, yet long prepared,
I see the genius of the modern, child of the real and ideal,
Clearing the ground for broad humanity, the true America,
    heir of the past so grand,
To build a grander future.

Whitman is outstandingly the poet of America and of the nineteenth century. No other place could have inspired him to write as he did; nor could any other time. "I know very well," he wrote in 1888, in "A Backward Glance o'er Travel'd Roads," "that my *Leaves* could not possibly have emerged or been fashion'd or completed, from any other era than the latter half of the nineteenth century, nor any other land than democratic America, and from the absolute triumph of the National Union arms." *Leaves of Grass* was founded firmly and realistically in the society of its time; but because of its dynamic, prophetic quality, it pointed to an ideal society. It was to be one made up of free men and women, free-bodied and free-thinking—a society arising from the great mass of average Americans.

For that great mass of people, *Leaves of Grass,* "the song of a great composite *democratic individual,* male or female," was to be both saga and revelation. Paradoxically, in this country, the people of whom and for whom Whitman wrote have not in large numbers accepted him. His greatest recognition has come not from the mass, but from the social and intellectual leaders.

Still another paradox the poet presents. In the realm of literature he has been a liberating influence, breaking down restrictions both of form and of subject. Yet his own work he wished judged less as art than as message.

"*Leaves of Grass* indeed (I cannot too often reiterate) has mainly been the outcropping of my own emotional and other personal nature—an attempt, from first to last, to put a *Person,* a human being (myself, in the latter half of the nineteenth century, in America,) freely, fully and truly on record. I could not find any similar personal record in current literature that satisfied me. But it is not on *Leaves of Grass* distinctively as *literature,* or a specimen thereof, that I feel to dwell, or advance claims. No one will get at my verses who insists upon viewing them as a literary performance, or attempt at such performance, or as aiming mainly toward art or æstheticism."

Yet both the source and the presentation of his views are emotional rather than logical; and the emotional is the material of poetry and of art. Poetry or prophecy? which is *Leaves of Grass?* At its noblest, it is both. But whether at its weakest, when it speaks neither with the music of the poet nor with the vision of the seer, or at its noblest, it is an avowal of faith in mankind, an exposition of human personality.

> Camerado, this is no book,
> Who touches this touches a man.

EMILY DICKINSON

O NE DAY in April 1862, in Worcester, Massachusetts, Thomas Wentworth Higginson, reformer, lecturer, writer, and author of the just-published "Letter to a Young Contributor" in the *Atlantic Monthly,* found in his mail a note which, enclosing four poems, asked the question, "Are you too deeply occupied to say if my verse is alive?" Other correspondents had asked similar questions, begging for literary advice and help; but invariably they had signed their names to their letters. This unknown writer, however, as though fearful of obtruding too much personality into the note itself, had left the letter unsigned and written the signature on a separate card. The name was Emily Dickinson.

Mr. Higginson was interested. The poems, not fulfilling the exact requirements of well-tailored verse, it is true, still held such stabbing ideas as "The nearest dream recedes, unrealized," and such colorful pictures as

> I'll tell you how the sun rose,
> A ribbon at a time.
> The steeples swam in amethyst,
> The news like squirrels ran.

He answered the letter, applying to the poem what she referred to as "surgery; it was not so painful as I supposed," and asking for more verse to read. But as much as interest in the poetry, curiosity about the poet prompted his reply. Her extreme diffidence made him wonder. It was his turn to ask questions. Who was she? How old? What was her life?

Her preparation for writing? Ten days later he received a second letter.

His question concerning the poet's age was left unanswered. "You asked how old I was? I made no verse, but one or two, until this winter, sir." About other things, however, the poet was more revealing.

"I had a terror since September, I could tell to none; and so I sing, as the boy does of the burying ground, because I am afraid.

"You inquire my books. For poets, I have Keats, and Mr. and Mrs. Browning. For prose, Mr. Ruskin, Sir Thomas Browne, and the *Revelations*. I went to school, but in your manner of the phrase had no education. When a little girl, I had a friend who taught me Immortality; but venturing too near, himself, he never returned. Soon after, my tutor died, and for several years my lexicon was my only companion. Then I found one more, but he was not contented I be his scholar, so he left the land.

"You ask of my companions. Hills, sir, and the sundown, and a dog large as myself, that my father bought me. They are better than beings because they know, but do not tell; and the noise in the pool at noon excels my piano.

"I have a brother and sister; my mother does not care for thought, and father, too busy with his briefs to notice what we do. He buys me many books, but begs me not to read them, because he fears they joggle the mind. They are religious, except me, and address an eclipse, every morning, whom they call their 'Father.'" [1]

That letter is an almost complete biography of Emily Dickinson. Dates and facts are missing. The identity, for example, of the "one more, but he was not contented I be his scholar" is still not indisputably or even satisfactorily estab-

[1] *Letters of Emily Dickinson,* edited by Mabel Loomis Todd, Harper & Brothers.

lished. One biographer insists that he was a young Amherst
student whom Emily's father forced her to renounce; another insists that he was the husband of one of her girlhood
friends; a third, that he was a married clergyman whom she
had heard preach in Philadelphia. But in spite of the omis-
sion of such factual information, the letter reveals the real
Emily Dickinson; it gives the clews to those influences that
created her personality, from which came her poetry: her
relation to her family and her friends, her education, her
attitude toward nature and religion, her unhappy love affair,
and her resort to poetry as a refuge from sorrow and fear.

The accidents of time and space could never explain
Emily Dickinson. More important than dates and places and
names are the intangible elements of her daily existence,
about which her letters form the richest source of information. To these elements alone can one look for the solution
of the greatest mystery of her life. That mystery is not that
of the name of some unidentified man; it is that of her personality and ability. What enabled her, shy, diffident, secluded, to touch by her poetry those whom she could not
and would not touch in life? How was she able to create out
of her restricted garden a complete universe with universal
truths? What gave her the power to recognize the two
worlds of fact and of intuition and made her aware that of
the two the latter is more important, that

> To make a prairie it takes a clover and one bee,—
> And revery.
> The revery alone will do
> If bees are few.

It was precisely this power to create through revery an
existence independent of the life about her that made Emily
Dickinson emerge from New England insistence and conformity instead of being overwhelmed by them. Other

women had lived lives similar to hers. They had had unhappy love affairs, had withdrawn into their homes, and had
become lost in the background as "eccentric spinsters."
Outwardly, Emily Dickinson conformed to the traditional
pattern. Inwardly, however, she rebelled. Her identity, instead of becoming lost, grew stronger and created of itself
a poet.

The traditional New England background entered into
Emily Dickinson's ancestry. The first Dickinson ancestor
had settled in Massachusetts in the early seventeenth century. Soon the family became identified with the community
about Hadley and Amherst. Samuel Fowler Dickinson, the
poet's grandfather, a graduate of Dartmouth College and a
lawyer, had been a moving force in providing educational
opportunities for Amherst. Largely through his efforts, Amherst Academy in 1814 and, a few years later, Amherst College were established.

His oldest son, Edward, was graduated from Yale in
1823. He became a member of the Governor's staff. He
studied law and was recognized as one of Amherst's leading
lawyers. In 1828, he married Emily Norcross of Monson,
Massachusetts, who was the daughter of a well-to-do family
and who had been educated at a school for young ladies in
New Haven, Connecticut. Three children were born to
them: Emily Elizabeth on December 10, 1830, Austin, and
Lavinia.

In this family, Edward Dickinson was the strongest force.
The mother seems to have been a faint, shadowy creature,
frequently ill and of so little effect that years later Emily
could say of her to Colonel Higginson, "I never had a
mother." It was the father who held the family together—
tightly, inexorably, even tyrannically. In the community he
was considered austere, coldly correct, his one endearing hu-
manizing quality being a love for fine horses. At home, he

was equally austere. "You know he never played," his daughter wrote of him. He made every effort to mold the family to his wishes, choosing their reading, supervising their education, ordering their lives. Yet it seems to have been a jealous devotion toward his children, rather than a simple desire to exercise authority, that motivated him. His difficulty lay in the fact that he was unable simply and openly to express his emotions. The keen joy, for example, that he derived from the letters of his son he was never able himself to convey to him. He loved his children intensely. His one way of showing it was to bind them closely to him, to insist upon their being near him.

The home naturally became the center of the family's activity. Authority and supervision were there; but so, too, were love and security. Emily's love for her home was profound. "Yes, Austin, home is faithful; none other is so true." At home, she was content; away from it, she was harassed by loneliness and nostalgia.

However close were the ties between Emily and her home, however secure she felt under her father's care, there was still not complete acceptance of her father's point of view. Her inner life could not yield entirely to his dictates; the rebellion was scarcely open, but it existed. "And we do not have much poetry," she wrote in 1852, "father having made up his mind that it's pretty much all real life. Father's real life and mine sometimes come into collision but as yet escape unhurt."

Yet it must not be assumed that the life in Amherst was one of conflict or of strain. It was the pleasant, peaceful one of a small New England college town; and Emily's life was that of any small New England girl. She attended classes at Amherst Academy. She learned to sew and wrote of embroidering bookmarks and slippers. She was taught cooking and housekeeping. She went to singing school and took piano lessons, learning to play "Grave of Bonaparte," "Lancers Quickstep," and "Maiden, weep no more." She had an outdoor garden and an indoor one, giving to her flowers tender care and devotion that lasted throughout her life. She had a number of friends to whom, when for one reason or another they left Amherst, she wrote long, vibrant letters, in which she poured out her rich affection.

At fourteen, she was an average little girl, with a little girl's interest and desires. She was no prig. "I expect," she wrote at 14 to her friend Abiah Root, a former schoolmate in the Academy, "you have a great many prim, starched up young ladies there, who, I doubt not, are perfect models of propriety and good behavior. If they are, don't let your free spirit be chained by them." For herself, she had plans and visions for the future. "I am growing handsome very fast indeed! I expect I shall be the belle of Amherst when I reach my 17th year. I don't doubt that I shall have perfect crowds of admirers at that age."

Ill health interfered with her regular attendance at the Academy. In 1846, she attended only the German recitations. But instead of books, she studied music. In the fall of that year, she left Amherst for a visit to an aunt in Boston. She saw Mount Auburn and Bunker Hill; she attended two concerts; she visited the Chinese Museum and the Horticultural Exhibit. The visit was a pleasant one; but it was extended so long that she was unable to enter the fall term of the Amherst Academy.

For two reasons that was to be regretted. In the first place, she was planning to enter the South Hadley Seminary the following fall and her preparatory studies were thus delayed. But in addition, the Academy had a new principal, Leonard Humphrey, who had just graduated from Amherst where he had been in the same fraternity as her brother, Austin. To have so young a principal was very much of an innovation and Emily was eager to study under him. Soon, however, she was back in the Academy, and immersed in algebra, geometry, and ecclesiastical history to fit herself for the new school.

In the fall of 1847, Emily went to South Hadley. There Mary Lyon, the noted educator, had established the Mount Holyoke Female Seminary. Designed to train women to be mates for missionaries, it was known facetiously as "Miss Lyon's Missionary Rib Factory." But jests did not affect Miss Lyon's scholastic standards. Her requirements were high; three days of preliminary examinations restricted to some three hundred the number of students at the school. The day's program was a long one. The curriculum included ancient history, chemistry, physiology, astronomy, and rhetoric. In addition to their studies, the scholars helped in the domestic routine of the institution.

Emily had no difficulty with her scholastic work; sufficiently prepared, she was able to enter the middle class of the school. But this first real absence from home was a terrific wrench. Though she roomed with a cousin, Emily Norcross, a senior, and though her first awful pang of loneliness soon was somewhat allayed, she longed constantly for home. "But I am now content and quite happy, if I can be happy when absent from my dear home and friends." The visits paid by her brother and her parents were hailed with delight. Her Thanksgiving vacation was eagerly awaited.

Any separation from home would have been difficult for Emily to bear. But at the Academy, especially, the atmosphere was not one of warmth and tenderness. Display of sentiment was frowned upon; the pleasant exchange of valentines was forbidden. The seriousness of life, the steadfast absorption in studies and in character training were stressed. The academic isolation of the school provoked Emily's irony. She wrote to her brother, "Won't you please to tell me when you answer my letter who the candidate for President is? I have been trying to find out ever since I came here, and have not yet succeeded. I don't know any thing more about affairs in the world than if I was in a trance, and you must imagine with all your 'Sophomoric discernment' that it is but little and very faint. Has the Mexican War terminated yet, and how? Are we beaten? Do you know of any nation about to besiege South Hadley? If so, do inform me of it, for I would be glad of a chance to escape, if we are to be stormed." [2]

But more disturbing than anything else was the religious insistence of the school. The times, in general, were marked by a strong revival of interest in religion; at the school particularly, the religious life was emphasized. Students who had not formally accepted their religious responsibilities, the "Impenitents," were lectured to and prayed over. Emily was unable to give herself up to the religious requirements. Her own father seems to have set her some example for nonconformity. For though he had always been a regular attendant at church and an active worker, he had not become a church member until 1850. Furthermore, he had never insisted that his daughter be christened. But Emily rebelled still further. The Sunday God of New England orthodoxy, distant, awful, cruelly stern, was not her God.

> Some keep the Sabbath going to church;
> I keep it staying at home,
> With a bobolink for a chorister,
> And an orchard for a dome.

If accepting Him meant rejecting this world, Emily could not accept. This world with its color and light and joy meant too much for her. The young girl who a year before had written, "I have perfect confidence in God and His prom-

[2] *Letters of Emily Dickinson.*

ises, and yet I know not why I feel that the world holds a predominant place in my affections," in spite of exhortation and prayers, in spite of the Mount Holyoke atmosphere, still found it "hard for me to give up the world."

Her stay at Mount Holyoke was, after all, not to be a long one. In the late winter, she had a severe cold and her parents insisted that she go back home until she was better. When she returned once more to school for the short spring session, it was with the knowledge that this was to be her last term there. Her father's decision that she was to remain no longer, a decision for which no definite reason has yet been given, she accepted with something of relief. "I have been quite lonely since I came back, but cheered by the thought that I am not to return another year, I can take comfort, and still hope on."

Restored once more to the family security, Emily was content. She reëntered Amherst Academy to study for another year. She contributed to the school paper, *Forest Leaves*, her sparkling humor giving her the reputation of being one of the school wits.

The school no longer had Mr. Humphrey as its principal. He had left his position the preceding year to study at Andover Theological. But now he was once more at Amherst, a tutor in the college. Between him and Emily grew a close and devoted friendship, which was to be cruelly broken by his sudden death in November 1850. Her friend who had "taught her Immortality," "ventured too near."

But meanwhile she had other friends, among them George Gould, who had entered Amherst in 1846 and who was also a member of Leonard Humphrey's and Austin Dickinson's fraternity. Life with her friends was most delightful. For serious moments there was the Shakespeare Society; for lighter ones, the P.O.M., seeking to conceal from forbidding elders that the letters were the initials of Poetry of Motion and that the group actually danced! There were numerous callers. There were parties, games, and "candy scrapes." There were college receptions, culminating each year in the Commencement Tea which her father, as treasurer, gave. And with the friends no longer at Amherst, there continued that joyous contact and outpouring through letters. Particularly with her brother Austin, the correspondence was a delight. He had graduated from Amherst in 1850 and had taught school at Sunderland, Massachusetts. From Boston, where he had next gone to teach school and then to study law at Harvard, came letters which she cherished. To Boston went letters in which Emily told all the events of the family and of the town, in which she expressed over and over again her sisterly devotion and her desire for her brother's return. Her longing for the complete home circle led her, she writes, to set the dinner table for five, "forgetting for the moment that we are not all here."

Home duties were now demanding more and more of her attention. She baked for the family and announced, "Twin loaves of bread have just been born into the world under my auspices." She did what she could "from a desire to make everything pleasant for father and Austin." For her mother was again not well. Emily cared for the invalid. One day "a friend I love *so* dearly" invited the young woman to ride with him. Because she felt her mother might need her, she had to refuse; and in her disappointment, she wept bitterly and heartbrokenly. Evidently she had not yet voluntarily renounced companionship.

The years from 1852 through 1854 are the years of mystery in Emily Dickinson's life. It is from this period that the facts are missing. What is known is that at this time began the process that changed her from an active, eager, alert young woman into a retiring, withdrawn recluse, shrinking almost to morbidity from contact with any but her most intimate friends. What seems apparent is that she suffered an unhappy love affair, and, in renouncing her lover, renounced the world of her fellow men and women. The nature of the love affair is not known.

According to some, George Gould, the Amherst graduate, wished her to marry him. But her father objected and made her give him up, either because he was doubtful of the possibility of her being happy married to a poor clergyman or, possibly, because he, himself, wished her not to marry at all and so keep his family group intact.

At all events, by 1854, Emily had already formed the habit of running away from people, and of going to church early so that the risk might be lessened of meeting people who would wish to talk. Her reluctance at leaving home was already known to her family. For in that year, her father, now a Congressman at Washington, asked Austin to bring his mother and Lavinia to the capital and suggested—suggested only—that Emily come too, if she cared to. Emily went and was gone from home for six weeks.

At Washington she saw the sights of interest. She met men of importance. She renewed her friendship with her old playmate Helen Fiske, now married to Major Edward Bissell Hunt. Her mind and understanding met those of Major Hunt. Her three weeks in Washington were followed by two in Philadelphia. There she heard the Reverend Charles Wadsworth preach, moved inexpressibly by his oratory. The two became lifelong friends. So much is fact. Supposition enters into the suggestion that she fell in love either with her friend's husband or with the elderly clergyman, who, too, was married; and, knowing the hopelessness of such love, renounced it.

With the return to Amherst, her lifelong retirement and seclusion began. Her life turned in upon itself. Her world was limited to her father's house and garden and to her brother's home next door. For Austin had married in 1856 and had been induced by his father to remain in Amherst, although he had wanted to go West with his bride. In time even the short journeys "a hedge away" to Austin's house were abandoned.

But as the physical limits of her universe grew more restricted, the spiritual ones enlarged. She discovered her own soul, its isolation, its independence. The small things about her grew large in meaning, a single leaf conveyed a forest. "Friday I tasted life," she wrote. "It was a vast morsel. A circus passed the house—still I feel the red in my mind though the drums are out."

Though withdrawn and shy, she did not become warped and misanthropic. For children, especially for her nephews and her niece next door, she was an engaging, entrancing personality. Mysterious notes, delightful packages went back and forth. Profound secrets were hinted at. She possessed magic; and somehow, though a grown-up, she appeared always as their friend and ally.

Something of this same self she was able to reveal in her letters. Timid, withdrawing from actual contact, in them she gave herself unstintingly. They carried the unbounded expression of her love and of her devotion. They contained the news of her intimate world. It was simply the world of affairs and of activity that she had given up. She had not given up living and her joy of life was keen. "I find ecstasy in living; the mere sense of living is joy enough." Her letters conveyed this joy. They were marked by her genius for choosing the essential trifles of her days and by her keen observation of things and of people. Her writing was vivid, sparkling. "The winds blow gay today and the jays bark like blue terriers." Her imagination was lively. "My heart grows light so fast that I could mount a grasshopper and gallop around the world, and not fatigue him any." "How

luscious is the dripping of February eaves! It makes our
thinking pink." Inevitably right were many of her expressions: "That bleeding beginning every mourner knows," for
example. With her sympathy and understanding, there
showed, too, a sparkling humor and ability to laugh at herself. When the family moved back to the ancestral mansion from which they had been away for some fifteen years,
she described the process: "I cannot tell you how we moved.
I had rather not remember. I believe my 'effects' were
brought in a bandbox, and the 'deathless me,' on foot, not
many moments after. I took at the time a memorandum of
my several senses, and also of my hat and coat, and my
best shoes—but it was lost in the *mêlée,* and I am out with
lanterns, looking for myself." [3]

Sometimes letters alone could not convey her thoughts or
her feelings. So there grew up the habit of sending some
flower from her garden or from her beloved little conservatory. And frequently she enclosed in her letter a small, tentative, unnamed poem.

The pattern of her life was set. It consisted, outside, of
her house and garden; inside, of her thoughts, her letters,
and her poems. Across this withdrawn existence flashed
briefly the drama of the Civil War. "War feels to me an
oblique place," she wrote. The first realization of war's import came with the news of the death of Frazer Stearns, the
son of Amherst's president. In some naval experiments that
he was conducting, Major Hunt died. Emily experienced
deep grief; vicariously she shared the sorrows of those who
lost dear ones in the war. It was this grief, this sorrow that
concerned her most—not political or social issues. Death,
not slavery, moved her.

From the existence which even war failed to alter, she
made throughout the rest of her life but two physical ex-

[3] *Letters of Emily Dickinson.*

cursions, both brief. The summers of 1864 and 1865 she went to Boston for treatment for her eyes, living with her cousins at Cambridgeport, a little way out from the city. A third visit to Boston, ordered by her doctor, she never made. "Father objects because he is in the habit of me"; and Emily was too strongly in the habit of heeding her father to think of disregarding his preferences.

But in one respect her father was powerless to restrain her. In that reserved, individual universe which she had created, her spirit, her imagination, her thoughts were completely free. Poetry became her spiritual escape. This freedom was signalized by the letter which, in 1862, she wrote to Colonel Higginson. How she finally reached the decision to submit her verse for criticism—and that, too, to a stranger—one does not know. But she did submit it, at the same time pledging Colonel Higginson to secrecy.

This critic, whose advice she sought, was unable completely to grasp her work. Her thoughts stimulated his interest; but the manner of her expression perplexed him. Her verse did not follow his neat standards of accurately measured feet or of exact, undeviating rhyme. He called it "spasmodic" and "uncontrolled." Whatever control he may have sought to exert she could not yieldingly submit to. She persisted in her own method, developed her own style. Yet she continued to look to him for advice and to rely on his judgment.

Some few people, besides Colonel Higginson, knew of her writing. She had sent poems to some of her closest friends. One of her poems, "The Snake," appeared in the *Springfield Republican* in February 1866, sent to the paper, one may be quite sure, not by the poet, herself. Another poem, "Success is counted sweetest," appeared in a collection of verse, *A Masque of Poets*. But she shrank from making her verse public. A request to contribute some poems to a charitable

cause, "to aid the world by my chirrup more," she immediately declined. Her old friend Helen Fiske, now Mrs.
Jackson by a second marriage, wished her to contribute to a
series of books published anonymously. This, too, she refused, feeling herself unworthy and unable. Yet because she
did not wish to hurt her friend and because she still had
not sufficient confidence in her own determination, she wrote
to Colonel Higginson asking him for support. "If you would
be willing to give me a note saying you disapproved it and
thought me unfit, she would believe you." Colonel Higginson was willing. Mindful of the awful responsibility of
print, mindful, too, of his pupil's violations of his rules of
prosody, he wrote that her decision was quite correct: "Such
being the majesty of the art you presume to practice, you
can at least take time before dishonoring it."

Had Emily wished her decision to be overruled? It seems
not likely. The act of publishing she had in one poem called
"the auction of the mind of man."

Her disinclination from print is totally in accord with her
temperament, her reticence, her withdrawal. So, during her
life, she remained unknown outside the circle of her friends.
Few knew she wrote; still fewer—probably no one—had
any idea of how much she had written.

To her contemporaries, particularly to her neighbors in
Amherst, Emily Dickinson was not a poet. She was a strange
recluse. When visitors called, she withdrew. Occasionally,
she would not retire, but would stand in the hall, talking to
them through the doorway. Only a very, very few would she
meet face to face, going to them diffidently as a child, offering them in silence a flower from her conservatory. From
contact with outsiders she retreated further and further into
the family group. Mr. Dickinson still dominated it. Mrs.
Dickinson was still ailing. Her brother Austin and his wife,
in the house next door, were pleasant companions. In her

own house, her sister Lavinia became closer and closer to her. Lavinia was protective; Lavinia could be relied upon; Lavinia acted as a buffer between Emily's tight little world and the world outside.

Then a change came to the family group. One June afternoon in 1879, Emily and her father spent together. She recalled, afterwards, how close they seemed to feel to each other; how, silently but almost embarrassingly, she became aware of the ties of affection that held them together. But nothing was spoken. The next day, her father was in Boston attending the session of the State Assembly. Arising to speak, he was stricken and a few hours later died. The daughter was overcome by grief. "Where is he? I can't find him!" she cried. She dreamed of him each night. Her main external reliance was gone. "Home is so far from home, since my father died."

Emily's devotion now centered on her mother, whose invalidism required constant attention. Exactly a year from the time of Mr. Dickinson's death, Mrs. Dickinson suffered a stroke of paralysis. For several years she lived, tended by her two daughters. In November 1882, she died, Emily writing of her death, "Our mother ceased."

During the years one and another of Emily Dickinson's friends "experienced the secret of death." Her letters, filled with tender consolation, were filled too with curiosity. How had this one died? Had this one suffered? Was the grief of the survivor too difficult to bear? The same interest manifested itself in her poem "To know just how he suffered would be dear."

Throughout these changes, the life of the poet remained unchanged. Her inner self, though gathering strength, remained secret. Outwardly, her pattern was the same. The habits of a lifetime were too strong to be altered. She and Lavinia, "grave, faithful, punctual" Vinnie, accepted unquestioningly the mold that had been set for them years before. Then one day in the spring of 1884, while Emily was at some household task, "a great darkness" came upon her. The doctor diagnosed her illness as mental exhaustion and prescribed rest. The threat of mental disorder she was able to fight off. But physically she grew weaker and weaker. One day toward the middle of May in 1886, she wrote a penciled note to her cousins, "Little Cousins,—called back. Emily." [4] On May 15, she died.

After her death, her devoted sister, going through her belongings, came upon innumerable pieces of paper, many of them torn scraps. Each bore some lines in Emily's handwriting, a poem in which she had expressed some part of her secret existence. She had written some 1,200 poems! They were gathered together, assorted, and edited by Mrs. Mabel Loomis Todd and by Colonel Higginson. In 1890 was published the first series of her poems, followed by others in 1891 and in 1896. In 1914 was published *The Single Hound,* made up of poems that had been sent to her sister-in-law, Mrs. Austin Dickinson. The interest evoked by the poems extended naturally to their creator. In 1894 her edited letters were published. Since then have appeared further collections both of her poems and of her letters; others remain to be edited and published.

In studying these poems and in using them as a basis for an understanding of the poet, several facts must be remembered. These poems were spontaneous, contradictory, reflecting some sudden and perhaps fleeting mood or thought. The editors dividing them into four large groupings—Life, Nature, Love, Time and Eternity—tried as best they could to arrange them chronologically within each group. But because this ordering cannot be accepted absolutely, one can-

[4] *Letters of Emily Dickinson.*

not hope to trace the logical, step-by-step development of a poet. It is rather the poet as she was from day to day, in one mood or another, that they reveal.

Emily Dickinson had her own test for poetry. She had told it to Colonel Higginson. "If I read a book and it makes my whole body so cold no fire can ever warm me, I know *that* is poetry. If I feel physically as if the top of my head were taken off, I know *that* is poetry. These are the only ways I know it. Is there any other way?" [5] She had, too, her own concept of a poet:

> This was a Poet—it is that
> Distills amazing sense
> From ordinary meanings,
> And attars so immense
> From the familiar species
> That perished by the door,
> We wonder it was not ourselves
> Arrested it before.

How did Emily Dickinson handle her medium? She had read some of the English poets; she had asked for literary criticism. But when she, herself, wrote, she broke the chains of poetic tradition. Her poetry is rhythmic, but it cannot be sorted into standardized verse-forms.

More striking, though, than her handling of meter is her individual solution of the problem of rhyme. Occasionally her verse contains rhyme exact enough to satisfy the most conservative critic. More frequently, it contains what might be best called a tonal harmony, something which, though neither rhyme nor simple assonance, still somehow satisfies all the requirements of the ear for sound agreement and return.

[5] *Letters of Emily Dickinson.*

The heart asks pleasure first,
And then, excuse from pain;
And then, those little anodynes
That deaden suffering;

And then, to go to sleep;
And then, if it should be
The will of its Inquisitor
The liberty to die.

In her refusal to be bound by traditional technique, in
her creation of her own manner, Emily Dickinson appears a
forerunner of those later poets, the creators of the "new
poetry" of the twentieth century. She seems to be, however, not so much a conscious rebel against old forms as one
who, thoroughly an artist, realizes that form must be sub-
servient to purpose.

Just as she modified meter and rhyme, so too she used
words as her tools. "For several years my lexicon was my
only companion," she had written. Those years must have
made her a connoisseur of words, one who loved them for
their own sake, one who delighted in their sound as a lover
of jewels delights in the colors of precious stones. "Penin-
sular," "stalactite," "amber," "plush," "juggler," such words
as words gave her infinite pleasure. Her imagination leaped
at the mere sound of distant places, "Peru," "Golconda,"
"Buenos Ayres." "The earrings of Pizarro" she used to
suggest untold wealth; but it is the name Pizarro, one feels,
that dictated her phrase. She used words delightfully, surprisingly:

If summer were an axiom
What sorcery had snow?

Who counts the wampum of the night
To see that none is due?

This flair for words, combined with her active imagination, filled her verse with phrases that are almost breathtaking in their startling aptness. Spring, "this whole experiment of green"; "punctual as a star"; "the least push of joy"; "dimity convictions"; "a few incisive mornings";

> A dog's belated feet
> Like intermittent plush—
>
> Before you thought of spring,
> Except as a surmise—

these are unforgettable phrases.

Equally unforgettable are the pictures which she created:

> When landlords turn the drunken bee
> Out of the foxglove's door.
>
> The leaves, like women, interchange
> Sagacious confidence.
>
> The twilight stood as strangers do
> With hat in hand, polite and new,
> To stay as if, or go.

and throughout all of that delightful poem, "The mushroom is the elf of plants."

Most ably, in the pictures she drew, did the poet present motion and atmosphere. A snake moves:

> The grass divides as with a comb,
> A spotted shaft is seen;
> And then it closes at your feet
> And opens further on.

A dream, as a bee:

> Dips—wades—teases—deploys.

Sunlight, shadows, the threat of storms, the play of light, these interested her and these she conveyed to her readers:

> There's a certain slant of light,
> On winter afternoons,
> That oppresses, like the weight
> Of cathedral tunes.

For such pictures of nature, Emily Dickinson did not go beyond her own house and garden. Need she go further to see the butterflies, about which she wrote the poems, "From cocoon forth a butterfly," and "A fuzzy fellow without feet"? or the snow, "It sifts from leaden sieves"? From her garden she could note the passing of summer:

> As imperceptibly as grief
> The summer lapsed away.

and the coming of autumn:

> These are the days when skies put on
> The old, old sophistries of June,—
> A blue and gold mistake.

From her garden, or even from her window, she could watch the sunset and reproduce those varied and fading lights which form some of the most vivid of her nature sketches:

> Night after night her purple traffic
> Strews the landing with opal bales;
> Merchantmen poise upon horizons,
> Dip, and vanish with fairy sails.

and

> She sweeps with many-colored brooms,
> And leaves the shreds behind;
> Oh, housewife in the evening west,
> Come back, and dust the pond!

You dropped a purple ravelling in,
You dropped an amber thread;
And now you've littered all the East
With duds of emerald!

And still she plies her spotted brooms,
And still the aprons fly,
Till brooms fade softly into stars—
And then I came away.

Nature, for Emily Dickinson, was the means for the enjoyment of the senses. It is what we see, it is what we hear, it is

what we know
But have no art to say.

Beyond that, she drew no deductions; she built up no philosophy of nature.

These pictures of an objective world are thoroughly satisfying. But even more interesting is the other world, the world of thinking and of living, to which she gave objectivity. She wrote herself into her poetry, as in "A little road not made of man," "My cocoon lightens, colors tease," and "I lived on dread; to those who know." In many poems she poured out her love, its depth, its delight, its sense of deprivation, and its constancy, as she does in her poem, "Alter? When the hills do." She played with her ideas as toys and of them made poems.

These poems are usually close-packed. They do not produce the effect of refined simplicity, with the poet refraining from expressing all that is in her mind. Elimination is present, it is true. But the impression produced is that there are so many thoughts to be conveyed that the thinker cannot take time to elaborate, explain, and simplify each one; she must choose and reject, suggest the flash of each thought and rely upon another's intuition for understanding. Furthermore, she speaks in a language of her own, using words in an individual way, filling them with new meaning. The result, in the case of many poems, is that of obscurity and abstruseness. But that is the judgment of a first reading and a hasty one. Whatever difficulty a poem presents is usually a difficulty arising from expression and not from complexity of idea. A willingness to complement the poet's thought with one's own thinking and to use the poet's own vivid vocabulary reduces the difficulty to solution. "The blunder is to estimate," "No other can reduce," "No romance sold unto,"— such poems should be allowed slowly to make their meaning clear. The poet's ability to strip her idea of non-essentials, to condense her thought into small compass, is exemplified in her poem:

> The soul unto itself
> Is an imperial friend,—
> Or the most agonizing spy
> An enemy could send.
>
> Secure against its own,
> No treason it can fear;
> Itself its sovereign, of itself
> The soul should stand in awe.

In the expression of her ideas, Emily Dickinson manifested a fondness for paradox:

> A death blow is a life-blow to some

or

> We miss a kinsman more
> When warranted to see
> Than when withheld by oceans
> From possibility.

This reconciliation of seeming contradictories suggests a duality in the poet's thinking. This would seem to be the natural outcome of the dual life the poet led. For her there were two worlds, the world of fact and that of intuition. Which was supreme?

> I bet with every Wind that blew, till Nature in chagrin
> Employed a *Fact* to visit me and scuttle my Balloon!

That was the Emily Dickinson of one mood. More frequently, however, she was the poet of intuition, of imagination:

> Much madness is divinest sense
> To a discerning eye.

This contradiction in thought is not the only contradiction in her poetry. One finds opposing, conflicting moods. The poet, in one mood, cries out with a sense of hurt and of despair, "I had been hungry all the years." There is a feeling of loss, of deprivation, as in "Except the heaven had come so near," and particularly in her love poems, as, for example, "Your riches taught me poverty." Then, in another, she is boldly daring:

> Is bliss, then, such abyss
> I must not put my foot amiss
> In fear I spoil my shoe?

At certain times, she is withdrawn, aloof. Her only reliance is herself; her one security, her own identity:

> A Soul admitted to Itself:
> Finite Infinity.

At other times, she is gayly debonair. This world, the world of the senses, delights her. "To live," she writes, "is so startling, it leaves but little room for other occupations, though friends are, if possible, an event more fair." The same feeling of joy and of power she expressed in her poem, "I'm sorry for the Dead today," and "To be alive is power."

In such a mood, the poet had no need of heaven. Indeed were it not for the death of her flowers and the death of dear friends "there were no need of other Heaven than the one below—and if God had been here this summer, and seen the things that I have seen—I guess that He would think His Paradise superfluous." A far cry, this, from the orthodox religion of New England. Emily Dickinson was familiar with the Bible; she read it frequently; its stately rhythm, its rolling words are echoed in her poetry. She was an attendant at church. But the church of her fathers did not satisfy her. The heaven to which her daily living was an approach was not the "heaven the creeds bestow." Her joy that she did not believe in the orthodox heaven, she sings in her poem "Going to heaven!" But, tolerant of others, she was equally glad that their faith solaced those who did believe.

She could not accept the time-worn tenets. "But I, grown shrewder, scan the skies"; she felt that she had outgrown the religion taught her in childhood. It is thus she writes in "I prayed at first—a little girl" and in "I meant to have but modest needs."

In her maturity, she criticized the terrors of orthodoxy.

> The Bible is an antique volume
> Written by faded men;

its spirit repels, rather than attracts. She even had the courage to become God's critic. "It's easy to invent a life" and in the carrying out of His plan, she felt, He is, at times, ruthless to man. Particularly, did she feel, as in "It always felt to me a wrong," the injustice of happiness suggested but withheld.

Her feelings well up; she will rebel. In a most delightful poem, "I never felt at home below," she resolves to run away from heaven, from God, from All! Then, in a sudden return of her childhood's teaching, in a flash of humor, comes the last line

> But—there's the Judgment Day!

and her rebellion subsides.

Colored by that humor, her God was no longer a distant cruel omnipotence.

> God's residence is next to mine,
> His furniture is love.

Kindly, then, becomes the face

> Of our old neighbor, God!

With such a One, the poet was at ease. In His kindliness, He will care for the small as well as the great; He will smile tenderly and enjoy a little fun. To Him one may address the plea:

> Papa above!
>   Regard a Mouse
> O'erpowered by the Cat;
> Reserve within thy Kingdom
> A "mansion" for the Rat!
>
> Snug in seraphic cupboards
> To nibble all the day,
> While unsuspecting cycles
> Wheel pompously away.

Emily Dickinson was not irreverent. She did discard her ancestral deity, it is true. But she worshiped her God, a tender, loving God, and she endowed Him with her own most precious possession, a sense of humor. Her humor gleams across her moods. She draws herself a sad, wistful creature; and then, in a moment, her eyes twinkle and her laughter sounds. She pokes fun at accepted ideas, at the emphasis, for example, upon somber sedateness. Because of the beauty of the butterfly,

> The circumspect are certain
> That he is dissolute.

Her humor can, at times, be pointed with satire. Again of the butterfly she writes:

> How condescending to descend,
> And be of buttercups the friend
> In a New England town!

But she was never bitter. Her humor includes herself.

So mercurial a person could scarcely be expected to evolve a consistent, coherent philosophy of life. She was aware of the hardships of life as well as of the joys. She seems to have recognized some balance existing between them:

> For each ecstatic instant
> We must an anguish pay.

Happiest is he who most simply accepts his destiny. With acceptance, however, there must be bravery, too. So she urges in "They say that 'time assuages.' " And finally, there must be sturdy self-reliance. But she realized, too, how inadequate are the powers of mankind to cope with all of mankind's problems. Knowing this incapacity, her philosophy is still not one of defeatism:

> Not what we did shall be the test
> When acts and will are done,
> But what our Lord infers we *would*—
> Had we diviner been.

Death was, for Emily Dickinson, the final seal; eternity, the solution of the conflicts of life. She hailed the inevitability and the universality of death as in "One dignity delays for all," in "It's coming—the postponeless creature," and in "This quiet Dust was Gentlemen and Ladies." Because of those who had died before, she writes in "You'll find it when you come to die," death is not difficult. Death was not far off. God was near her and heaven was about her. So eternity was a present friend:

> No friend have I that so persists
> As this Eternity.

Death held the solution for which life was the seeking. Emily Dickinson, in her life, looked to beauty for an answer to existence, feeling that beauty was truth.

> I died for beauty, but was scarce
> Adjusted in the tomb,
> When one who died for truth was lain
> In an adjoining room.
>
> He questioned softly why I failed?
> "For beauty," I replied.
> "And I for truth!—the two are one;
> We brethren are," he said.
>
> And so, as kinsmen met a night,
> We talked between the rooms,
> Until the moss had reached our lips,
> And covered up our names.

Death was the solvent for Emily Dickinson. It reconciled into unity her two worlds, her two selves. And in a paradox, appropriate to her, it did not destroy, it created her. The New England spinster would have faded out unnoticed. Death released her poems and through her poems gave her life. The life that is measured by dates she lived in nineteenth century America. She was a product of her time and of her place, made by her New England past and present. But the result was not what New England had expected. Outward conformity turned into an inner rebellion. The external New Englander, only one of many, became a supreme individualist. It is useless to talk of Emily Dickinson's Americanism. Death, which gave the real Emily Dickinson to the world, removed her from the world's geographical limitations.

SIDNEY LANIER

His song was only living aloud,
His work, a singing with his hand!

How closely did Sidney Lanier approach this identifi-
cation of life and song which he, himself, declared
to be the ideal goal of every poet? For him life was "the
hottest of all battles," but one to be entered upon gallantly
and bravely. "To die, consumed by these heavenly fires,"
he wrote to a friend, "that is infinitely better than to live
the tepid lives and love the tepid loves that belong to the
lower planes of activity; and I would rather fail at some
things I wot of, than succeed at some others." [1] Was he able
to transmit this indomitable spirit to his verse? Could he
transform his life into poetry?

Lanier was born in Macon, Georgia, on February 3, 1842.
His father was Robert Sampson Lanier, a lawyer; his
mother, Mary Jane Anderson, the daughter of a Virginia
planter. The home, which Lanier was to share with a brother
Clifford and a sister, was one of culture and of gentility, of
religious piety, and of strong family ties. The household
boasted a well-used library, made up of the classical books
that were the foundation of every gentleman's collection:
Shakespeare, Froissart, Addison, Scott. There was, furthermore, from the Lanier side of the family, the tradition of
musical ability. For the Laniers, settling in Virginia in the
early eighteenth century, seem to have been derived from
a Huguenot family which, in the time of Elizabeth, had fled

[1] *Letters of Sidney Lanier*, Charles Scribner's Sons.

from France to England and there, for several generations, had provided musicians for the English court.

Literature and music—these were the two strong strains in Lanier. The child attended school, little one-room schools of the South. More important, however, than the schoolroom, both because of his own interest and because of the effect on his later life, were the books in his father's library and the music which he, himself, was soon able to create. At seven he made a flageolet. One Christmas brought him a flute as a present. While he was teaching himself to play, he organized among his playmates quartets and bands.

At fourteen the boy entered the Sophomore class of Oglethorpe College, a small Presbyterian college at Midway, Georgia. Here Lanier studied Greek, and Latin, and mathematics. He became interested in philosophy and in science. His scientific interest was undoubtedly stimulated by James Woodrow, the professor of science who had, himself, studied under Agassiz and who manifested a deep and tender interest in the young Lanier. Professor and student together went on long walks, during which Lanier became more closely acquainted with the beauties of nature; they engaged in long, earnest talks, discussing the mysteries of science and of life.

The new and widened outlook gained from this association did not shut out Lanier's earlier interests. With his college friends he read widely, discovering new delights in Tennyson, Carlyle, Keats, Shelley, and Chatterton. His music, too, continued. He had brought his flute with him and by his playing refreshed himself and charmed his hearers.

These interests were not permitted to interfere with his college work; for, in spite of an absence in 1858-1859 as a post-office clerk, he graduated in 1860 at the head of his class. But before his graduation, the problem of his future had bothered him. Unquestionably, music was his soul's delight. Yet he had no certainty that this could be made his life's work. Some of his perplexity, some of the sincerity with which he approached his problem, is suggested in an entry made at this time in his notebook.[2]

"The point which I wish to settle is merely by what method shall I ascertain what I am fit for as preliminary to ascertaining God's will with reference to me; or what my inclinations are, as preliminary to ascertaining what my capacities are—that is, what I am fit for. I am more than all perplexed by this fact: that the prime inclination—that is, material bent (which I have checked, though) of my nature is to music, and for that I have the greatest talent; indeed, not boasting, for God gave it me, I have an extraordinary musical talent, and feel it within me plainly that I could rise as high as any composer. But I cannot bring myself to believe that I was intended for a musician, because it seems so small a business in comparison with other things which, it seems to me, I might do. Question here: 'What is the province of music in the economy of the world?' "

A temporary solution was reached with the aid of Professor Woodrow. At the latter's suggestion, Lanier returned to Oglethorpe as a tutor. During this year at his Alma Mater, he made vague plans for study at a German University as preliminary to some still vaguer professorship in an American college.

All such plans, however, were abandoned with the outbreak of the Civil War. The South glowed with patriotic fervor. It dreamed dreams of a rich future. Macon saw itself as a Southern center of learning and culture. Imbued with patriotism, fired with zeal, Lanier—as did almost the entire university—volunteered in the Confederate Army. He, with his brother Clifford, in the summer of 1861, en-

[2] Quoted in *Sidney Lanier*, by Edwin Mims, Houghton Mifflin Co.

listed in the Macon Volunteers and, with flute and note-
books in his knapsack, went off to join them where they
were stationed near Norfolk, Virginia. Here he enjoyed the
"pleasures and sweet rewards—of—toil consisting in agues
which played dice with our bones, and blue-mass pills that
played the deuce with our livers." He soon saw actual fighting, taking part in two battles. Then, in the late summer of
1862, he was transferred to the signal corps and became part
of a mounted field squad. In the following spring he enjoyed a brief furlough. Returning to Macon for two weeks,
he met there a Miss Mary Day. Thereafter "Macon was my
two weeks' dream." In 1863 and 1864, he and his brother
served as scouts along the James River.

But even in war, music and literature were his companions. He visited the mansions of the neighborhood, playing
for his hosts—and more particularly for his hostesses—tender tunes upon his flute. He read widely in the English and
German poets. And about this time, he definitely decided to
begin a literary career. He wrote to his father: "Gradually
I find that my whole soul is merging itself into this business
of writing, and especially of writing poetry. I am going to
try it; and am going to test, in the most rigid way I know,
the awful question whether it is my vocation."

Poetry, however, for a time, had to wait upon war. In
August 1864, Lanier was transferred to Wilmington, North
Carolina, as a signal officer on blockade-runners. In November, his boat *Lucy* was captured; Lanier was taken prisoner
and sent to Point Lookout prison. Four months of prison
life undermined his health, making him a ready victim to
tuberculosis. Thereafter illness and, later, poverty were the
constant foes against which he was forced to battle. The
hardships of prison existence, however, he bore bravely.
His flute cheered him and his fellow prisoners. His further
release he found in poetry. During this period he translated

German poems into English: "The Palm and the Pine" from Heine, and "Spring Greeting" from Herder.

March 1865 saw Lanier back in Macon. His illness continued for several months. Scarcely had he recovered, when his mother died of tuberculosis.

The Civil War was over. The South was impoverished. Lanier recognized the Southern situation, "the mortal stagnation which paralyzes all business here." What could the future hold for him? For a short while he was a tutor on a large plantation on Mobile Bay. Then for a time he served as clerk at the Exchange Hotel in Montgomery, Alabama, which was owned by his grandfather and his uncle. But always he clung to his dream of achievement through music and writing. He played the organ at the Presbyterian Church in Montgomery. He formed a literary club; and, eager to make literary contacts, he subscribed to *The Round Table,* a New York publication. That magazine in 1867 and 1868 published some of his first poems, "Tyranny," "Life and Song," "Resurrection," "Barnacles," "The Tournament." The last ends on a note typical of Lanier:

> Then Love cried, "Break me his lance, each knight!
>   Ye shall fight for blood-athirst Fame no more!"
> And the knights all doffed their mailèd might
>   And dealt out dole on dole to the poor.
>
> Then dove-flights sanctified the plain,
>   And hawk and sparrow shared a nest
> And the great sea opened and swallowed Pain,
>   And out of this water-grave floated Rest!

By this time he had completed *Tiger Lilies,* a novel in which he used his observations in the Southern mountain countryside and his experiences in the Civil War. The war left Lanier with no bitterness and no resentment. He realized and sympathized with the plight of the South; but he recognized the weaknesses in the Southern system and urged that they be overcome. Once the war was ended, he transformed his dream of an idealized South into one of a peaceful and united nation. Loyally devoted to his own section of the country, he nevertheless felt that whatever chance he might have of national literary fame must come first from the North. So in 1867 he visited New York and secured the publication of his novel, which was well received.

That same year, on December 21, he married Mary Day, the young woman he had met on his Macon furlough. To her he wrote his tender poems, "Laus Mariæ," "Acknowledgment," "My Springs":

> Dear eyes, dear eyes and rare complete—
> Being heavenly-sweet and earthly-sweet,
> —I marvel that God made you mine,
> For when He frowns, 'tis then ye shine!

Their married life was to be one of complete tenderness and devotion. With the four sons born to them they lived a domestic life that would have been a completely happy one had not the twin enemies, poor health and poverty, unrelentingly pursued them.

In the year 1867-1868 several hemorrhages gave evidence of tuberculosis, from which Lanier suffered all the rest of his life and from which he died. Poetry, his solace, could very possibly provide him escape from his own personal sufferings; but it could not provide him with the means of supporting his family. In "June Dreams in January," one finds the echo of his despair:

> Why can we poets dream us beauty, so,
> But cannot dream us bread?

By the end of 1868 Lanier realized that he must make some decision about his future. In the South, literature was not yet acceptable as a career; furthermore, it was not sufficiently remunerative. Of Lanier's vague plans for a professorship nothing had materialized. He had before this expressed his doubt about music. Finally, he decided to study law, influenced unquestionably by his father's example and urging. It was, after all, a decision of despair. "I have not," he wrote to a friend, "ceased my devotion to letters, which I love better than all things in my heart of hearts." But it was a decision to which he clung. In November 1869, he wrote to his brother, "It is best that you and I make up our minds immediately to be lawyers, *nothing but lawyers, good* lawyers, and *successful* lawyers; and direct all our energies to this end." From 1869 to 1873 he practiced law in his father's office. His work, office rather than trial work, he accomplished with absolute accuracy and meticulousness.

The period of his legal career was broken up by frequent trips in a search for health. He visited Tennessee, Virginia, and Georgia, where deeply and more deeply developed his love for nature and his knowledge of the Southern countryside. It was in Georgia, at Brunswick, that he saw the marshes that inspired his "Hymns of the Marshes," which include among their number the very well-known poem, "The Marshes of Glynn." Some of his travels took him North, to New York, where his passion for music was to some extent satisfied. He went to the opera; he went to concerts; he went to the opening concert of Theodore Thomas's orchestra in Central Park Garden "and tonight I came out of what might have been heaven." Finally on a visit to San Antonio, Texas, in 1872, during which he was in close contact with a group of German musicians, he came to the conclusion that music and literature meant so much more to him than law that he must of necessity give the latter up and devote himself to an artistic career. In a letter to his father, November 29, 1873, he announced his decision: "Then, as to business, why should I, nay, how *can* I, settle myself down to be a third-rate struggling lawyer for the balance of my little life, as long as there is a certainty almost absolute that I can do some other things much better? Several persons, from whose judgment in such matters there can be no appeal, have told me, for instance, that I am the greatest flute-player in the world; and several others, of equally authoritative judgement, have given me an almost equal encouragement to work with my pen." [3]

Several months before writing this letter, Lanier had been in Baltimore and had played one of his own musical compositions for Asger Hamerik, the director of the Peabody Conservatory of Music. Hamerik held out to him hopes of a position as first flutist with the Peabody Orchestra, then being formed. By November, final arrangements were made. Although the salary was not so large as Lanier had first hoped it would be, he gladly accepted the position. He felt that the schedules of rehearsals and concerts would give him time not only to supplement his salary but also to continue his writings; and that his association with the Peabody Institute "will give me a foothold, which I can likely step from to something better—for the Peabody is a literary as well as a musical institution."

From the end of 1873 until March 18, 1876, when Lanier played in his last concert, his life was filled with music. He gave it his passionate devotion. He was untiring at rehearsals. At his public appearances, he evoked ardent enthusiasm. He was, himself, interested particularly in orchestral music and formulated plans for a small group that could carry such music to communities removed from large or-

[3] "Memorial" by William Hayes Ward in *Poems of Sidney Lanier*, Charles Scribner's Sons.

chestras. His love for music, his complete understanding of it, he was able to translate into words, as in his description of the tuning-up of the orchestra: "and presently the others begin to flourish also, and here we have it, up chromatics, down diatonics, unearthly buzzings from the big fiddles, diabolic four-string chords from the 'cellos, passionate shrieks from the clarionets and oboes, manly remonstrances from the horns, querulous complaints from the bassoons, and so on."

It was the artist in words as well as in music who thus described the orchestra. The artist in words, of necessity, sought some outlet in addition to his flute. Music helped earn him a living; but literature was not abandoned. In the first few months of his orchestral connection, his only poems were those written to his absent wife. But soon the desire to write became more and more insistent. "My head and my heart are both so full of poems which the dreadful struggle for bread does not give me time to put on paper, that I am often driven to headache and heartache purely for want of an hour or two to hold a pen."

The summer of 1874 brought him a reunion with his family and some little leisure. In August, he was at Sunnyside, Georgia, where he was struck by the pathos of deserted farms. The abandoned farmlands gave him the inspiration for his poem, "Corn," which, in February 1875, appeared in *Lippincott's Magazine,* a Northern publication.

> I wander to the zigzag-cornered fence
> Where sassafras, intrenched in brambles dense,
> Contests with stolid vehemence
> > The march of culture, setting limb and thorn
> > As pikes against the army of the corn.

One stalk of corn, however, the corn-captain, stands out above the others and, as a symbol of the poet-soul, speaks to the South, urging it to recognize the fact that its salvation lies in agriculture, not in industry and trade:

> Lo, through hot waverings of the August morn
> Thou givest from thy vasty sides forlorn
> Visions of golden treasuries of corn—
> Ripe largesse lingering for some bolder heart
> That manfully shall take thy part,
>> And tend thee,
>> And defend thee,
> With antique sinew and with modern art.

The poem was most enthusiastically received. Among its admirers were Gibson Peacock, the editor of the Philadelphia *Evening Bulletin,* and Bayard Taylor, the poet, both of whom became Lanier's close and devoted friends. Heartened by their encouragement, Lanier wrote more copiously and more surely. In June 1875, *Lippincott's* published a second poem by him, "The Symphony," wherein various musical instruments decry the evils of national life and unite in praising love as the universal panacea:

> "And ever Love hears the poor-folks' crying,
> And ever Love hears the women's sighing,
> And ever sweet knighthood's death-defying,
> And ever wise childhood's deep implying,
> But never a trader's glozing and lying."

By now the poet was finding his own method of expression. In 1875, he wrote,[4] "In this little song I have begun to dare to give myself some freedom in my own peculiar style, and have allowed myself to treat words, similes, and metres with such freedom as I desired. The result convinces

[4] Quoted in "Memorial" by W. H. Ward, preface to *The Poems of Sidney Lanier,* Charles Scribner's Sons.

me that I can do so now safely." He now was sure of his own poetical gifts.

These were called upon in national service in 1876. The nation was celebrating at Philadelphia the hundredth anniversary of its founding. For the opening of the Centennial a cantata was to be sung. Bayard Taylor suggested to the chairman of the Centennial Committee that Lanier, because of his poetic and musical ability, was peculiarly fitted to write the words. The suggestion was accepted. Lanier, told by Taylor, "It's a great occasion—not especially for Poetry as an art, but for Poetry to assert herself as a power," applied himself to the task. He realized that the essence of a cantata is its singability and that words and thoughts must lend themselves to the musical score. The resulting poem was one quite different from Lanier's characteristic verses. "Somehow all my inspirations came in these large and artless forms, in simple Saxon words, in unpretentious and purely intellectual conceptions." Published prematurely without its musical setting, it called forth by its stark simplicity no little criticism. But its success in Philadelphia was instantaneous. Lanier, a Southerner, had voiced his faith in the nation and had served as a symbol of the healing of the breach between North and South. With some sense, then, of his acceptance nationally as a poet, he brought out, late in 1876 but bearing an 1877 date, his first volume of collected poems.

This appeared, however, during a period of deepest despair. Ill health during 1876 and 1877 had again taken him South. He had severed connections with the orchestra. His finances were so low that family silver had to be sold to raise money. Worry about his daily existence interfered with the writing of his poetry. In a letter to his friend Peacock, he voiced his position: [5]

[5] *Letters of Sidney Lanier,* Charles Scribner's Sons.

"I long to be steadily writing again. I'm taken with a poem pretty nearly every day, and have to content myself with making a note of its train of thought on the back of whatever letter is in my coat-pocket. I don't write it out, however, because I find my poetry now wholly unsatisfactory in consequence of a certain haunting impatience which has its root in the straining uncertainty of my daily affairs; and I am trying with all my might to put off composition of all sorts until some approach to the certainty of next week's dinner shall remove this remnant of haste, and leave me that repose which ought to fill the artist's firmament while he is creating."

A temporary regaining of his health had brought him back to Baltimore. From there he sought some official appointment at Washington, applying for the very humblest positions, clerkships paying $75 a month. But he had no success. In one forlorn cry, he sounded his desperation: "Altogether, it seems as if there wasn't any place for me in this world, and if it were not for May I should certainly quit it, in mortification at being so useless."

His courage, however, soon returned. In 1877, his family joined him in Baltimore. The family, united and established in a home of its own, filled him with happiness. He wrote a buoyantly joyous description of himself as a householder:

"I confess I *am* a little nervous about the gas-bills, which must come in, in the course of time; and there are the water-rates, and several sorts of imposts and taxes: but then, the dignity of being liable for such things! is a very supporting consideration. No man is a Bohemian who has to pay water-rates and a street-tax. Every day when I sit down in my dining-room—*my* dining-room!—I find the wish growing stronger that every poor soul in Baltimore, whether saint or sinner, could come and dine with me." [6]

[6] *Letters of Sidney Lanier*, Charles Scribner's Sons.

Poverty still stalked the household. "I'm making some desperate efforts to get steady work, of any kind; for I find I cannot at all maintain our supplies of daily bread by poetry alone." There had some time before been an effort to augment his literary earnings by a book on Florida, "a spiritualized guide book." Now he found a further source of income in some books for children. He had delighted his own sons with his versions of old legends. From the tales which he had retold grew the four books: *The Boy's Froissart, The Boy's King Arthur, The Boy's Mabinogion, The Boy's Percy.*

Still another activity engrossed him. From his young manhood he had read widely and deeply in the poets, particularly in the English ones. Out of his accumulated knowledge he prepared a series of lectures on the Elizabethan Poets, which he gave in 1878 at the home of a Baltimore woman. The following year he gave a course under the auspices of the Peabody Institute; and he drew up plans for "Schools for Grown People," a forerunner of present-day schemes for adult education. His early hopes for a professorship had evidently never been completely abandoned.

As a matter of fact, in 1877, he had applied for a fellowship at the then newly established Johns Hopkins University in Baltimore. The scientific interest awakened in his own college days at Oglethorpe had continued and this he had applied to his own field of poetry. In outlining his plans for study, he proposed work in the general science of mineralogy, botany, comparative anatomy and in French and German literature; all this was to be subordinated to the main purpose of his work, research in the physics of musical tone.

The fellowship was not given to him. But the success of his Baltimore lectures led to his appointment in 1879 as a lecturer in English literature at Johns Hopkins. He was a systematic student, one imbued with the spirit of research.

His point of view toward the study of literature, however, was not that of purely objective academic scholasticism. In his plans for graduate courses he wrote, "That they keep steadily in view, as their ultimate object, that strengthening of manhood, that enlarging of sympathy, that glorifying of moral purpose, which the student unconsciously gains, not from any direct didacticism, but from this constant association with our finest ideals and loftiest souls. . . . I am so deeply interested in this matter—of making a finer fibre for all our young American manhood by leading our youth in proper relations with English poetry."

His program was a heavy one. He set himself the task of giving each week two public lectures at the University, two in the closed University classes, and six at private schools. His frail health broke; he became weaker. But unrelentingly he continued his activity. In December 1880, while sick with a fever of 104 degrees, he composed his poem, "Sunrise." In January 1881, he resumed his lectures at Johns Hopkins, his strength scarcely sufficient to carry him through each session. The course was shortened from twenty to twelve lectures. In April, it came to an end.

Immediately at its conclusion, he paid a brief visit to New York to arrange for the publication of his books for children. Then he went to North Carolina in a vain pursuit of health. His family was with him: wife and children and, for a time, father and brother. The rich, affectionate family life was darkened only by the shadow of his illness. In spite of that illness, Lanier's desire to write poetry persisted; to those attending him he dictated lines, fragments of verse, ideas for poems. Then he grew weaker, too weak even for dictation. On September 7, he died.

The life that ended had been characterized by a tenderness and an idealism that suggested the knightliness of the Middle Ages. Friends who knew him well spoke always of the freshness of his spirit, the purity of soul that he presented to a not always hospitable world. Nor was his goodness of the pale and passive sort. Two characteristics prevented that.

One was his sense of humor, a sense of humor that he exercised even in the things closest to him. However serious were his literary desires, however much poetry meant to him, he could still use refreshingly humorous phrases in describing his work. "About four days ago," he wrote, "a certain poem which I had vaguely ruminated for a week before took hold of me like a real James River ague, and I have been in a mortal shake with the same, day and night ever since." Even the grinding poverty that at times seemed unbearable, at other times was faced with a smile. "The poem is the only piece of work I have. I suppose God intends me to feed on blackberries all summer."

The other saving characteristic was the intensity of his feelings, fervor which he in turn transmitted to his actions. Events did not passively occur in Lanier's life; he rushed to meet them with all his being. His philosophy of art itself was based upon morality, but upon a morality of ardor. "He, in short, who has not come to that stage of quiet and eternal frenzy in which the beauty of holiness and the holiness of beauty mean one thing, burn as one fire, shine as one light within him, he is not yet the great artist."

The rush of feeling, the overflowing of emotions, that characterized his life is present in his poetry. His characteristic poetic manner is headlong, unrestrained, undampened.

Basic to his poetic technique is his theory of poetry which, through the study of English poetry from its beginning, gave him the material for his lectures at Johns Hopkins and, in its final form, produced his book, *The Science of English Verse*. With the detachment and objectivity of a scientist,

he studied and analyzed examples and reached the conclusion that the "sound-relations which constitute music are
the same with those which constitute verse." His theory
that it is length of sound rather than stress that is fundamental to poetry is not wholly tenable. But for himself the
result of his theory was that he based his poetry on musical
form and so produced verse lovely in the variety of its
movement. A short phrase is balanced against a short
phrase, then developed, then expanded into a longer one,
just as a musical phrase is built up into a composition.

> Once on a time a soul
> Too full of his dole
> In a querulous dream went crying from pole to pole—
> Went sobbing and crying
> For ever a sorrowful song of living and dying,
> *How life was the dropping and death the drying*
> *Of a Tear that fell in a day when God was sighing.*
> And ever Time tossed him bitterly to and fro
> As a shuttle inlaying a perilous warp of woe
> In the woof of things from terminal snow to snow,
> Till, lo!
> Rest.

The exposition of his theory of tone-quantity takes up
the larger part of his book. A second section considers tune
in verse, intonation and inflection. A final section is devoted
to "The Colors of English Verse." This for Lanier embraces
those poetic devices that supplement rhythm and rhyme:
alliteration, assonance, and the harmonious combination of
consonant sounds.

Lanier shows himself the complete master of rhyme. "If
the rhyme is not perfect," he admonishes, "if it demands any
the least allowance, it is not tolerable; throw it away."
With nimble dexterity he employs triple rhyme, as in

> If business is battle, name it so:
> War-crimes less will shame it so,
> And widows less will blame it so.

and

> Knowledge of Good and of Ill, O Lord! she hath given thee;
> Perilous godhoods of choosing have rent thee and riven thee;
> Will's high adoring to Ill's low exploring hath driven thee—
> Freedom, thy Wife, hath uplifted thy face and clean shriven
>   thee!

The third line of the last quotation illustrates still another of Lanier's favorite devices, internal rhyme.

> Oh, rain me down from your darks that contain me

> While the riotous noon-day sun of the June-day long did
>   shine

> Vanishing, swerving, evermore curving again into sight

The use of internal rhyme is frequent. But it is not monotonous. The rhyming words vary in their position in the line so that the device in Lanier's hand is a flexible one, something more than two short rhyming lines printed as one.

The ear that was so nicely attuned to rhyme was equally well attuned to other effects to be derived from letter-sounds. Alliteration, obvious in a line like

> To wheel from the wood to the window where

becomes something more delicately patterned in a passage like

> Ye lispers, whisperers, singers in storms,
> Ye consciences murmuring faiths under forms,
> Ye ministers meet for each passion that grieves,
> Friendly, sisterly, sweetheart leaves.

Assonance, too, the similarity of vowel-sounds other than in rhyme, is frequent in Lanier's verse. The sounds of *o* in the following lines, for example, add a richness additional to rhyme:

> And if I were yon stolid stone,
> Thy tender arm doth lean upon.

The use of refrain, the repetition with but slight variation of final lines of stanzas, as the repetition in "Song of the Chattahoochee" of

> Far from the hills of Habersham
> Far from the valleys of Hall

is a by no means unusual device. Lanier, however, introduces into his use of repetition somewhat different, somewhat less obvious effects. Words are repeated, phrases are repeated, as are motifs in music. "A Song of the Future" illustrates the certainty with which this device is used.

> Sail fast, sail fast,
> Ark of my hopes, Ark of my dreams,
> Sweep lordly o'er the drownèd Past,
> Fly glittering through the sun's strange beams;
> Sail fast, sail fast.
> Breaths of new buds from off some dying lea
> With news about the Future scent the sea:
> My brain is beating like the heart of Haste.
> I'll loose me a bird upon this Present waste;
> Go, trembling song,
> And stay not long; oh, stay not long:
> Thou'rt only a gray and sober dove.
> But thine eye is faith and thy living is love.

There is at times, one must admit, too little restraint in the use of the technical devices of a poet. One notes, too, an indulgence in mannerisms that detract from, rather than add to, beauty. One finds, almost too frequently, compound words like "burly-back'd man-bodied Tree," "one-desiring dove," "curious-hill'd and curious-valley'd Vast." Personification, as in "my lord Sun," studs his verse with capitals. The use of the plural form of abstract nouns becomes insistently noticeable; "glooms of the live-oaks," "all shynesses of film-winged things." Word forms that are remnants of a now discarded "poetic diction," mark his lines: "passeth, drownèd Past, blood-shotten eyes." Lines descriptive of a robin:

> And thrid the heavenly orange-tree
> With orbits bright of minstrelsy.

reveal that stylistic and obviously poetic use of words against which a later generation of poets rebelled.

The rich embroidery of Lanier's poetry is one indication of the fervor of his spirit. So, too, is his exuberance of fancy. Fate becomes "the Course-of-thing, shaped like an Ox"; it tramples the fields and devours flowers, the flowers symbolizing poets! Thus is the early morning pictured:

> If haply thou, O Desdemona Morn,
> 　　Shouldst call along the curving sphere, "Remain,
> Dear Night, sweet Moor; nay, leave me not in scorn!"
> 　　With soft halloos of heavenly love and pain;—

Almost startling in imagery are the lines from "Sunrise":

> Now a dream of a flame through that dream of a flush is
> 　　uprolled:
> 　　To the zenith ascending, a dome of undazzling gold
> Is builded, in shape as a bee-hive, from out of the sea:
> The hive is of gold, undazzling, but oh, the Bee,
> 　　The star-fed Bee, the build-fire Bee,

Of dazzling gold is the great Sun-Bee
That shall flash from the hive-hole over the sea.

Something in the richness of Lanier's poetry, something
in the imagery, the meticulous attention to detail suggests
a medieval tapestry. Nor is this figure entirely inappropriate
when one recalls how great an influence was exerted upon
him by his studies of the poets of tapestry-making generations. But though his technical knowledge was grounded in
the past, his poems are not derivative. They reveal Lanier,
not some antiquated predecessor.

To Lanier, technique was but a tool; the message of the
poem, important. Indeed, with his insistence upon the place
of morals in art, he made the poet an artist with a purpose.
"The poet is in charge of all learning to convert it into wisdom," he said; and again, in a lecture at Johns Hopkins, "In
short,—and here I am ending this course with the idea with
which I began it,—in short, it is the poet who must sit at the
centre of things here, as surely as some great One sits at the
centre of things Yonder, and who must teach us how to control, with temperance and perfect art and unforgetfulness
of detail, all our oppositions, so that we may come to say
with Aristotle, at last, that poetry is more philosophical than
philosophy and more historical than history." [7]

Whatever the poet is to reveal must be based upon his
immediate knowledge and his interests. So it is to be expected that the two major sources from which Lanier drew
his poetry are nature and music. "To Richard Wagner" and
"To Beethoven" are the direct acknowledgment of his debt
to music. But more important than such use of musical
subjects is the manner in which music underlies his poems.
It may furnish a symbol, a figure, as in "Opposition":

[7] Quoted in *Sidney Lanier*, by Edwin Mims, Houghton Mifflin Co.

> The lute's fixt fret, that runs athwart
> The strain and purpose of the string,
> For governance and nice consort
> Doth bar his wilful wavering.

Or it may, as in "The Symphony," reveal itself, consonant with Lanier's basic belief, as the language of the soul.

Just as the soul of man speaks through music, so, according to the poet, does God speak through nature. "A Florida Sunday," a vivid picture of nature in that Southern state, is the revelation of God to Man:

> I am ye,
> And ye myself; yea, lastly, Thee,
> God, whom my roads all reach, howe'er they run,
> My Father, Friend, Belovèd, dear All-One,
> Thee in my soul, my soul in Thee, I feel,
> Self of my self.

The nature that Lanier knew and that entered into his poetry was not the nature of poet-cultivated English gardens. It was that of his native Southern countryside, lush and luxuriant. It was one, not of imported and poetically accepted birds, but of mocking-birds, robins, pelicans, woodpeckers, blue-jays; it was one of corn, and of sassafras, one in which

> Palmettos ranked, with childish spear-points set
> Against no enemy—rich cones that fret
> High roofs of temples shafted tall with pines—
> Green, grateful mangroves where the sand-beach shines—
> Long lissome coast that in and outward swerves,
> The grace of God made manifest in curves—

Of all the manifestations of nature, none inspired him more than did the marshes which he first saw about Brunswick;

in nothing did he show more skill than in depicting the play of Southern sunlight upon those marshes.

MARSH HYMNS—BETWEEN DAWN AND SUNRISE

Were silver pink, and had a soul
 Which soul were shy, which shyness might
A visible influence be, and roll
 Through heaven and earth—'twere thou, O light;

O rhapsody of the wraith of red,
 O blush but yet in prophecy,
O sun-hint that hath overspread
 Sky, marsh, my soul, and yonder sail.

Lanier's close identity with the South manifests itself, too, in those poems written in Southern dialect, "A Florida Ghost," "Nine from Eight," "Thar's More in the Man Than Thar Is in the Land"; and in those in negro dialect, written in collaboration with his brother, "Uncle Jim's Baptist Revival Hymn," "The Power of Prayer: or, The First Steamboat Up the Alabama."

His vital concern with the economics and the politics of the South, a concern voiced in "Corn," in "Raven Days," and in "Laughter in the Senate":

In the South lies a lonesome, hungry Land

is very deep and earnest. It is not, however, the revelation of a narrow sectionalism. With the end of the Civil War, the whole nation became his country. As he could voice that nation's feelings in the "Cantata" for the Centennial, so he could vision its whole sweep in "Psalm of the West." The indomitable steadfastness of spirit revealed in the Columbus episode, *"hold straight* into the West," the abiding faith of the *Mayflower* episode, the patriotism of the Revolution, all these culminate in nation-wide love and liberty:

Dear Love, Dear Freedom, go with me!

There can be no question of Lanier's contact with the life
about him. He was essentially an American, of his time and
of his place. Influenced in his point of view by his environment and by his individual personality, how did he translate
"knowledge into wisdom"? What was his philosophical contribution? The answer is to be found in his poems, both in
his completed ones and in those tentative poem-suggestions,
published as *Poem Outlines*.

Fundamental to all his philosophic thought is his sympathy with oppressed humanity. He was alert to the social
questions of his day: to the plight of the small farmer, as
in "Nine from Eight"; to the forlorn state of agriculture
in the South, as in "Corn"; to the devastating effect of
mechanized industry, as in "The Symphony":

> Thou Trade! thou king of the modern days!
>> Change thy ways,
>> Change thy ways:
> Let the sweaty laborers file
>> A little while,
>> A little while
> Where Art and Nature sing and smile.

In his hope of a kindlier, a more humane world, he did
not envision one of passivity, one without effort. He, himself, was of too proud a nature, too forceful and too brave, to
ignore the beneficial results of struggle:

> Of fret, of dark, of thorn, of chill,
>> Complain thou not, O heart; for these
> Bank-in the current of the will
>> To uses, arts, and charities.

Throughout his poems of endeavor runs the thread of duty:

Downward the voices of Duty call—
Downward, to toil and be mixed with the main.

This call to duty is the message of nature. In its adherence, regardless of hurt, to the divine plan, nature sets the pattern for man's approach to the Deity:

Tolerant plains, that suffer the sea and the rains and the sun,
Ye spread and span like the catholic man who hath mightily
    won
God out of knowledge and good out of infinite pain
And sight out of blindness and purity out of a stain.

A deeply religious feeling permeates Lanier's poems. They reveal an abiding faith in God. Lanier's God is, however, not one of restricting creed:

Prim Creed, with categoric point, forbear
To feature me my Lord by rule and line.

He is a universal God, a God to be worshiped by boundless love:

O let me love my Lord more fathom deep
Than there is line to sound with; let me love
My fellow not as men that mandates keep:
Yea, all that's lovable, below, above,
That let me love by heart, by heart because
(Free from the penal pressure of the laws)
I find it fair.

Love was to Lanier the solvent of the difficulties and despairs of this world. Love characterized his personal relationships. Deep and vibrant was his love for his children and his wife, a love that produced so tender a lyric as "An Evening Song":

Look off, dear Love, across the sallow sands,
   And mark yon meeting of the sun and sea,
How long they kiss in sight of all the lands,
   Ah! longer, longer, we.

Now in the sea's red vintage melts the sun,
   As Egypt's pearl dissolved in rosy wine,
And Cleopatra night drinks all. 'Tis done,
   Love, lay thine hand in mine.

Come forth, sweet stars, and comfort heaven's heart;
   Glimmer, ye waves, round else unlighted sands.
O night! divorce our sun and sky apart,
   Never our lips, our hands.

Including, but transcending, the personal emotion was the love that embraced mankind; the sympathy and understanding between man and his fellow that must underlie industry and trade and art:

And Love be known as the marriage of man with the All.

This message of an inclusive love was the message that Lanier sang for the South, for America, and for mankind. It was meant not merely for his own time, but for all time.

Love, tenderness—these are the keynotes to Lanier's life and to his poetry. Harmoniously, his two interests, music and poetry, merged. With his music he comforted himself and others; in his poetry, his music gained voice. "Music is Love in search of a word," Lanier had said. Surely in his poems, Love found it.

EUGENE FIELD

IT IS well to acknowledge at the outset that Eugene Field was not a great poet and that no one of his poems is a great poem. No note of apology, however, need accompany that statement. For, though denied a place among the great, Field was not without significance. A generation younger than the New England group of poets, he represented not only a time but a part of American life that they could never have represented. The America that Field interpreted was not fixed simply by his geographical residence in the Middle West. Compared with the America of the New Englanders, it was fresher, less intellectualized; one with feelings more easily stirred, one interested in people and in gossip rather more than in social movements and philosophy. Moreover, Field was one of the forerunners of much of our current American verse, best exemplified, perhaps, by that of the newspaper columnists of today. Through him can be traced that school of writing which has developed in many ways: in those of the sentimentalist, the humorist, the "wise-cracker," the topical rhymester, the self-analyst who draws his own portrait for the delight of his readers.

The writings of such a person must inevitably reflect his temperament and personality. So Field, the man, becomes important. The "Good Knight Sans Peur et Sans Monaie" he called himself and in so doing gave an intimate self-revelation. Field was one who refused completely to grow up. He retained a childlike love for pranks and for fooling; a joy in collecting curious odds and ends; a strange combination of feelings made up of irreverence toward tradition

and commonly accepted authority together with a sentimental reverence toward women, both equally boylike. The
self-chosen title suggests his escape into make-believe; the
assumption of knightly dignity reveals his interest in the
past, an interest, particularly in the medieval, that he expressed in his verse.

In the development of such a personality, both West and
East entered. "I am a Yankee by pedigree and education,"
Field once wrote, "but I was born in that ineffably uninter-
esting city, St. Louis." The Field family traced its ancestry
to John Field, a London astronomer of the sixteenth century, whose grandson Zachariah settled in Massachusetts in
the early 1600's. From Zachariah descended General Martin
Field, born in 1807, the poet's grandfather. General Field,
a lawyer and something of a naturalist, lived in Newfane,
Vermont. Besides a daughter Mary, he had two sons, Roswell Martin and Charles Kellogg. Roswell Martin Field, the
poet's father, was a brilliant and precocious child; he entered Middlebury College at the age of eleven, was admitted
to the bar at seventeen, represented his state in the General
Assembly, and was for a time State's Attorney. Such eminence was reached contrary to his father's expectation. For
while he and his brother were at college, they were suspended for some misdemeanor. General Field, much disturbed, predicted their ruin; and in a letter written to their
sister said, "The boys' conduct has already brought a disgrace upon our family which we can never outgrow. . . . I
am convinced that an education will only prove injurious to
them." Their strain of mischievousness led them frequently
to take the opposing side to their father in his law cases, a
course which not infrequently resulted in a decision against
the elder.

It was a curious episode that caused Roswell Field to
leave his New England home. A sudden romance with a

young lady who had come as a visitor from Windsor, Vermont, resulted in a hasty and secret wedding. Immediately after the marriage, the young woman returned to her home and, a short time later, went through a second ceremony with a former suitor. Roswell Field contested the legality of the second marriage; but in the final courts a decision, based possibly on sympathy for the woman rather than on strictly legal grounds, was rendered against him. Field left Vermont and went to St. Louis, Missouri.

There he continued his practice of law, gaining national prominence by his part on the side of the negro in the Dred Scott case. In May 1848, he married Frances Reed, whose family, too, had come originally from New England. Of the six children born to the couple, only two survived babyhood, Eugene and his younger brother, Roswell.

Eugene was born in September 1850, but whether on the second or on the third of the month is not certain—an uncertainty by no means displeasing to Field, who accepted it as a basis for double celebrations of his birthday. When Eugene was six, his mother died. How much of her he recalled, how close were the ties between them, one can never know. But the mother-child relationship Field used frequently as the subject of his verse. The memory of his mother, the memory coupled with the wish for the security of childhood, became the theme of his poem "To My Mother":

> How you have loved me, mother,
> I have not power to tell,
> Knowing full well
> That even in the rest above
> It is your will
> To watch and guard me with your love
> Loving me still.
> And, as of old, my mother,

I am content to be a child,
By mother's love beguiled
From all these other charms;
So to the last
Within thy dear, protecting arms
Hold thou me fast,
My guardian angel, mother!

It must have been with a feeling made up of sorrow, loneliness, wonder, and curiosity that the two little boys of six
and of five left their St. Louis home for the East. For their
father had decided to entrust them to his sister Mary who,
with her unmarried daughter Mary Field French, was living
in Amherst, Massachusetts. Upon the latter, their grown-up
cousin, a strong-minded woman of culture and graciousness,
fell the chief responsibility for the two boys. An acknowledgment of the love and devotion which she lavished upon
them Field made in the dedicatory poem of one of his books,
"To Mary Field French."

It was in 1856 that Eugene returned to the New England
atmosphere and influence of his father's family. The effect
of this was intensified by a visit which he made to his grandmother's home in Vermont. From that visit he often recalled
the memory of attending his grandmother at church, of carrying a small stove to keep her feet warm, of watching her
nibble lozenges while he had to remain still and, presum-
ably, dry-mouthed and hungry.

Contact with the church of his fathers led him to prepare
notes for a sermon on "Good Understanding giveth favor;
but the way of the transgressor is hard." The sermon was
to develop, among others, this point: "The life of a christian is often compared to a race that is hard and to a battle
in which a man must fight hard to win, these comparisons
have prevented many from becoming christians."

But one must not picture the youthful Eugene Field as being completely absorbed in religion or in the state of his soul. The country about him, his pets—dog, cat, bird, goat, squirrel, and chickens, each with its name and its special form of speech—the games that boys everywhere delight in, these occupied much of his time. A picture of his boyhood is suggested in "Long Ago":

> I once knew all the birds that came
>   And nested in our orchard trees,
> For every flower I had a name—
>   My friends were woodchucks, toads and bees;
> I knew where thrived in yonder glen
>   What plants would soothe a stone-bruised toe—
> Oh, I was very learned then,
>   But that was very long ago.

The love of animals remained with Field throughout his life. In his *Auto-Analysis,* a jumble of biographical fact and fiction, he made this statement, which was a true reflection of his feelings: "If I had my way, I should make the abuse of horses, dogs and cattle a penal offense; I should like to abolish all dog-laws and dog-catchers, and I would punish severely everybody who caught and caged birds." To this same love of animals may be traced his first known poem, that written about a dog:

> Oh, had I wings like a dove I would fly
>   Away from this world of fleas!
> I'd fly all around Miss Emerson's yard
>   And light on Miss Emerson's trees.

Field's education under his cousin's guidance seems not to have been a very formal one. When he was fifteen, however, it was decided that he should have a more organized training. At the same time, the needs of his mischievous temperament were recognized. So the decision was reached, that, instead of being sent to a large boys' school where, the presumption was, he would get into trouble, he be sent to the home of the Reverend James Tufts at Monson, about twenty-five miles from Amherst.

With five other boys, Field lived in the clergyman's house and was taught by him. His teacher found him not very much interested in books; a certain immaturity of mind and a suggestion of frail health seemed to preclude complete devotion to his studies. But he was lively and witty. He shone in declamations delivered in a rich, flexible voice. He devised all sorts of games and activities, including the building of a moated castle in the woods. He drew pictures of his playmates, of his pets, and of fanciful creatures of his own imaginings. He was, in short, a prime favorite with his fellows. Yet something of the academic did affect him; for in the last months of his stay at Monson, he caught a little of the spirit of the Latin classics, of Virgil and of Horace.

In September 1868, with a few conditions, he entered Williams College. But before the year was over, President Hopkins informed the Reverend Mr. Tufts that it might be better for Williams and for the young student if Eugene Field left college. He was not expelled: he was not suspended; but in April 1869 he returned to Monson.

A few months later, the illness of his father called him to St. Louis. Within a week, the elder Mr. Field had died. Evidently, Field experienced no desire to return to the East. New England was definitely abandoned.

Through the influence of his guardian, Professor John William Burgess, Field entered Knox College, Galesburg, Illinois, in 1869. His stay there was limited to a year. In 1870, he entered the Junior class of the University of Missouri, where his brother Roswell was a student. That institution, too, held him for but a year. His brief exposures to college atmosphere had little scholastic effect upon Field. His time seemed to be occupied with devising all sorts of pranks to be played upon the college and town and with the writing of humorously exaggerated accounts of college activities for local newspapers.

After leaving college, Field made his home in St. Louis with Melvin L. Gray, an executor of his father's will. One of the heirs to his father's moderate estate, Field did not seem overwhelmed by financial worries; yet the question of a livelihood was one that had to be answered. College and an academic or professional career were, through his own indifference, out of the question. The stage attracted him— and throughout his life continued to attract him. But his desire to be an actor was discouraged by Edwin Forrest, the leading tragedian of his time; and a two weeks' season of a dramatic company, organized by Field, was far from being successful. Finally, he decided upon journalism as his future work, a decision no doubt fostered by the reporting he had done at Knox College for the local press.

But several events of importance were to occur before Field entered upon his career. Field had accepted an invitation to visit at St. Joseph, Missouri, the home of Edgar V. Comstock, who had been one of his college classmates. On his visit, he fell in love with his friend's sister Julia, a girl of fourteen. His love was returned. But because of the extreme youth of his fiancée, her father urged that the marriage not take place for several years.

Meanwhile, on reaching twenty-one, Field had received some money from the sale of some of his father's property. With this he planned a trip to Europe, taking with him his friend and future brother-in-law. The two, with another Comstock sister, left for New York, whence the young men were to sail. Before the sailing date, Field made a flying trip back to Missouri, pleading a business call which was, un-

questionably, simply a desire to say one more good-by to his
fiancée. In the fall of 1872, he sailed, "spending six months
and my patrimony in France, Italy, Ireland, and England."

The money was soon exhausted. Field returned with a
number of memories and a heterogeneous store of useless
souvenirs.

In June 1873, Field began work on the St. Louis *Evening
Journal*. Assured now of a means of earning a living, Field
felt that he could undertake the responsibilities of married
life. He persuaded Mr. Comstock to reconsider his original
decision that the young people wait until his daughter
should be eighteen; and on October 16, 1873, he married the
sixteen-year-old Julia.

The love between Field and his wife was a life-long and
devoted one. Year after year, Field sang it in verse. Each
year, almost without exception, produced its poetic valentine, a poem like "A Valentine to My Wife":

> What though these years of ours be fleeting?
>   What though the years of youth be flown?
> I'll mock old Tempus with repeating,
>   "I love my wife and her alone!"
>
> And when I fall before his reaping,
>   And when my stuttering speech is dumb,
> Think not my love is dead or sleeping,
>   But that it waits for you to come.

When, in later years, worn and sick, Field was in London,
his memory went back lovingly to the days of his courtship
in St. Joseph:

> Saint Jo, Buchanan County,
>   Is leagues and leagues away;
> And I sit in the gloom of this rented room,
>   And pine to be there today.

Yes, with London fog around me
    And the bustling to and fro,
I am fretting to be across the sea
    In Lover's Lane, Saint Jo.

I would have a brown-eyed maiden
    Go driving once again;
And I'd sing the song, as we snailed along,
    That I sung to that maiden then;
I purposely say, "as we *snailed* along,"
    For a proper horse goes slow
In those leafy aisles, where Cupid smiles,
    In Lover's Lane, Saint Jo.

From the time of his marriage, Field's professional career was made up of work now on one paper, now on another. He filled editorial positions on newspapers in St. Louis, St. Joseph, Kansas City, Missouri; and in Denver, Colorado, on the *Tribune*. Finally, in 1883, he went to Chicago to work for the *Morning News*, later *The Record*. In the letter accepting this final position, he wrote, "An attempt at honesty in the profession has kept me gloriously hard up, with a constantly increasing family."

He had done much writing before he went to Chicago, both his prose and his verse attracting general attention. He had inaugurated newspaper columns, called variously in successive papers "Funny Fancies" and "Odds and Ends." These contained paragraphs, highly simplified, exaggeratedly moralized, that were later to be made up into *The Tribune Primer*. Typical of these paragraphs was the one on peaches that began with the statement "The Peach is hard and green" and, after suggesting the dire results of eating unripe peaches, ended with "If there were no green Peaches there would not be so many Children-sizes of Gold

Harps in Heaven." The columns held, too, short quips about local events and personages. And, finally, they were the vehicle for the verse that he was beginning to write. Only three or four of these early poems are worthy to outlast the ephemeral fame of a daily newspaper; but these few are typical of the kinds of verse which Field was later to write in great number.

On "Christmas Treasures," Field later made the comment: "The first piece of serious verse I ever wrote. It was printed in the St. Louis *Morning Journal*, December 25, 1878. I regard it as one of my best pieces of work." In that poem, one finds the germ of his later, somewhat sentimentalized poems about children, particularly the suggestion of "Little Boy Blue." Some little while before, his first-born son had died at the age of two months. This loss, intensified by the death later of other children, seems to have colored his whole life; undoubtedly, it must have suggested the ending of "Christmas Treasures":

> They came again one Christmas-tide—
>   That angel host, so fair and white;
>   And, singing all that glorious night,
> They lured my darling from my side.
>
>   .   .   .   .   .
>
> But if again that angel train
>   And golden-head come back for me,
>   To bear me to Eternity,
> My watching will not be in vain.

A startling contrast to this poem was the widely popular "The Little Peach" which, with stark simplicity, told the same story as did *The Tribune Primer* lesson: A green peach grew in an orchard.

John took a bite and Sue a chew,
And then the trouble began to brew,—
Trouble the doctor couldn't subdue.
    Too true!

Under the turf where the daisies grew
They planted John and his sister Sue,
And their little souls to the angels flew,—
    Boo hoo!

"The Wanderer" is a third poem of this period.

Upon a mountain height, far from the sea,
    I found a shell,
And to my listening ear the lonely thing
Ever a song of ocean seemed to sing,
    Ever a tale of ocean seemed to tell.

How came the shell upon that mountain height?
    Ah, who can say
Whether there dropped by some too careless hand,
Or whether there cast when Ocean swept the Land,
    Ere the Eternal had ordained the Day?

Strange, was it not? Far from its native deep.
    One song it sang,—
Sang of the awful mysteries of the tide,
Sang of the misty sea, profound and wide,—
    Ever with echoes of the ocean rang.

And as the shell upon the mountain height
    Sings of the sea,
So do I ever, leagues and leagues away,—
So do I ever, wandering where I may,—
    Sing, O my home! sing, O my home! of thee.

This poem appeared in Field's column over the name of the Polish actress Modjeska. Attributing, in this manner, to wholly innocent and unsuspecting people poems which he had, himself, written was simply one of the many forms which Field's prankish humor took. A public impersonation of Oscar Wilde; his appearance on Chicago streets in the depth of winter, dressed in linen duster and straw hat; a seatless office chair which he offered to visitors; telegrams and letters pursuing absent friends—all these helped to create the legend of the irrepressible Eugene Field.

His Chicago newspaper activity gave Field ample opportunity to indulge his humorous interests and to make them the subject of his writings. In his tiny cubby-hole of an office—above his desk a sheet of tin on which he could summon messengers or signal others of the staff for silence—Field was host to all sorts and conditions of men; from the office flowed daily a column of observation, criticism, or suggestion. Printed first under the name of "Current Gossip," the column after August 31, 1883, was called "Sharps and Flats." In it appeared notes—usually much exaggerated or else entirely fictitious—on the men and women he knew; comments on baseball, of which he was an ardent fan; reports of music and of plays, in which his interest was always keen. His criticisms of Chicago's cultural crudities were gathered together and, in 1887, printed in book form as *Culture's Garland; Being Memoranda of the Gradual Rise of Literature, Art, Music, and Society in Chicago and Other Western Ganglia*. Glowing local industrial or agricultural reports he satirized in comments such as this: "A substantial new bridge has been built over Crow creek, four miles south of Tolusa. During a freshet in August a heavy cornstalk from the Bennington farm floated down and loosened the foundations of the bridge." In politics Field seldom took an active partisan position; but he wrote with a sharply pointed pen on political subjects. The refrain of his poem:

> But jest 'fore election, I'm as good as I can be!

was a satiric thrust at political candidates and their pre-election promises. The marriage of President Cleveland in 1886 inspired a whole series of "White House Ballads." In all this writing, both of prose and of verse, there was manifest a sympathetic interest in people, an interest made up of knowledge and of edged—but always friendly—criticism.

Field's column became widely quoted. His quips and jests circulated freely. But a new high note of popularity was struck with the publication in 1888 of his poem, "Little Boy Blue." The dusty toy dog and the rusted tin soldier became immediately the symbols of loss for all who mourned some dead child. In the poem undoubtedly entered the grief that Field had experienced in the death of his infant children; in it there very probably entered some of his own unrecognized longing for the return of his own childhood.

At about the time of the writing and publishing of "Little Boy Blue," a Dr. Frank W. Reilly became a member of the staff of Field's newspaper. Through him Field extended his interests in still one more direction, that of books. He became both an avid reader and an enthusiastic collector. One of the "Saints and Sinners," a group of book-lovers who made McClurg's book store in Chicago their headquarters, he chronicled their real or imaginary adventures in the collecting of old and curious books. News of books began to appear in his column; advice was given to book buyers, such advice as:

> So buy what finds you find today—
>   That is the safest plan;
> And if you find you cannot pay,
>   Why, settle when you can.

The books that he, himself, read and loved best were those that carried him into the past: Percy's *Reliques of English Poetry*, Bede's *Ecclesiastical History*, Marco Polo's *Travels*, *The Compleat Angler*, *Father Prout's Reliquies*, fairy tales, and—a harking back to an earlier interest—Horace. This renewed interest became intensified and resulted in his popularized and modernized translations which, together with those of his brother Roswell, were collected in book form as *Echoes from the Sabine Farm*.

Before the publication of this book in 1892, however, Field's health, never very strong, had broken down. In the hope of recovery, he sailed with his family in 1889 to Europe. The children went to school in Germany while Field spent most of his time in London. In that city his antiquarian heart found delight, which was modified only by his impecunious condition.

O ye that hanker after boons that others idle by—

he says in "Dear Old London":

Ye only can appreciate what agony was mine
When I was broke in London in the fall of '89.

Europe, however, failed to restore his health. Furthermore, he felt lonely away from his work and his friends, a homesickness that he voiced in "John Smith":

And so, compatriot, I am proud you wrote your name today
Upon the register at Lowe's "John Smith, U. S. A."

To the unhappiness at the general failure of the European sojourn was added the deep sorrow of his eldest son's death. Tenderly, sadly, he wrote to his next oldest boy, "Melvin knows all the great mysteries now. He sees us and loves us just as of old; perhaps, unseen, he will join you in your play. Who knows but that God will appoint him to be your guardian angel?" [1]

After his return to America, Field continued his newspaper work; but, because of his constantly failing health, much of his writing was done at home instead of in his office. His never adequate income he increased by lectures, at which he occasionally appeared with James Whitcomb Riley and George W. Cable. In 1893, after an attack of pneumonia, he went west to the Pacific Coast and as far south as New Orleans.

During these years, Field's family had grown. His newspaper salary, even though increased by lectures and by the royalty from his books, had been barely enough for his needs, certainly not enough for his desires. But finally he saw the way clear to obtaining one of his deepest wishes, the ownership of his own home. In July 1895, he moved into a remodeled house, "provided with all the modern conveniences, including an ample porch and a genial mortgage," a house which he called "Sabine Farm." Humorous accounts of the various stages of purchase, remodeling, and occupying appeared in his column and were collected as *The House; an Episode in the Lives of Reuben Baker, Astronomer, and of his Wife Alice,* and published posthumously in 1896.

The writer's enjoyment of his home had been brief. On November 4, 1895, in his sleep, he died.

After his death was published also his last piece of work, still unfinished, *Love Affairs of a Bibliomaniac.* Collections, too, were made of his poems and of his prose articles. His first book of poems had appeared in 1889, *Little Book of Western Verse.* From then on, his volumes of poetry were: *Echoes from the Sabine Farm, With Trumpet and Drum,*

[1] Quoted in *Eugene Field's Creative Years,* by Charles H. Dennis, Doubleday, Page and Co.

Second Book of Verse, Love Songs of Childhood, Sharps and Flats, and *A Little Book of Tribune Verse.*

Of this quantity of verse, probably but few poems will find a long lasting place in American poetry. But the poems, both those destined to be remembered and those destined to be forgotten, reveal not only the poet Field, but also the early forms of much of our current lighter verse.

Field in his poetry expounded no deep philosophy either of life or of esthetics. His poetry was the simple singing of the fancies that came to him:

> So, joyous friend, when you and I
>   Sing to the world our chosen theme,
> Let's do as do the birds that fly
>   Careless o'er woodland, wold, and stream:
> Sing Nature's song, untouched of art—
>   Sing of the forest, brook, and plain;
> And, hearing it, each human heart
>   Will vibrate with the sweet refrain.

The force of Field's simple emotional appeal came from a certainty of technique developed through study of the older poets. He had read Herrick, Suckling, and Skelton for variety of verse form. His reading of foreign poets resulted in translations, like those of the French poet Beranger and, particularly, those of Horace.

If, in the case of the latter, a classicist might object on the ground of accuracy, still, written as they might have been had Horace, himself, used the American idiom, the poems have unquestionably caught the spirit and tone of the Latin poet:

Seek not, Leuconoe, to know how long you're going to live yet,

What boons the Gods will yet withhold, or what they're
    going to give yet.

Ode 22, Book I, the familiar "Integer vitæ," is an illustra-
tion of a more serious, but no less rich, translation:

> Fuscus, whoso to good inclines,
>   And is a faultless liver,
> Nor Moorish spear nor bow need fear,
>   Nor poison-arrowed quiver.

The ability to catch the essential spirit of another writer
and to modify it with a humorous touch is suggested by
"The Human Lad," [2] a parody of Isaac Watts, in which
little boys are told not to harm flies or to pull dogs' tails
because

> The little fly howe'er so frail
>   Was made on Rover's hide to prey;
> And faithful Rover's honest tail
>   Was made to brush the flies away.
>
> So let each bird and beast enjoy
>   The vain, brief life which God has given,
> Whilst I my youthful hours employ
>   In works that fit the soul for heaven.

Field's technical skill is apparent both in his metrics and
in his rhymes. A glance through his collected works is sufficient to show the variety of his verse forms; and these are
unerringly and gracefully handled. Almost any poem, taken
at random, shows his rhyming facility: internal rhyme, as
in:

[2] Quoted in *Life of Eugene Field*, by Slason Thompson, D. Appleton
and Co.

Now, wit ye well, it so befell, that when the night grew dim,

or

And that on dress I lay much stress I can't and shan't deny;

double—rather triple—rhyme, as in:

> Oh, but it takes agility
> Combined with versatility
> To run a country daily with appropriate ability!

One finds no false, no tortured rhymes in Field's verse. Those perfectly obvious mispronunciations necessary for rhyme, which are to be found and in great numbers, are used for the sake of humor. *To us,* for example, is rhymed with *superfluous*—spelt *sooper-floo-us; horizon* is rhymed with *pizen.*

His own facility with rhyme made him somewhat impatient with those poets who used an unrhymed meter. The meter of Longfellow's "Evangeline," for example, is satirized in the last lines of "The Peter-Bird":

This is the legend of old, told in the tumtitty metre
Which the great poets prefer, being less labor than rhyming
(My first attempt at the same, my *last* attempt, too, I
    reckon!);
Nor have I further to say, for the sad story is ended.

Doubtless, such a protest was as much an evidence of his general irreverence of spirit as it was the enunciation of an artistic canon. One principle, however, Field did insist upon: [3] "To young writers everywhere: Attend diligently and patiently to your work and atmosphere will come to you. You can no more subsist upon the 'atmosphere' of an-

[3] Quoted in *Eugene Field's Creative Years,* by Charles H. Dennis, Doubleday, Page and Co.

other than you can do your breathing with another man's lungs."

In adhering to this principle of self-expression, Field showed one curious manifestation. A strange duality existed in his choice of diction: a use of forms of speech with an archaic flavor that linked him to the poets of the past, and a use of current idiom that connected him with the poets that were to write in the future. The poems written in archaic diction reflected his interest in the medieval. Sometimes the device was employed primarily for the purpose of humor, as in "A Proper Trewe Idyll of Camelot." But frequently it was used to convey the spirit of the past: something more than quaint spelling, odd words, and age-flavored figures.

MEDIÆVAL EVENTIDE SONG

Come hither, lyttel childe, and lie upon my breast tonight,
For yonder fares an angell yclad in raimaunt white,
And yonder sings ye angell as onely angells may,
And his songe ben of a garden that bloometh farre awaye.

To them that have no lyttel childe Godde sometimes sendeth
   down
A lyttel childe that ben a lyttel angell of his owne;
And if so bee they love that childe, he willeth it to staye,
But elsewise, in his mercie, he taketh it awaye.

And sometimes, though they love it, Godde yearneth for ye
   childe,
And sendeth angells singing, whereby it ben beguiled;
They fold their arms about ye lamb that croodleth at his
   play,
And beare him to ye garden that bloometh farre awaye.

I wolde not lose ye lyttel lamb that Godde hath sent to me;
If I colde sing that angell songe, how joysome I sholde be!

For, with mine arms about him, and my musick in his eare,
What angell songe of paradize soever sholde I feare?

Soe come, my lyttel childe, and lie upon my breast tonight,
For yonder fares an angell yclad in raimaunt white,
And yonder sings that angell, as onely angells may,
And his songe ben of a garden that bloometh farre away.

From the use in a poem of this language of a time gone
by, Field could turn and use equally well the conversational
tones and words of the men and women and children about
him.

Let critic folk the poet's use of vulgar slang upbraid,
But, while I'm speaking by the card, I'll call a spade a
  spade.

Slang, idiomatic speech, mispronunciations—all these Field
used tellingly, as, for example, in "Picnic-Time":

It's June ag'in, an' in my soul I feel the fillin' joy
That's sure to come this time o' year to every little boy;
For, every June, the Sunday-schools at picnics may be seen,
Where "fields beyont the swellin' floods stand dressed in
  livin' green";
Where little girls are skeered to death with spiders, bugs,
  and ants,
An' little boys get grass-stains on their go-to-meetin' pants.
It's June ag'in, an' with it all what happiness is mine—
There's goin' to be a picnic, an' I'm goin' to jine!

This language of everyday—sometimes, indeed, illiterate
—speech was not confined to humorous poems. Field used
it in some of his serious, sentimental verses, as he did in
"Marthy's Younkit":

The camp is gone; but Red Hoss Mountain rears its kindly
    head,
An' looks down, sort uv tenderly, upon its cherished dead;
'Nd I reckon that, through all the years, that little boy
    which died
Sleeps sweetly an' contentedly upon the mountain-side;
That the wild-flowers uv the summer-time bend down their
    heads to hear
The footfall uv a little friend they know not slumbers near;
That the magpie on the sollum rocks strange flutterin' shad-
    ders make,
An' the pines an' hemlocks wonder that the sleeper doesn't
    wake;
That the mountain brook sings lonesome like an' loiters on
    its way
Ez if it waited for a child to jine it in its play.

"Marthy's Younkit" is one of Field's Red Hoss Mountain
poems. These, written in dialect, give pictures of the Colorado of his time. Highly sentimentalized pictures these may
be, pictures wherein the portraits are far from life-like. But
they give the spirit that has come to be accepted as that of
the West, a spirit made up of humor, rough actions, and
tender feelings; a spirit new, and fresh, young in attitude
and outlook:

Your ancient history is a thing the Coloradan hates.

However conventionalized this picture may by now have
become, it was a more original one when Field wrote
"Casey's Table d'Hôte," "The Conversazzhyony," "Prof
Vere de Blaw," and "Our Lady of the Mine."

Field's use of the rich material of the Coloradan scene,
alone, would mark him as an essentially American writer.
But his Americanism consisted of something more than this;

it embraced both his subject matter and his point of view. There was, to be sure, in Field's writing some influence of books and of various literatures; but even this influence was modified by the life about him, in which he was by turn enthusiastic observer and active participant. The events and people of his day gave him suggestions for his verse: the performance of a great actress, for example, as in "Modjesky as Cameel"; the widespread power of a journalist, in "Mr. Dana, of the New York Sun" and "The Great Journalist in Spain"; politics in "The Political Maud" and the previously mentioned "White House Ballads"; the death of Grant, in "Grant":

> His was the sword that from its scabbard leapt
> To cleave the way where freedom could be won,
> And where it led a conquering army swept
> Till all was done.

No respect for authority, no loyalty toward tradition restrained Field in his treatment of the subjects of his choice. Wit, impishness, insouciance, all entered into the turning of any matter, however serious, into a lively jest.

Toward one subject alone, Field permitted himself no irreverence. To him women as women seemed something sacred, something not to be touched by his humor. To some extent this worshipful attitude may have been the result of contact with Western life, where there were so few women that they became something wonderful and to be treasured. To a greater extent, however, it was the only conceivable attitude of the America of his time, an attitude that made women a race apart, not altogether human. Occasionally, it is true, Field jested about some feminine characteristic: women's inability to understand the masculine collector's point of view; or their worrying concern for their children.

But the jesting was always tenderly done; beneath even it lay the sentimentalized, not wholly real, portrait of woman, as in "Our Lady of the Mine":

Do you wonder that that woman's face consoled the lonesome critters?

In this mingling of the humorous with the sentimental and pathetic, Field is representative of the large number of Americans with free and easily touched emotions. His sentiment may vary from the tenderness of "Telling the Bees," to the more obvious one—heightened, one must feel, by imagination rather than by actual feeling—of the last stanza of "Good-by—God Bless You!"

> She let no tear bedim her eye,
> For fear *that* might distress me,
> But, kissing me, she said good-by,
> And asked our God to bless me.

This, in turn, may become something almost as maudlin as the present popular crop of "Mammy Songs," as it does in "Father's Letter":

For when I went away from home, the weekly news I heard
Was nothing to the tenderness I found in that one word—
The sacred name of mother—why, even now as then,
The thought brings back the saintly face, the gracious love
again,
And in my bosom seems to come a peace that is divine,
As if an angel spirit communed awhile with mine;
And one man's heart is strengthened by the message from
above,
And earth seems nearer heaven when "mother sends her
love."

Humor, on the other hand, may save a poem from the extreme of the sentimental. "Grandma's Prayer" is an example:

> I pray that, risen from the dead,
>   I may in glory stand—
> A crown, perhaps, upon my head,
>   But a needle in my hand.
>
> I've never learned to sing or play,
>   So let no harp be mine;
> From birth unto my dying day,
>   Plain sewing's been my line.
>
> Therefore, accustomed to the end
>   To plying useful stitches,
> I'll be content if asked to mend
>   The little angels' breeches.

Field's humor is, for the most part, the humor of the incongruous. "A Proper Trewe Idyll of Camelot," for example, projects against the medieval past the phrases and incidents of what was Field's present; "The Conversazzhyony" presents a contrast between the ambition for sophistication and an unsophisticated background; in "The Delectable Ballad of the Waller Lot" the contrast lies between the simple incident and its epic telling. The humor may, as in "Mr. Dana of the New York Sun," be derived from some incident which helps point the jester's finger at mankind. Or it may be touched with irony, as it is in "An Imitation of Dr. Watts":

> The dumb shall never call on me
>   In vain for kindly aid.

Field's poetry reveals swift play of feeling. From one extreme to another, from bright humor to deep pathos, he varied; and in this variability, he suggested the uncontrolled emotions of a child. Always he retained something of the childish spirit. This spirit entered into his verse and made him preëminently a poet of children and of childhood.

"We are not going to have a fine American fiction," he wrote, "until we have encouraged, trained, and cultivated in our children the God-gift, fancy." He, himself, created a land of fairy and of imagination; a wonderful land of dinkey-birds, of flimflams and gluglugs, of Fly-Away horses, of gingham dogs and calico cats.

However fancied this world, the children of his poetry are real children. The strange goodness that envelops children toward the end of December, could that be better described than it is in "Just 'Fore Christmas"? It is any little boy—every little boy—who voices his ambitions in "The Limitations of Youth":

I'd like to be a cowboy an' ride a firey hoss
  Way out into the big an' boundless West;
I'd kill the bears an' catamounts an' wolves I came across,
  An' I'd pluck the bal' head eagle from his nest!
    With my pistols at my side,
    I would roam the prarers wide,
An' to scalp the savage Injun in his wigwam would I ride—
    If I darst; but I darsen't!

"The Night Wind" expresses the awfulness of childish fears:

    Suppose you ask, "Who has been bad?"
      And then you'll hear what's true;
    For the wind will moan in its ruefullest tone:
        "Yoooooooo!
        Yoooooooo!
        Yoooooooo!"

Because he knew and understood children, he knew what desolation was brought to parents by their early death. His own experience, too, had taught him. Out of his own sorrow, he voiced the sorrow of others and sought to console them. The theme runs throughout his poetic years, from the early poem "Christmas Treasures," through "Marthy's Younkit," "Little Boy Blue," "To the Passing Saint":

> O dear saint, that blessest men
>   With the grace of Christmas joy,
> Soothe this heart with love again,—
>   Give me back my little boy!

In so far as religion entered into his consolation, it was a religion of childlike faith and trust, the religion of "The Divine Lullaby":

> Speak on—speak on, dear Lord!
> And when the last dread night is near,
>   With doubts and fears and terrors wild,
> Oh, let my soul expiring hear
> Only these words of heavenly cheer,
>   "Sleep well, my child!"

Of all his poems of childhood it is, indeed, the lullabies which seem to express Field's deepest feelings. He himself appeared always to be seeking

> The Dreamland that's waiting out yonder,

the winding path to which is made easier by a mother's song. All the tender love and care that a mother holds for her child is sung in "Balow, My Bonnie," "The Rock-A-By-Lady," "A Lullaby." In his lullabies of various nations, Field expresses universal mother love and universal child trust: in "Wynken, Blynken, and Nod"; in the Japanese "Little Blue Pigeon":

Sleep, little pigeon, and fold your wings—
  Little blue pigeon with velvet eyes;
Sleep to the singing of mother-bird swinging—
  Swinging the nest where her little one lies;

"Norse Lullaby"; the Cornish "Gold and Love for Dearie";
"Armenian Lullaby":

If thou wilt shut thy drowsy eyes,
  My mulberry one, my golden sun!
The rose shall sing thee lullabies,
  My pretty cosset lambkin!
And thou shalt swing in an almond-tree,
With a flood of moonbeams rocking thee—
A silver boat in a golden sea,
  My velvet love, my nestling dove,
    My own pomegranate blossom!

The road to sleep—to glamor and to surcease from care—
was the road that Field constantly sought. For him it led to
the past, to the security of childhood. So he sought it
through his pranks, his boyish enthusiasms, his wistful
clinging to youth. His very poetry was his groping effort to
recapture it. All his longing, all that the man hoped for, all
that his poetry said, is suggested in "Long Ago":

I know it's folly to complain
  Of whatsoe'er the fates decree;
Yet, were not wishes all in vain,
  I tell you what my wish should be:
I'd wish to be a boy again,
  Back with the friends I used to know.
For I was, oh, so happy then—
  But that was very long ago!

THE END